The State of UK
Higher Education

The State of UK Higher Education

Managing Change and Diversity

Edited by
David Warner and
David Palfreyman

The Society for Research into Higher Education
& Open University Press

Published by SRHE and
Open University Press
Celtic Court
22 Ballmoor
Buckingham
MK18 1XW

email: enquiries@openup.co.uk
world wide web: www.openup.co.uk

and 325 Chestnut Street
Philadelphia, PA 19106, USA

First published 2001

A catalogue record of this book is available from the British Library

ISBN 0335 20833 9 (pb)   0335 20659 X (hb)

Library of Congress Cataloging-in-Publication Data is available

Typeset by Graphicraft Limited, Hong Kong
Printed in Great Britain by St Edmundsbury Press, Bury St Edmunds, Suffolk

To Mike Shattock who taught us all a lot of what we know

Contents

Notes on Contributors

Suzanne Alexander is Director of the International Office at the University of Birmingham. She joined the Registry at the University of Warwick after a period teaching English in Paris. At Warwick Suzanne undertook a number of generalist roles before moving to the Business School where she acquired her own MBA.

Allan Bolton is the General Manager of Leeds University Business School, having previously worked for 12 years as the Administrator of the Lancaster University Management School. He joined the Registry at Warwick immediately after completing his university studies. While at Warwick Allan gained an MBA from Aston University, and has subsequently held a Fulbright Fellowship. He is the author of *Managing the Academic Unit* in the 'Managing Universities and Colleges' series for the Open University Press.

Robert Burgess is Vice-Chancellor of the University of Leicester. He was Senior Pro-Vice-Chancellor and Director of CEDAR (Centre of Educational Development, Appraisal and Research) and Professor of Sociology at the University of Warwick until August 1999. Robert's main teaching and research interests are in social research methodology, and the sociology of education. He was President of the British Sociological Association, President of the Association for the Teaching of the Social Sciences and Founding Chair of the UK Council for Graduate Education. Robert is currently a member of the Council and Chair of the Postgraduate Training Board of the Economic and Social Research Council.

David Caldwell is the recently appointed Director of the Committee of Scottish Higher Education Principals (COSHEP). After his education in Scotland, David originally joined the University of Warwick as a lecturer in Politics, but then moved to the Registry in 1976. In 1984 he was appointed Secretary of the then Robert Gordon's Institute of Technology (now Robert Gordon University).

Steve Cannon is the Secretary and Director of Operations at the University of Aberdeen. He began his higher education management career in the Registry at the University of Warwick before returning to his native Scotland to become Financial Manager at Ninewells Hospital and Medical School in Dundee. During the next decade Steve moved rapidly up the promotion ladder as Secretary of Duncan of Jordanstone College of Art, Deputy Secretary of Dundee University and then Secretary and Director of Finance Strategy and Corporate Affairs at the Scottish Higher Education Funding Council.

John Gledhill is Academic Registrar at the University of Coventry. He joined the Registry at the University of Warwick, after gaining a PhD on Dutch spelling at the University of London and working for a couple of years at the then Hatfield Polytechnic (now University of Hertfordshire). After 18 years at Warwick, John moved to Coventry in 1992. He is the author of *Managing Students* in the Open University Press's 'Managing Universities and Colleges' series.

Philip Harvey is the Academic Secretary of the University of Exeter. He studied at Oxford Brookes University and the Universities of Oxford and Durham before beginning his career in higher education management in the Registry at the University of Warwick. During his ten years at Warwick, Philip held a wide range of posts including positions in personnel, quality assurance and the secretaryship of the Graduate School.

John Hogan is Registrar and Secretary of the University of Durham. He gained a Doctorate in History at the University of Sussex before starting his career in the Registry at the University of Warwick. John moved to Durham in 1993 initially as Academic Registrar.

David Holmes is Registrar of the University of Oxford, a Professorial Fellow of St John's College and an Honorary Fellow of Merton College. He joined the Registry of the University of Warwick in 1970, leaving 12 years later to go to the University of Liverpool where he held a series of posts culminating in that of Deputy Registrar. In 1988, David was appointed as the first unitary Registrar of the University of Birmingham before moving to Oxford.

Anthony McLaren is Deputy Chief Executive of the Universities and Colleges Admissions Service (UCAS). He began his career at the University of Warwick in 1985, where he held a variety of posts including that of Admissions Officer in the Registry. In 1992 Anthony moved to the University of Hull as Academic Registrar and was then appointed Acting Registrar and Secretary immediately prior to his departure to UCAS.

Russell Moseley is Director of Open Studies at the University of Warwick having previously worked in the Registry. Before joining Warwick he worked for the Council for National Academic Awards and, prior to that, was Lecturer and Research Fellow at the Universities of Aston and Sussex respectively. Russell has served as the Administrative Secretary, Editor and as a member of the Executive Committee of the Universities Association for Continuing Education.

Jonathan Nicholls, who contributed the bibliography, succeeded Michael Shattock as Registrar of the University of Warwick in October 1999 having previously been the University's Academic Registrar. He was educated at the University of Bristol and at Emmanuel College, Cambridge where he studied for a PhD on medieval courtesy books. Immediately prior to joining the Registry at Warwick in 1982, Jonathan spent a year at Harvard on a Fellowship and has also had a period of exchange at the University of Sydney.

David Palfreyman is the Bursar and a Fellow of New College, Oxford. After a brief period writing a company centennial history, David joined the University of Liverpool in 1976. He then moved to the Registry of the University of Warwick and was one of the first HE administrators in the UK to gain an MBA. This resulted in him moving to Warwick's Finance Department and thence to Oxford. David teaches and writes widely on higher education management issues including with David Warner being the General Editor of the Open University Press series 'Managing Universities and Colleges'. David is the Director of the Oxford Centre for Higher Education Policy Studies (OxCHEPS), of which David Warner is the Deputy Director.

Tony Rich is Registrar and Secretary at the University of Essex. He joined the Registry of the University of Warwick in 1984 after gaining a PhD and having worked as a writer and researcher for the Longman Group. At Warwick, Tony helped launch the part-time degrees programme and the flourishing student recruitment operation in Kenya. He left Warwick in 1989 to work at the University of Sheffield, before moving to the post of Academic Registrar at the University of East Anglia.

Jim Rushton is Deputy Registrar at the University of Warwick having previously worked earlier in his career at the University of Wales, Bangor. Jim has undertaken training and consultancy work for government bodies and universities in Nigeria, Namibia, Poland, Ethiopia, Malaysia, Romania and Argentina and served as a member of the 1996 Presidential Commission of Enquiry into the University of Guyana. Since 1982 he has been Joint Director of the prestigious University of Warwick and University of Oxford Management Programme for international university administrators.

Peter Scott is the Vice-Chancellor of Kingston University. Prior to this appointment in 1998, he was Pro-Vice-Chancellor, Professor of Education and Director of the Centre for Policy Studies in Education at the University of Leeds. Peter was Editor of *The Times Higher Education Supplement* from 1976 until 1992. His books include *Higher Education Re-formed* (Falmer Press, 2000), *The Globalization of Higher Education* (Open University Press, 1998), *Governing Universities* (with Catherine Bargh and David Smith, SRHE/Open University Press, 1996), *The Meanings of Mass Higher Education* (SRHE/Open University

Press, 1995) and *The New Production of Knowledge* (with M. Gibbons, H. Nowotny, C. Limoges *et al.*, Sage, 1984).

Rosemary Stamp is Riley's National Director for Education and Marketing and the Director of Riley Consultancy, the company's consultancy and strategic marketing division. Prior to joining Riley, she was responsible for student recruitment marketing, communications and research in the Registry at the University of Warwick. Rosemary is a governor of a Further Education college in the Midlands. She is a graduate of the Universities of Birmingham and York and the Nottingham Business School, and is a member of the Institute of Public Relations and the Chartered Institute of Marketing.

David Warner is the Principal and Chief Executive of Swansea Institute of Higher Education. After studying at the University of Warwick, both as a mature undergraduate and a postgraduate, he joined the Registry in 1971. A couple of years later, David moved to the University of East Anglia and then returned to the Warwick Registry for a further period. During the spells at Warwick he also taught in the Politics Department and on extramural programmes. In 1985, David moved to the then Birmingham Polytechnic (now University of Central England in Birmingham) to a post which finally metamorphosed into that of Professor and Pro-Vice-Chancellor. He writes and edits extensively on higher education management, primarily for Open University Press.

Selected Abbreviations

ABS	Association of Business Schools
ACPs	admissions criteria profiles
ADAR	Art and Design Admissions Registry
AMBA	Association of MBAs
AoC	Association of Colleges
APR	age participation rate
APT&C	administrative, professional, technical and clerical
AUT	Association of University Teachers
BTEC	Business and Technology Education Council
CAT	college of advanced technology
CBI	Confederation of British Industry
CE	College of Education; continuing education
CEDAR	Centre for Educational Development, Appraisal and Research
CEO	chief executive officer
CI	central institution
CIHE	Council for Industry and Higher Education
CNAA	Council for National Academic Awards
COSHEP	Committee of Scottish Higher Education Principals
CPD	continuing professional development
CSCFC	Conference of Scottish Centrally Funded Colleges
CSM	Camborne School of Mines
CSU	Careers Service Unit; Central Students' Union (of Oxford)
CSUP	Committee of Scottish University Principals
CUCO	Commission on University Career Opportunities
CVCP	Committee of Vice-Chancellors and Principals
CVE	continuing vocational education
DBA	Doctor of Business Administration
DipIBA	Diploma in Business Administration
DENI	Department of Education for Northern Ireland

DES	Department of Education and Science (replaced originally by DfE and then DfEE)
DfEE	Department for Education and Employment
DTI	Department of Trade and Industry
EAS	electronic application system
E&G	Estimates and Grants (Committee)
ESRC	Economic and Social Research Council
EU	European Union
FE	further education
FEFC	Further Education Funding Council
FHE	further and higher education
FTEs	full-time equivalent students
GDP	gross domestic product
GNVQ	general national vocational qualification
HE	higher education
HEFCE	Higher Education Funding Council for England
HEFCW	Higher Education Funding Council for Wales
HEI	higher education institution
HERoBaC	Higher Education Reach-out to Business and Community
HESA	Higher Education Statistics Agency
HEQ	Higher Education Quality
HHEW	Heads of Higher Education in Wales
HMG	Her Majesty's Government
HNC	higher national certificate
HND	higher national diploma
ICT	information and communication technology
IIMD	International Institute for Management Development
INSEAD	European Institute of Business Administration
IT	information technology
JCR	junior common room
JRF	junior research fellow
KCL	King's College London
LSE	London School of Economics and Political Science
MBA	Master of Business Administration
MIT	Massachusetts Institute of Technology
MP	member of parliament
NAB	National Advisory Body
NABCE	non award-bearing continuing education
NATFHE	National Association of Teachers in Further and Higher Education
NEWI	North East Wales Institute
NHS	National Health Service
Nimby	'not in my back yard'
OECD	Organisation for Economic Co-operation and Development

OST	Office of Science and Technology
OUP	Oxford University Press
PAC	Public Accounts Committee
PCAS	Polytechnics Central Admissions Service
PCFC	Polytechnics and Colleges Funding Council
PhD	Doctor of Philosophy
PI	performance indicator
PVC	pro-vice-chancellor
QAA	Quality Assurance Agency
RAE	Research Assessment Exercise
RDA	regional development agency
RDG	research development grant
SCoP	Standing Conference of Principals
SCUE	Standing Conference on University Entrance
SFEFC	Scottish Further Education Funding Council
SHEFC	Scottish Higher Education Funding Council
SIHE	Swansea Institute of Higher Education
SLC	Student Loans Company
SME	small and medium-sized enterprise
SORP	statement of recommended practice
SSRC	Social Sciences Research Council
SRHE	Society for Research into Higher Education
SUCE	Scottish Universities Committee on Entrance
SWAS	Social Work Admissions System
TEC	Training and Enterprise Council
TQA	total quality assessment
UCAS	Universities and Colleges Admissions Service (formed by a merger between UCCA and PCAS)
UCCA	Universities Central Council on Admissions
UCL	University College London
UCNS	Universities Council for Non-teaching Staff
UEA	University of East Anglia
UFC	Universities Funding Council
UfI	University for Industry
UGC	Universities Grants Committee (replaced by UFC)
UHI	University of Highlands and Islands
UMIST	University of Manchester Institute of Science and Technology
USR	Universities Statistical Record (replaced by HESA)
WCMD	Welsh College of Music and Drama

1

Introduction: Setting the Scene

David Warner and David Palfreyman

Genesis of the book

It will not be long before observant readers spot that all but one of the chapters in this book have been written by people who have spent some part of their career at the University of Warwick. Furthermore, all but one of these Warwick people, including the joint editors, have worked, or are still working, in the Registry at that institution. Why is this? The phenomenon could, of course, be attributed to sloth in 'networking' on the part of the joint editors. In fact, the real answer is rather more interesting.

From time to time in almost every discipline taught, or area of activity practised, in higher education there coalesces a grouping which proceeds to have a significant influence on its domain. Sometimes this group, which may be focused upon a methodological approach, a philosophical position, an individual, an institution or, more likely, a combination of two or three of these, becomes completely dominant. It may then start to function rather like a Kuhnian paradigm.[1] Sometimes two or more groupings compete on more or less equal terms and so the domain may become bitterly divided. One of the joint editors has, himself, experienced the situation where, until quite recently, philosophy in United Kingdom (UK) departments was in thrall to the analytical tradition of Austin and Ayer[2] and continental system building was eschewed. Similarly, some politics departments displayed allegiance to the rationalism of Oakeshott,[3] while others (including that of Warwick) were permeated by the Manchester tendency. Readers will speedily provide other examples.

UK higher education (HE) administration or management[4] also displays this phenomenon intermittently. During the 1960s, when the profession was relatively young, the Northern universities, bound by the Joint Matriculation Board, seemed to provide every new Registrar. Manchester alone was the early home of such legendary names as Currie, Lockwood, Bosworth, Walsh and, of course, the then doyen of the business – Knowles.[5] Burchnall, as Registrar of Liverpool in the 1970s and early 1980s, next provided a generation of new Registrars at Newcastle, Sheffield, Brunel . . . During the last decade or so, Warwick has gradually moved to assume the position of spider at the centre of a similar powerful web of influence. The biographies of our current contributors are impressive, but even so there are other former Warwick colleagues holding senior positions who could have contributed. These include the Academic Registrar at Aberdeen University, the Secretary and Registrar of the University of Manchester Institute of Science and Technology (UMIST), the new Director of Finance at the University of Cambridge and the Assistant President of the University of Science and Technology in Hong Kong. This international perspective provides another dimension of Warwick influence because, since the early 1980s, the Warwick Registry team has run an annual development programme for senior staff from overseas higher education institutions (HEIs) and the total of its graduates, who are distributed throughout the world, now exceed some 350. If you add to this the fact that the editors are also the joint directors of the Annual Management Development programme for HE Administrators run by the Committee of Vice-Chancellors and Principals (CVCP), then the earlier claim about Warwick's influence on UK HE management gains some credence – a claim reinforced by the editors' book *Higher Education Management: The Key Elements* which has now spawned the first seven of a projected 20-volume 'good practice' series, 'Managing Universities and Colleges' (Open University Press, 1999 onwards).

All of this must be attributed to one man – Michael Shattock, the former Registrar of Warwick, and the only person whom anyone in the profession has ever met who, it is anecdotally said, has always wanted to be a university manager from early childhood. Later chapters in this book will refer in more depth to the precise nature of his contribution on the local, national and international stages, both as a practitioner and a thinker about HE management. Suffice it to say that it is his appointees from the 1970s onwards who form what we jokingly call the 'Warwick Mafia'! It therefore seemed fitting that when Mike announced his retirement in order to take up a Visiting Professorship at the Institute of Education in London (and, no doubt, to do lots of other things as well because it is hard to imagine him staying at home tending his roses or keeping bees!) that we should mark the occasion with a personal tribute. And what more appropriate, given Mike's own considerable writings, than a book?

The scope and use of the book

This book is not intended, however, as merely a *festschrift*. Rather it collects together a series of essays written by senior managers who share a common work experience and have reacted to that experience in differing ways. The common thread is the belief in the dynamism of HE and the role of managers in helping to achieve the continuous improvement, relevance and development of the system.

The essays as a whole provide almost, but not quite, comprehensive coverage of the state of UK HE. The first and largest section covers the various categories of institutions which have evolved during the last 50 years. The only major omissions are perhaps those of the technological universities which derived in the 1960s from the colleges of advanced technology (CATs), and a reference to the federal University of London. However, it should be remembered that not all of the 'CATs' (colleges of advanced technology) became universities directly and one of the authors works at an HEI (Coventry University) which followed the less favoured polytechnic/modern university route. Moreover, it is particularly pleasing to have chapters on both Scotland and Wales, thereby avoiding the common fault of complete Anglocentrism. The exclusion of Northern Ireland is only excused by the fact that the Vice-Chancellor of Queen's University is a former Warwick academic and his spouse worked in the Warwick Registry, so even the most distant parts of the UK are not beyond Warwick influence.

The second section is an eclectic pot-pourri of perspectives from those who sit around the edge of the HE lake or occupy somewhat beleaguered islands in its midst. This extended simile may not be a particularly good description of Suzanne Alexander's contribution, but what she has to say needs to be said and it could be argued that there are significant parallels between the alienation felt by business schools, continuing education departments and women in HE, at least from time to time. It was the original intention of the joint editors to include a view of UK HE from overseas in this section, but this proved so difficult to confine and so challenging in content that it may now form the core of another book.

The third section attempts to distil the essence, effect and impact of the Warwick way of doing things. Inevitably, the descriptors 'entrepreneurial' and 'innovative' spring to mind, but there is far more to it than just those epithets. The conclusion comprises an urbane, overarching essay by Peter Scott whose work needs no 'puffing' here. He is the sole contributor not to have faced the Warwick experience first hand and, as such, provides a counterweight of objectivity.

Along the way (as illustrated by the wide scope of the index) the contributors have managed to flag up the essential themes of UK HE over the past 25 years, and to identify the likely key issues with which the system will need to grapple over the next 25. The territory covered includes the following, in no special order of priority:

- 'massification', accountability and audit: the Research Assessment Exercise and quality assurance
- access and social equity
- collegiality versus managerialism
- academic autonomy and financial autonomy
- income generation
- 'elites' and an emerging 'Ivy League'
- 'top-up' academic fees

- the costing and pricing of HE courses
- globalization and 'e-degrees'
- HE as a 'lifestyle' product
- strategic positioning and niching
- HE as 'the last of the nationalized industries'
- performance indicators and the teaching 'black box'
- 'spin-off' companies and 'the entrepreneurial university'
- 'dumbing-down' and standards
- caring for the alumni: 'lifelong learning' as 'after-sales service'
- 'regionalization' and serving the local economy (recalling the circumstances of the creation of the big civics in the late nineteenth century)
- the 'casualization' of the academic labour force
- the student as client/customer/consumer
- the retreat of the taxpayer from HE funding combined (paradoxically) with an enhanced state inspection regime
- quality control of 'the learning experience'
- the use of information technology (IT) in teaching
- the refinement of 'student satisfaction' surveys
- the increased incidence of student complaints and the related threat of litigation
- the search for a credible internal procedure for handling student grievances
- the recruitment and promotion of female academics
- universities as administered or managed institutions
- the crumbling physical plant and infrastructure of HEIs (back to being 'the last of the nationalized industries'!)
- the recent emphasis on staff development and training
- the role and effectiveness of the Committee of Vice-Chancellors and Principals (CVCP)
- benchmarking
- collaboration: partnership and franchising
- mergers and, especially within the big conurbations where several HEIs nestle cheek by jowl, the potential revival of the live-at-home-and-commute students (so prevalent in other national HE systems, and once common in the UK)
- the drivers of and the management of change
- the role of HEIs in society and their function within the economy
- the relationship between HE and further education (FE)
- the creation of new HEIs
- the community university
- the niche-marketing of HEIs: 'brand value' and 'corporate personality'
- the setting of HEI entry requirements . . .

This very long list has somewhat surprised the editors because in essence the book has begun to nibble away at such key questions as 'What is higher education?', 'What is a university?', 'How is the concept of higher education and the nature of higher education institutions changing?' and 'What might they become by 2025?'

Yet, in identifying this breadth of issues within the complex world of HE management, our group of contributors also demonstrate the diversity of approaches shown by the wide range of institutions of which they have experience. Such diversity can only be organizationally healthy in ensuring that there is steady innovation within and across UK HE, in establishing a creative tension among the many HEIs, and in allowing individuals to maximize their personal contributions to the various institutions in which they will work over a career of three decades or so. Perhaps, above all, the chapters indicate the rich diversity of the responses within differing institutions to similar drivers of change, the management of the change process varying according to the organizational culture and history of the HEI. The chapters also illustrate the key role played by university administrators (or rather managers) such as Mike Shattock in formulating and implementing these institutional responses.

The brief for each author was very simple: write a little bit about the past of your chosen topic, show how the current situation has derived from it, and then speculate about the near future. Each author has treated this brief idiosyncratically and the editors have not attempted to harmonize the chapters. Some contributors have attempted to provide readers with a panoramic snapshot including all of the key features, while others have concentrated on a definite and partial angle. The most notable exemplar of this latter approach is John Hogan who, perhaps stung by an early editorial exchange which described Durham University as 'old and sleepy', has written a powerful piece about the success of the new campus at Stockton. Similarly, Phil Harvey was probably not overly happy with the description of Exeter University as 'nice' and has responded with a chapter emphasizing the regional role of the university and the probable development of a 'University of/in Cornwall'. *Needless to say, each contributor is writing in a personal capacity and is not expressing views which can in any way be construed as belonging to those of the organization for which he or she works.*

The book is consequently of value at a variety of levels. It can be read straight through and the chapters will form an intriguing and rich mosaic of the current state of UK HE. Alternatively, individual chapters can be selected and each will provide an excellent starting point for the topic under consideration. Finally, the forward-looking elements of the book can be combined to create a view of the future. A view which, in due course, may become the present and then the past . . . and then it may not.

Final thoughts or a word of advice

The birth of this book was trailed in the house journal of the Association of University Administrators.[6] In that article, it was argued that HEI managers have nothing to fear in putting pen to paper as they have much of import to say. The actual production of this book has done nothing to blunt those views. However, it has reinforced the previous experience of the editors that in general it is easier to write a book oneself than to edit one. In particular, it is very unwise to work primarily with colleagues and friends. Keeping these (admittedly busy) people to deadlines has been a nightmare and the excuses they use for failing to deliver on time are always imaginative and at times eccentric, but on occasion they have tended to be expressed in a way that could be said to lack subtlety! One nameless and shameless contributor actually blamed the editors because he had thrown away the letter which prescribed the referencing system which we had decided to use; illnesses increased in proportion to the proximity of deadlines; but the most common line was, 'You know me, I never write anything until after the last minute' (so much for the myth of the cool university administrator always thoroughly prepared well in advance . . .). Budding editors: you have been warned.

Notes and References

1. See T.S. Kuhn (several editions) *The Structure of Scientific Revolutions.* London/ Chicago: University of Chicago Press.
2. Several books and essays helped to establish this tradition, but in particular J.L. Austin (originally the William James Lectures, 1955) *How to Do Things with Words.* London: Oxford University Press, and A.J. Ayer (originally published 1936) *Language, Truth and Logic.* London: Gollancz.
3. Again, several books and essays formed this position, but see particularly M.J. Oakeshott (originally published 1962) *Rationalism in Politics and Other Essays.* London: Methuen.
4. The editors have written elsewhere on this debate in *Higher Education Management: The Key Elements* (1996, pp. 2–3. Buckingham: Open University Press) and come down firmly in favour of the term 'management' as the title of the book implies. See also Eliot (1909); Hudson (1995); Cuthbert (1996); Lewis and Altbach (1996); Eggins (1997); Thorley (1998); Birnbaum (2000).
5. Warner and Palfreyman (1996), op. cit., pp. 6–9.
6. D. Warner (1999) An academic and/or an administrative career, *Perspectives: Policy and Practice in Higher Education*, 3 (1): 16–18.

Part 1

The Institutions

2

The Ancient Collegiate Universities: Oxford and Cambridge

David Palfreyman

Introduction

The desire to group or classify British universities gives us a rather small category known as 'the ancient universities' and also as 'the collegiate universities', comprising just two institutions: Oxford (established 1167) and Cambridge (1209).[1] In fact, it has to be confessed that this chapter is really about Oxford rather than Oxford *and* Cambridge, and this is mainly because it is based on the recently published book *Oxford and the Decline of the Collegiate Tradition*,[2] which in turn elaborates on the journal article 'Continuity and change in the collegial tradition'.[3] That said, much of what is asserted here about Oxford probably applies to Cambridge as well, and also gives a feel for how both of the ancient collegiate universities compare with the wider range of British universities. In essence, the chapter looks at the Oxford of the early twenty-first century, considers its exceptionalism within a mass higher education system, and speculates on what the Oxford of 2025 will be like.

The questions

Oxford and Cambridge remain, each at around 15,000 students (10,000 undergraduates and 5000 postgraduates), relatively large universities by British standards, but they are no longer the largest as they were until some 15 years ago when 'massification' began (cf. Manchester Metropolitan at 25,000 students: see Table 3.2, page 34). Indeed, their relative weight in terms of their share of the national number of students within UK HE has steadily declined throughout the twentieth century as other universities have been created.

But do they punch above their weight? If so, why? Might it be just their historical accumulation of endowment assets (kash) and the evolution of an 800-year 'brand image' (kudos) which leaves them, at present, outperforming other 'elites' on the Research Assessment Exercise (RAE) and total quality

assessment/Quality Assurance Agency (TQA/QAA) criteria? Are they, therefore, living on borrowed time as competition from UCL and Imperial
stiffens, and as upstarts like Warwick snap at their heels? If Warwick, Edinburgh, UCL and Nottingham had Oxbridge's extra cash from endowment
income and greater taxpayer funding in the form of college fees, would
they be more productive with it and soon eclipse Oxbridge in the RAE
scores? What if 'the big civics' as sleeping giants for the past 50 years awake?
Just how well placed are Oxford and Cambridge to be truly internationally
competitive, firmly in the same league as Harvard, Yale, Princeton and
Massachusetts Institute of Technology (MIT)? (But note the recent Cambridge–MIT link-up and the Oxford-Princeton-Stanford e-link . . .) What is
the Oxbridge recipe for success? Can it be copied for use elsewhere? Will it
continue to ensure perfectly baked and employable undergraduates emerging from the academic oven, and continue to provide solid scholarship and
fruitful research?

The model

Let's consider Oxford in terms of an inputs–processes–outputs performance
indicator (PI) model . . .

INPUTS	$\rightarrow$	PROCESSES or 'THE BLACK BOX'	$\rightarrow$	OUTPUTS
$\uparrow$		$\uparrow$		$\downarrow$
students (academic achievement/potential *and* 'social capital')		'the tutorial'		employable graduates + research
+ staff		+ 'peer pressure'		+ 'a wider social role'
+ infrastructure (including the concept of 'the collegiate university')		+ 'collegiality'		
+ money (extra taxpayer funding plus endowment income)				

We will take each ingredient of the recipe (the four inputs), then consider
the results (the three outputs), and finally explore the management theory
of what happens (the three processes) inside Oxford's listed building, stone-
faced, oak-beamed black box as the truly mysterious part of any set of
performance indicators! The detailed data supporting the assertions made
summarizing the statistics of inputs/outputs are to be found in the comparative information on UK HEIs published by the Higher Education Funding
Councils (HEFCs), Higher Education Statistics Agency (HESA) and CVCP,

as also used to compile the growing number of 'good university' guides (e.g. *Financial Times, Guardian, Times, The Higher,* etc.).

In the case of Oxford, however, it needs to be remembered that the resources of the colleges, in terms of an input to 'the black box', are not generally included in the data since their income and expenditure statements (the 'Franks Accounts' in a format dating from the 1960s) are not consolidated with the University accounts based on the 1990s HEFCE statement of recommended practice (SORP), and hence it is difficult to compare Oxford precisely with, say, Bristol or Birmingham. Similarly, not all outputs are captured in the published data. Thus, college spending on library books, IT, college lecturers, junior research fellows (JRFs), travel grants, vacation residence grants, book grants, housing allowance, cheap mortgages, joint purchase housing equity schemes, medical insurance, and research allowances may be unseen as inputs to 'the student teaching experience' or 'the remuneration package' for academics, just as the research output of entirely college-funded academic staff (mostly JRFs) may not be always fully credited within the RAE. In broad terms the published data will underestimate inputs at Oxbridge and hence inflate productivity, relative to other HEIs, until University and college accounts are properly combined for PI purposes. This is likely soon to happen, but at the time of writing there are some 'Keepers of the Flame' of the sanctity of the Franks Accounts who yet need persuading that even Oxford must move into the age of transparency and accountability, and that swift and decisive voluntary progress in the form of embracing the HEFCE SORP is better than being pushed and prodded towards reality! The days of delighting in Oxford's obfuscation are coming to an end. Many colleges will, in fact, rely on their own version of a set of management accounts, producing the statutory, archaic and obscurantist Franks Accounts only because they have to. (The college accounts position at Cambridge is even more amateurish: but radical change is also in the offing in 'the other place' . . .) Those against accounting changes fear that revealing all could encourage charges that Oxford has too much money, but any intelligent scrutiny would show that the yield taken on capital as 'the spend-rate' is in line with how the major US universities handle endowment, while the demonstrable infrastructure costs (including the need for costly refurbishment) of running 'the collegiate university' are probably in excess of Oxford's capital base: i.e. Oxford is *under-capitalized* for the volume of operational activity at 15,000 students it currently supports (and certainly compared with its US global competitors).

Inputs

Students arrive at Oxford in the traditional form: aged 18; 3 'good' A levels with entry points at an average of over 29 out of 30 (3 grade As at 10 points each); from resolutely middle-class backgrounds as revealed by home address postcodes; selected at college interview the previous December largely on academic achievement-to-date and interviewers' attempts to assess 'potential' as the tie-breaker among so many applicants of similar achievement-to-date, family and school background. How different is this undergraduate intake from that at other UK HEIs, and especially at other 'elite' universities? Entry A level scores drop away to 10 or 12 at the far end of the range of 100 or so HEIs, but the other 'elites' log in at around 25 or more: hardly dramatically lower than for Oxbridge. Similarly, most of the other 'elites' are not distinctly different in terms of the undergraduate intake analysed by state–independent school or according to residential area (postcodes) – Oxford, Cambridge, Imperial, Bristol, Edinburgh, UCL all admit fewer from state schools than their statistical 'benchmark' would expect, and take fewer from 'less affluent residential areas'. That said, 'nice' universities such as Oxford Brookes, and those in 'nice' places like Exeter and Bournemouth, also admit more than their fair share of students from private schools or from 'good' state schools in 'nice' areas. So much for widening participation, despite Oxford's increasing, sincere, imaginative (recruitment 'gigs' at the Manchester United ground!) and strenuous efforts at broadening 'access'. Access is rather more balanced at some 'elites' such as York and Warwick.

Will Oxford's attempts at access ever be immune to the allegation that they amount to little more than empty rhetoric or committed but ineffectual gestures? The cynic will argue that well-intentioned committees can deliver very little when the actual decision about whom to admit is atomized, with no guarantee of University policy being implemented at college level let alone at that of individual subject dons selecting their brood for next year.[4] Some dons (incidentally, not a widely used term in Cambridge, and less frequently heard in Oxford nowadays) will go in for a little 'social engineering' here and there; others will want an easy life and are hardly going to select candidates from little-known sixth forms whom they *may* think will need remedial teaching on arrival; one or two will unconsciously select in their own image; the naïve few will allegedly be taken in at interview by 'public school bullshitters' . . . (Indeed, as Mellanby speculates, this supposed bullshit factor may also partially explain 'the gender gap' in Oxford finals, whereby women do less well than men in scoring firsts in certain subjects; *Oxford Magazine* No. 176, pp. 2–4, Hilary Term 2000; see also Ryan, *Guardian*, 24 May 2000 and Dukes, *Oxford Magazine*, Week 4, pp. 5–8, Trinity Term 2000.) That said, the aggressive use of the European Convention on Human Rights as now to be fully assimilated into English Law by the Human Rights Act 1998, perhaps especially by way of 'horizontal effect', *may* severely challenge Oxford's admissions process (*Financial Times*, 3 October 2000): it would certainly challenge college culture and college bureaucracy to have to keep the *detailed* paper trail on why dons X and Y selected candidates A, B and C (and not E, F and G), and thereby *convincingly* and *retrospectively* demonstrate how the selection process carefully and *consistently* implemented an entirely rational and *plausible* admissions policy.

Perhaps, as far as interventionist-minded would-be reformers are concerned, until the admissions process is linked to taxpayer funding (or unavoidably haphazard selection by interview improved or ended!) nothing much will change in Oxford. If, and when, it does, there will be a need for colleges concerned about 'access' to provide (at their own expense using their charity funds for this charitable purpose) intensive summer schools staffed by experienced schoolteachers to prepare their 'freshers' from state schools so that they too can hit the academic deck running at the same speed as the best-prepared entrant from well-resourced sixth forms in independent schools where spending per child has been three times as much. Otherwise, with minor adjustments, Oxford will overall continue faithfully to serve Middle England, whether living in 'New Labour' Islington, 'Lib-Dem' Richmond or 'Portillo Tory' Woking, and whether educated at 'nice' state schools or at private schools, just as it always has done. The heads of independent schools have little to worry about: private schooling will remain a well-oiled fast track to Oxford and, less so, Cambridge (but also to most other 'elites'), and thence to solid careers – even if nowadays only for the academically able with 29 points.[5] Thus, applicants to Oxford educated in an independent system catering for less than 10 per cent of children will continue, despite the access rhetoric now slowly and painfully becoming meaningful action, to monopolize more than their statistical share of the fresher intake.

The conservative reader may well feel that is as it should be: it is not Oxford's job belatedly to try and correct the deep deficiencies of UK state education which has a spend per pupil at secondary level some £500 pa less than the EU average of £3145 on 1998 OECD figures; nor the proper concern of government to lean on elite universities to distort their admissions in the name of political correctness. Similarly, when Chancellor Brown hits out in a surprisingly Old Labour way at Oxford's 'scandal' of an admissions system (*Times*, front page, 26 May 2000 and, for example, *Sunday Times*, 28 May 2000 and 4 June 2000), the true scandal is ignored: the refusal of New Labour after several years in power properly to fund UK state schools. Those concerned with social equity, however, will be disturbed that UK HE (and especially at the elite end) is very largely a middle-class (virtually) 'free good' funded disproportionately by working-class taxpayers whose children finish education at 16 – see the *Times*, 10 April 2000, for a scathing critique of social exclusion at 'leading universities' in the front page lead article, in an editorial, and in an article by Peter Lampl as the Chair of the Sutton Trust. Mr Lampl pulls no punches: 'a scandalous waste of talent' and 'a mindless waste of talent' which 'if anything is getting worse' despite efforts by the Sutton Trust 'to overcome social inequality in education'. Thus the age participation rate (APR) at 18 for the children of the AB professional and managerial classes has risen to around 85 per cent with the massification of UK HE over the past 15 years, while the APR for the offspring of the manual workers has remained stubbornly stuck at around 15 per cent. So, while the middle classes complain about paying more tax and their student children protest about university tuition fees, they monopolize the best of UK HE just as they grab the best of NHS healthcare (as noted by Freedland in 'Closing the Privilege Gap', *Guardian*, 31 May 2000).

Anyway private schooling and a 'good' postcode mean enhanced 'social capital' on entry,[6] and Oxford's undergraduates (high achievers, self-motivated, well-connected, worldly-wise) go on to become highly employable graduates in City law firms, in 'the City' itself, in management consultancy, and in accountancy. The vice-chancellor of a Thames Valley or a Derby may well then ask whether this translation from middle-class upbringing to middle-class careers is not preordained and hence what 'added value' Oxford provides with all its resources, compared with the teaching and learning (stained concrete) 'black box' in his HEI which also produces II(i)s (assuming, of course, a degree is a degree is a degree . . .), and does so on a staff–student ratio of half that at Oxbridge!

Staff, or Oxford's dons, are increasingly difficult to recruit and retain: unlimited port in the Senior Common Room by a roaring log fire after a fine dinner in Hall does not make up for a feeble academic salary or help pay the mortgage in a city where house prices rival those in fashionable London suburbia in the catchment area of its few 'good' (defined as achieving entry to elite HEIs!) state secondary schools. The attractions are clear: working in a world-class university alongside stimulating colleagues; a supply of good research students; teaching bright undergraduates; slightly better pay than (wage-for-age) the salary scales at other UK universities; varying levels of perks at different colleges. (NB: Cambridge academics are generally paid less than their Oxford counterparts, and receive fewer of the perks within 'the college package' as referred to above.)

But the downside is a tutorial teaching load in colleges of 12 hours per week for a full 24-week teaching year for arts academics, and six hours per week for science academics (and hence with a greater departmental teaching load than for arts colleagues). This 12-hour teaching load is probably higher than for colleagues at other elite universities, and in addition Oxford academics in tutorial teaching have to teach across a wider range of the degree subject than will usually be expected elsewhere; also Oxford's academics are generally more research active (a higher percentage of them were entered into the last RAE than for any other UK HEI), and they probably carry more minor administrative duties than colleagues elsewhere. They are thus, thanks more to peer pressure and self-motivation rather than being managed within a formal academic hierarchy, arguably worth their small extra premium in salary/allowances. Indeed, some would argue that Oxford's productivity could be improved in the humanities departments not by convoluted changes in governance nor by massive expenditure on faculty/departmental office blocks, but by the simple expedient of relieving its arts academics of Noddy administrative tasks which they perform amateurishly, and instead having them undertaken more cheaply, more competently and at less opportunity cost by junior administrators and clerical officers.

Yet, as the modern academic profession becomes increasingly specialized and segmented, even fragmented, research counts for far more than teaching, and so the challenge to 'the collegiate university' is whether academics want to be bothered with a heavy undergraduate teaching load and the (petty?) burdens of college business, compared with seeking out a research professorship at another elite university. Will Oxford (and indeed other UK elites) end up with undergraduates being largely taught by graduate students, as is allegedly the case at top US universities where the famous-name academics are too busy being famous to teach routine first-degree courses? Or might the academic profession's enthusiasm for the cult of research be indulged by a refinement in 'the joint contract' (University lectureship plus college fellowship) to allow for some academics to be relieved of teaching duties while they are most productive in RAE terms, while others beyond their RAE sell-by date can pursue a rewarding, *and well-rewarded*, career as a college tutorial teacher (while, of course, keeping up their 'scholarship')? If, however, Oxford can't offer the right package to recruit and retain good academics (and its half-baked, one-off, meagre merit-pay scheme floated for consultation in mid-2000 – and now wisely junked – is certainly not a sign of Oxford getting its managerial act together; see Palfreyman in *Oxford Magazine* No. 180, p. 10, Trinity Term 2000), then how quickly might things wind down once the third or fourth choice applicants have been appointed in the face of refusals from the preferred candidates? How long before mediocre appointments at professorial level appoint juniors unlikely to challenge or embarrass them? Could Oxford's reputation as a world-class university be lost in a generation, by 2025, if it does not soon tackle its remuneration package and the working conditions for its academic staff? And universities are not just collections of academics in different subject groups united solely by a common grievance over car parking or by a shared central heating system and email server – universities also need competent support staff (technicians, librarians, secretaries), who also must cope with Oxford house prices and hence the University will increasingly face the same recruitment and retention problems that the Oxford hospitals face in relation to nurses or Oxford schools in relation to teachers.

Infrastructure is the next key input. The University may be a mass of splendid listed buildings in an historic city, but they are expensive to maintain, some are not easily adapted to modern uses, sites for new buildings are increasingly scarce, and getting planning permission for new building is a fraught process in a city full of well-off Nimbies (not in my back yard!). Certainly the civics in major conurbations with 'brownfield' development land, and the 1960s campus universities surrounded by 'greenfield' development land, are better placed for expansion. Will Oxford split into a core undergraduate teaching university at the heart of the dreaming spires, and a series of research institutes in rural locations? Unless Oxford University succeeds in competing with private housing and commercial uses to purchase the redundant Radcliffe Infirmary site in the city centre for £75 million or so from the Hospital Trust, it is difficult to see how such a core–satellite model for the future of Oxford can be avoided. On the other hand, academic staff working at satellite sites may prefer the convenience of an easy car journey to work and of free parking to the temptation of deserting the laboratory and strolling to college for a free lunch! On balance, Oxford's historic infrastructure is probably a plus in input terms compared with other UK elites, but it is not necessarily going to remain so in the face of a potential polarization into the Liberal Arts teaching undergraduate collegiate university and the Big Science research graduate departmental university.

Money, however, is clearly the key differential as an advantageous input compared with other UK elites, even if there are additional costs in operating within the architectural charms and quirks of the listed building infrastructure. The extra money comes from two sources: an academic fee premium paid mainly by the UK taxpayer, and income from charitable endowment assets. Combining the two provides an example of the creative mixing of public and private funding currently so trendy as 'the third way'. Oxford, of course, also receives very substantial research grant and contract income, but this is not meant to generate a profit or to be used to subsidize teaching. Indeed, if anything, the reality is that such research activity is a drain on the other sources of income, since the grants come with little allowance for overheads. In this respect Oxford is no different from most research-driven HEIs.

The extra taxpayer funding takes the shape of the college fee of around £3500 per undergraduate student per year of the three/four year degree course, and about £1500 a year for a postgraduate. This fee for undergraduate UK/EU students is now paid by the University to the colleges using additional money from the Higher Education Funding Council for England (HEFCE) transferred to it by the Department for Education and Employment (DfEE). In fact, because HEFCE already reduced the University block grant by some 40 per cent of the college academic fees hitherto collected by colleges directly from LEAs in the name of undergraduates, the nett extra taxpayer funding to Oxford and Cambridge is about £2000 per UK/EU undergraduate each year over other British universities (although London institutions also get special treatment). This amount is due to be reduced by one-third over ten years.[7]

The justification for any extra funding at all is the fact that Oxford and Cambridge function inside a museum of architectural history with unavoidable inefficiencies and inevitably higher costs, and that colleges do from their own endowment resources provide junior research fellow posts which contribute to the nation's quantum of academic activity. Plus, if in one small island, we want to continue to have two of the half-dozen world-class universities, somebody has to pay up, be it Mr Taxpayer, the student consumer and his/her proud parents, impending employers, or kindly benefactors. If the last, preferably – as Lord Beloff once put it – dead medieval bishops rather than an interfering Mr Maxwell![8]

These founder/benefactor-created endowment resources are the other main source of income for the colleges side of 'the collegiate university'.

Each college, as an autonomous, eleemosynary, chartered, perpetual corporation aggregate and exempt charity run by the quasi-trustee fellows as the Governing Body,[9] has permanent endowment capital, the bulk of which will probably date back to its foundation and the assets with which it was endowed by its founder. The total value (at 1999 valuations) of the income-earning endowment assets held within the Oxford colleges is around £2 billion, the richest college tipping in at close to £150 million and the poorest at less than £10 million. Cambridge's overall figure is similar, but there the richest comes in at around £450 million[10] – although that very wealthy charitable corporation (Trinity) is remarkably generous to its poorer Cambridge brethren, as well as funding the Newton Trust which stimulates research activity across the University. These are crude estimates, the capital values not being revealed in the Franks Accounts (as would be required under the Charities SORP for any perpetual charity needing to be registered with the Charity Commissioners, and not being an exempt charity), and hence one can only extrapolate from the Endowment Income figure on the basis that a prudent college will take an annual yield of around 4 per cent as its 'spend rate'.[11]

The University itself has much less (around £500 million) by way of endowment and most of that figure is held on trust for specific purposes X, Y, Z, with, as it were, strings attached, *not* being 'free' money for use entirely at the University's discretion. In 1998/99 the University itself had a total income of £320 million, of which only 9 per cent was from endowment; for the colleges the figures were, respectively, £145 million and 30 per cent. Thus, Oxford as 'the collegiate university' (University plus colleges), along with Cambridge, is the only UK HEI with any serious amount of the long-term endowment needed to provide at least some insulation from over-dependence on the state. By US standards, however, neither Oxford nor Cambridge is well-endowed, each at, say, £2.5 billion, compared with Harvard, Yale, MIT, Princeton, etc., all at rather more, and exceeding £10 billion for Harvard. That said, Oxford has its Oxford University Press (OUP) as a successful £250 million turnover trading operation, generating around £25 million a year profits which can be ploughed back into the parent body, the University itself.[12]

In short, Oxford is rich by UK and European HEI norms, but not rich by US elite university standards (or rather, Oxford would feel richer if it were smaller and did not dilute its endowment across twice as many undergraduates than, say, Princeton!). One major problem for its competing with the US Ivy League is that UK elites are unable to charge 'top-up' academic fees.[13] To remain competitive more money has to go in, and in a low(ish) tax political climate the only source of such extra funding has to be higher student fees charged by the elites (thereby, sadly but inevitably, (re)introducing into UK HE the same public–private divide that characterizes the schools' end of the UK's education system). Moreover, in considering the cost to the student of UK HE, we have to note that it is relatively high by EU standards partly because the courses are shorter and hence more intensive and with less scope for the student to be in part-time paid employment while study-ing full-time, but also partly because the Oxbridge residential model has become dominant. This is the idea of HE as not merely the earning of a degree but also as a lifestyle experience, as a rites-of-passage process for the 18–21 year old, as Newman's nineteenth-century Oxford created civilised young gentlemen.[14] And this extra cost of the residential accommodation makes the introduction of even a modest charge for the academic content seem too much of a burden, while, of course, no other OECD country barely tries to fund a decent quality mass HE system solely via the taxpayer.

Although there will be management problems in fixing the price of de-grees from elite to elite (and possibly even subject by subject within each elite), and although (rightly) Oxford will need to redeploy some of its new fee income in the form of loans and bursaries to allow for 'needs-blind' selection of students in order to achieve fair access, the end result should be more nett cash with which to run the University. If there is not more nett cash, then the introduction of top-up fees will merely have meant the students of 'rich' families paying three times so that those from 'poor' families need pay only twice while Her Majesty's Government (HMG) tax-payer funding can be reduced still further. The taxpayer will have to con-tinue to put in funding at the standardized 'university voucher' rate, with some transfer from 'rich' to 'poor' via fee-financed bursaries as also supple-mented from charitable endowment assets, but with *all* students being of-fered extra loan capacity to enhance the HMG 'nationalized' Student Loans Company (SLC) 'cap' to student borrowing. And that extra loan money could come from a pool of corporate bond capital borrowed at a fine rate of interest by the elites collectively on behalf of their student clientele who in turn will borrow from 'ivyleaguestudentloans.com' at a margin above that fine rate to allow for bad debt. In short, the existing US student fund-ing package! Thus, Tom Brown and Jude *will* go to Oxford, and preferably not as 'servitors' earning their scholarships by waiting at Hall table on their rich aristocratic fellow undergraduates.[15] But whether Tom and Jude need to be given grants and bursaries is debatable: making available private loan capacity to top-up government loans and to be repaid when they duly emerge as well-paid management consultants and City lawyers may suffice, *providing* the loan debt is written off *if* they enter poorly paid careers such as school teaching and academe.

Given Oxford's kudos perhaps a premium price over other elites to reflect the value of a premium product can be commanded also from students themselves as it currently is from the taxpayer by way of college fees – but then there will be the issue of 'quality control' over the idiosyncratic tutorial system as students paying serious fees become empowered consumers demanding value-for-money. Thus, given this extra fee revenue, Oxford's money input will be even more favourably skewed relative to most other UK HEIs. The key question is, then, whether its outputs reflect that level of financial input, or whether other HEIs, perhaps with better black-box pro-cesses, could achieve more output given that higher level of financial input.

Outputs

Employable graduates is Oxbridge's key output, whatever academics may feel about the value of their research activity, in terms of the need for the University to serve society and the economy. Oxford's graduates remain immensely employable, given the mix of intelligence, motivation, achievement at school, 'social capital' networking before and while at Oxford and (crucially if the Oxford teaching process is to add anything to that already potent mix) of being worked hard and consistently in the intensive tutorial teaching system (three essays each fortnight of 3–4000 words for arts/social studies students). The graduate output emerges as oven-ready for the world of work as any HEI is likely to get them and hence duly finds its way into well-paid careers within City law firms, 'the City' itself, management consultancy, accountancy, and, among rather lesser paid professions, apprenticeship for academic life in the form of PhD study. A few, as with elite US HEIs, once moved quickly into 'dot-com' business ventures – or even launched them while still undergraduates (*Guardian*, 8 February 2000). One or two publish their first novel while still at college and get a substantial advance for the next! Compared with the 1970s, few 1990s Oxford graduates found their way into the public services, especially school teaching.

It is debatable, therefore, whether Oxford should tinker too much with the content of and teaching techniques for its degrees in an attempt to add 'transferable skills' as currently and vaguely defined by such as the Confederation of British Industry (CBI), lest in doing so it dilutes the rigour of the degrees' academic core values by trying to do what it has neither the real inclination nor the resources and expertise to achieve. If employers want Oxford's English or modern languages graduates to have a working knowledge of statistics, business economics and marketing terminology, then it is for *their* induction programmes to impart the skills. If what employers mean by 'transferable skills' is the ability to relate to a wide range of fellow human beings, to 'problem solve', and to work within teams, then they must test the applicants in relation to their pre-Oxford experience, their involvement in extra-curricular sporting and cultural activity at Oxford, and their performance in appropriate interviews.

Research is, however, clearly what the Oxford branch of the clerisy cares most about and, as Table 3.1 in David Holmes's chapter shows, they are very successful in getting research funding, but are they properly productive in their utilization of this largesse? Certainly in terms of the RAE they are successful, but more so than the output other elites could have achieved with the same money? Johnes and Taylor[16] have explored this in that, 'using regression models to estimate the output that each university could be expected to produce given the inputs available to it' (p. 172), they *tentatively* suggest that Oxford should be doing rather better with its research output than it actually manages given the generally privileged flow of inputs from which it benefits (Table 10.1, p. 176). Thus, instead of the actual position on the 1989 (*sic!*) UGC research ratings of 1st and 2nd, respectively, for Cambridge and Oxford, the revised rating is 22nd and 21st, with other universities like Aston, Bradford, Essex, UMIST and Strathclyde surging up the table – while, of course, Warwick slips assuredly into first place! That said, Johnes and Taylor themselves would not want too much read into this one PI, or indeed any PI and anyway 1989 is now a rather long time ago!

It has to be recognized, therefore, that the Oxford RAE output is indeed impressive, especially given the demands of tutorial teaching and of college duties on the core joint contract university lecturer/college tutorial fellow academic staff. Moreover, both Oxford and especially 'silicon-fen' Cambridge have been immensely active and successful in spinning off profitable high-tech companies within certain academic areas, creating millionaire dons and juicy windfalls for each of the two ancient universities. The Oxford colleges are now joining in via a multi-million pound innovation investment fund channelled through the University's existing venture-capital operation. Thus, beneath seemingly fuddy-duddy cloistered calm lurks cutting-edge science shrewdly and profitably applied.

'*A wider social role*' is an emotive issue to discuss in a supposedly egalitarian society, but if higher education (like Premier League football or Olympic-level sport) is necessarily elitist then Oxford (together with a handful of other UK elite HEIs) has the job of taking the best students (*carefully and fairly selected*) and coaching them (*in a very demanding and intensive way*) using academic staff who are themselves the best available. It is still, and always has been, a nursery for the nation's leaders, in most if not all walks of life; a finishing school for proto-leaders. It would fail the talent sent to it, and in turn the nation, if it were staffed by second-rate academics on third-rate salaries, and failed to demand of those talented students less than total commitment and prolonged hard work in order to earn the Oxford degree, which, clearly, must never be 'dumbed-down'. Fine words: but sustainable concepts? And anyway, how readily does a robust commitment to academic rigour fit with the government's agenda on 'social inclusion'?

Processes

The tutorial is the key feature of this demanding and intensive learning experience vital to the proper use of that talent. Occasionally it does not work: academically sub-standard tutors, weak tutors, lazy tutors, boring tutors, alcoholic tutors, not prepared to or able to demand a vigorous pace from their tutees; or lazy students, dim students, alcoholic and 'substance abusing' students, not able to keep pace. It certainly does not work if the academics lose interest in teaching 'the young', or if they retreat to the research closet, or if they lack the intellectual nerve and agility to teach across a reasonably broad range of the degree discipline's spectrum and instead have the confidence and desire to teach only their increasingly narrow specialism based on their research expertise. It is unlikely, however, that teaching at other HEIs, given that they lack the financial resources to provide Oxford's favourable staff–student ratio, could generate from students the same amount of written work produced on a regular basis, thereby inculcating not only the ability to cope with a sustained volume of work set to deadlines which is needed for any high-powered career but also a competence in the process of assimilation–distillation–expression so necessary for success in almost every walk of life, and perhaps even more so in an 'information age'.

It is a pity, therefore, that Oxford's lip-service to the value of the sacred-cow tutorial system is rarely backed up by a proper analysis of its pedagogy: for example, note the absence of such an analysis in the North Report, 1997, Oxford's latest effort at organizational navel-gazing.[17] Perhaps Oxford's new HEFCE-funded Institute for the Advancement of University Learning will be better able to articulate the pedagogy of the Oxford tutorial as a key feature of the University's version of 'the learning experience'? If it does not, Oxford is left spluttering with indignation, but rather ineffectually, when confronted with allegations that the tutorial jewel in its pedagogical crown is mere paste.

It is a further pity that Oxford's archaic examination system is only slowly catching up with more sophisticated norms elsewhere, as an article in the *Oxford Magazine* noted in calling for an increase in 'both the diversity and the spread of assessment' to provide a fairer means of testing the student learning experience: 'It is absurd that a university possessing, in tutorial teaching, the world's finest educational system, should choose to assess the academic quality and achievements of its pupils by asking them to regurgitate as much as they can remember of the tutorial essays nearest in subject to the [exam] questions at furious handwriting speed, over half a dozen or more three hour sessions spanning just a few days . . .' (Tom Kemp, 'Widening the Range and Spreading the Load', *Oxford Magazine*, No. 175, Hilary Term 2000). If there is any value at all for Oxford in the bureaucracy of QAA visitations, then at least the presence of academics from other universities might challenge the insularity regarding assessment methodology within some (not all) of Oxford's subject areas, which can suffer from the incestuousness of appointing faculty drawn substantially from Oxford or Cambridge and with little or no experience of teaching and examining elsewhere in the system. (Cambridge, in contrast, has a wider range of assessment methods and has annual exams rather than 'Big Bang' Finals.)

Peer pressure is an important element within the black box, both in terms of motivating academics (especially in competition over research) but also in respect of students maintaining 'internal' standards. Thus, occasionally a whole year group in subject X or Y at college A or B can seemingly go off the boil academically, a virus spreading among them creating a 'get away with the minimum' attitude that is not always firmly dealt with by the relevant tutors (backed up by the senior tutor and the head of house) declaring fiercely that this minimum just will not do! In the end, all the TQA, QAA and RAE audit, assessment and inspection in the world in relation to faculty similarly going off the boil is but a cumbersome, expensive and ineffective substitute for truly rigorous self-policing among a vigorous profession which retains its self-respect and intellectual integrity intact – a difficult process at any time as all professions tend to drift towards being lazy conspiracies against the laity, but especially so when UK academics have been systematically devalued by politicians and a wider society for 20 years or more.[18]

Collegiality as a feature of the black box takes several forms, the first as the usual interaction among faculty in going about their routine professional lives. Here for humanities and social studies academics there may be *less* collegiality at Oxford than for colleagues at other universities, given that Oxford does not generally have departmental buildings except those in the sciences. Thus, for example, history academics at Oxford are scattered among the colleges; they meet periodically at the Faculty Board; they have a departmental/faculty secretary and only a few rooms for professors; they are not all gathered together along a corridor of offices on the third floor of the Arts Block as at, say, Warwick; and they have no easy coming-together over coffee or around the departmental photocopier. It is doubtful, moreover, that there is much reality in the compensatory view that the theoretical synergy of, say, chemistry dons lunching or dining next to physics dons or engineering dons in the colleges gives rise in practice to exciting interdisciplinary initiatives less able to spring forth at other places.

The second form of collegiality is as academic *demos* (one don, one vote). Here Oxford scores: the academics really are in charge; the academic lunatics *do* run the University of Oxford asylum! Unlike every other UK HEI, except Cambridge, the academics *are* the University. En masse in Congregation they are the sovereign body as 'the dons' Parliament'. The rank-and-file 'back-bencher' dons really can challenge and control the vice-chancellor and Council as their executive: they can and indeed do say 'non placet' to proposals from the University's 'great and good', such as the ill-fated and ill-judged recommendation that Mrs Thatcher should get the usual Honorary Degree awarded to an Oxford alumnus serving as Prime Minister.[19] There is no lay majority control via Council, and only very recently as part of the North reforms any lay members of Council. Similarly, Cambridge recently rejected in its Regents' House an executive proposal to have even a token lay presence, but see Edwards, *Cambridge University Reporter* 901 (21 June 2000), for a warning that Cambridge is well on the way to destroying its 'traditional democratic processes' now seen by 'management' as merely 'a disposable luxury'!

Yet if all this means Oxford has only itself to blame for allegedly poor management, there is still an amusing tendency for its academics at the chalkface to talk of 'They', as if there really were a set of aliens imposing their will on hapless academics.[20] At college level the governance position on a much smaller scale is even clearer: the 40 or so fellows *are* the corporation aggregate and (subject to the Charter and Statutes) sovereignty *does* really lie with them when in Governing Body chaired by the warden/principal/ president that they elect as 'first amongst equals' (see Notes 9 and 26).

In essence, it is the debate about where the optimal position is for an *effective* (as opposed perhaps to an efficient and economical!) HEI on the collegiality–managerialism governance spectrum (in US terms, shared-values–corporatist). How is the right balance achieved between, on the one hand, consultation and participation and, on the other, decisiveness, responsiveness, flexibility and agility? As Roger Brown, Principal of South-ampton Institute of Higher Education, expressed it in a lecture at Goldsmiths College (11 March 1999): 'All institutions operate in an uneasy equilibrium between would-be managerialism and supposed collegiality.' In Oxford, at present, collegiality is more real than supposed – but for how much longer?[21]

Third is collegiality as college life,[22] 'the cult of collegiality' so strongly represented in the genre of the university novel and in TV drama such as 'Inspector Morse';[23] its physical manifestation is the quadrangle and the staircase, the chapel and the gargoyles, the clipped lawns and polished silver on High Table.[24] (Incidentally, for the University of Warwick, thinly disguised in novel form and also turned into TV drama, see the two novels by Andrew Davies,[25] and for Oxbridge colleges in recent fiction the essen-tial references must, of course, be Snow,[26] with Sharpe,[27] and Stewart.[28]) But do busy RAE and QAA dons have time for this form of collegiality: for serving on college committees, for minding the college silver, for being Seneschal of Hall or the Outrider (*sic!*) at New College, for taking on a major college office such as senior tutor or dean? Is this aspect of collegiality merely a Victorian leftover; an anachronism which is charming but costly, quaint and quirky but questionable in an age of accountability and value-for-money?

Finally, and fourth, there is collegiality as a way of breaking up a large university into human-sized chunks of 250–450 undergraduates, giving them college identity and endless opportunity to enhance their CVs by 'officering' the 30-plus college junior common rooms (JCRs), drama societies, boat clubs, tiddlywinks teams, etc., as well as providing the tutorial teaching already discussed. Would these 'junior members', however, be happier with grander discos, larger bars and cheaper booze in a lavish, centrally located, University-provided Students' Union?

But, whatever form collegiality takes and especially in terms of collegiality as colleges, and even if much of the extra cost of collegiality is covered from private charitable endowment rather than by public money or students personally paying academic fees and accommodation charges, the ques-tions will always be there (and rightly so). Is collegiality, as expressed within the colleges' side of the collegiate university, value-for-money? Does it add value? Or should that £2 billion of endowment capital locked within the colleges be redeployed to the departmental University, used to buy better labs and more kit for the scientists, to provide departmental corridors and coffee lounges for the arts dons so as to stimulate that first dimension of collegiality? Or, as Pattison proposed way back to the second nineteenth-century Royal Commission on Oxford and Cambridge, should the colleges become the faculty centres – New College as the History or Law College/Department? Or should Oxford simply become another big civic, reducing the colleges to merely listed building halls of residence, stripped of their teaching role, of their autonomy, and of their endowment? Certainly Robert Stevens, Master of Pembroke College, Oxford, sees the Oxbridge colleges as already doomed, their fate sealed by Baroness Blackstone building on 'the centralizing tendencies of Mrs Thatcher' and nationalizing them in 1998: 'Within 10 or 20 years, colleges will be glorified halls of residence, even if most dons have yet to notice. For the Oxbridge colleges "top-up" fees will come too late . . .' (*Financial Times*, p. 23, 5 April 2000). Clearly, the ultimate questions are: 'So what?' and 'Who cares?'!

Of course, all this discussion about the future of 'the collegiate university' may seem very parochial. So consider another 'big issue' for Oxford and Cambridge (and indeed for all the other UK elites with a global brand image): coping with the globalization of HE and the emergence of the cyber-university. Should they capitalize on their international kudos by offering their degrees on the Internet? And, if so, how? By joining forces with a commercial media organization such as Pearson willing to match its investment 'kash' to their academic 'kudos' in the way that universities such as Michigan and Colombia have linked with the likes of TimeWarner and Microsoft? Or by collaborating with their major US competitors to carve up the market place – witness 'Worldwide Universities Network' and 'Universitas 21' already emerging to challenge the University of Phoenix, Jones University and Western Governors University competition? Where would an Oxford e-degree from 'learning@oxon.com' leave the requirement for undergraduate residence in a college? Could 2025 see the need for a virtual-reality e-college in the form of 'cybercoll@new.com'? Indeed, a *Financial Times* article ('Online university challenge', 17 June 2000) mused that, ironically, the Oxbridge federal University–colleges model, currently out of fashion and threatened, might be the way forward for the e-university of 2025! Or, e-branding aside, and like the UK motor industry, will Oxford and Cambridge survive simply and happily as the last special niche viable bits after the globalization of UK HE? Oxford as a solid and stylish Land Rover, Cambridge as the sleek Jaguar with 'go-faster strips', leaving room for a Morgan or two, and perhaps scope downmarket for a Reliant Robin!

Conclusion

Clearly I'd like to think that the colleges add value; that as a further dimension to this complex organism, 'the university', they provide another source of initiative and creativity; that the research departmental University and the teaching colleges are in a state of creative tension, and that thereby at micro-level Oxford has the same rich diversity the UK HE system needs nationally to adapt constantly to and flourish within a complex and ever-changing wider world. But as Oxford, following the 1997 North Report,[29] introduces full-time 'heads of division' (deans) to be installed in a tasteful bunker on St Giles, allocates HEFCE money to the colleges on the basis of a 'contract' between University and colleges, redraws its committee organogram in an attempt to be managerially efficient, and rewrites the University/college joint academic contract, the jury must remain out as to whether all this simply means rearranging the deckchairs on the Titanic. Or signals a shift to a more (better?) managed University operating along HEI normal (top-down?) lines. Or means throwing out an (unappreciated?) collegial baby with the (over-valued?) managerial bathwater. Or means that Oxford will reinvent itself and the collegial tradition in a robust new format well able to face the twenty-first century as it has survived, and at times flourished, for the past eight centuries. Tapper and Palfreyman[30] in their Postscript put money on the last route as the way things will shape up by 2025. If so, collegiality would remain a valuable component process within Oxford's black box, and Oxford's exceptionalism would not just be based on its extra inputs by way of money, student talent and faculty strength.

Between now and then the members of the present generation of academic *demos* bear a heavy strategic, managerial and custodial burden as they struggle to get the crucial balance between 'top-down' and 'bottom-up', to facilitate creativity, to recruit and retain able academics, to fend off intrusive 'control-freak' government, to keep Oxford world-class as, in effect, a first-rate US Liberal Arts undergraduate teaching university (the colleges)[31] embedded within a strong research university (the departments). If all these objectives could be achieved simply by a plentiful supply of well-meaning, committed, honest committee folk, all 'sound chaps' and each equipped with a pair of 'safe hands', then Oxford will be fine – except that the surfeit of safe hands on the governance deck of the 'SS Oxford' has had hitherto an unfortunate tendency to steer the elegant vessel most decisively into the midst of any doldrums to be found! Certainly Cambridge in recent years appears to have trounced Oxford in the image stakes, presenting itself in the media as the quality university blessed also with strategic vision, and with a charismatic vice-chancellor at the helm. So, if managerial competence, tactical flair, and strategic vision are also required, Oxford faces a challenge, and a new batch of less 'grey', less 'sound', less 'safe', and less 'clubby male' talent needs to find its way into all corners of the committee organogram and of Wellington Square (and indeed into the colleges where a robust vision and sound leadership are also needed); style and culture must change as much as structure and organization. In essence, Oxford needs more grit in its decision-making system in order to avoid the inertia and complacency that characterizes a committee system dominated by the stuffy and somnolent 'great and good'. Happily there are some signs that this is beginning to happen[32] . . . So watch out Warwick, for Oxford – newly energized as the Wellington Square centre adds value by *crucially* not managing but merely facilitating existing widespread creativity and competence at the departmental and college periphery – might reopen that gap which you have so assiduously and successfully narrowed over the last 20 years . . .

So, Oxford in a nutshell for budding management consultants? Seemingly utterly uneconomic and inexorably inefficient, but in reality eerily effective. *Utterly uneconomic* – all those expensive-to-maintain listed buildings: sell off to Disneyland as a theme park and relocate to the redundant US Air Force base at Upper Heyford 20 miles away? *Inexorably inefficient* – all that one-to-two undergraduate teaching: exploit the brand image to the full by going all out for the cyber-degree delivered by a small core of (casual-contract) academic staff based at Upper Heyford? *Eerily effective* – make a note to try and work out which bits of the 800-year-old recipe for success are the vital ones before tinkering and defenestrating academic babies with managerialist bathwater . . .

Notes and References

1. A. Cobban (1988) *The Medieval English Universities: Oxford and Cambridge to c1500*. Aldershot: Scolar Press.
2. T. Tapper and D. Palfreyman (2000) *Oxford and the Decline of the Collegiate Tradition*. London: Woburn Press.
3. T. Tapper and D. Palfreyman (1998) Continuity and change in the collegial tradition, *Higher Education Quarterly*, 52 (2): 139–61. See also A.H. Halsey (1992) *Decline of Donnish Dominion*. Oxford: Clarendon Press; T. Tapper and B. Salter (1992) *Oxford, Cambridge and the Changing Idea of the University: The Challenge to Donnish Domination*. Buckingham: SRHE/Open University Press; and J. Rose and J. Ziman (1964) *Camford Observed*. London: Victor Gollancz.
4. See T. Tapper and D. Palfreyman (2000) op. cit., Chapter 4.
5. For Oxford's shift to a meritocratic intake see Chapter 2 of J.A. Soares (1999) *The Decline of Privilege: The Modernisation of Oxford University*. Stanford, CA: Stanford University Press.
6. P. Ainley (1994) *Degrees of Difference: Higher Education in the 1990s*. London: Lawrence and Wishart; P. Brown and R. Scase (1994) *Higher Education and Corporate Realities*. London: UCL Press. For discussion of access issues in US higher education see T.J. Kane (1999) *The Price of Admission: Rethinking How Americans Pay for College*. Washington, DC: Brookings Institution Press, and New York, NY: Russell Sage Foundation. The US has the same problem of 'lower' classes being under-represented in HE.
7. For discussion of how 'the ancient universities' ably lobbied to defend their privileges, see pp. 298–303 of N. Annan (1999) *The Dons*. London: HarperCollins.
8. For the story of how the University got Lord Nuffield to endow a college full of economists and sociologists when he'd hoped to have engineers, see B. Harrison (ed.) pp. 647–8 of *History of the University of Oxford: Volume VIII, The Twentieth Century* (1994). Oxford: OUP.
9. D. Palfreyman (1995/96) Oxbridge fellows as charity trustees, *Charity Law and Practice Review*, 3 (3): 187–202; D. Palfreyman (1998/99) Oxford colleges: permanent endowment, charity trusteeship and personal liability, *Charity Law and Practice Review*, 5 (2): 85–134; D. Palfreyman (1999) Is Porterhouse really 'a charity'?, *Charity Law and Practice Review*, 6 (1): 75–87.

10. For 1997 figures see pp. 192 and 194 of D. Hobson (1999) *The National Wealth: Who Gets What in Britain.* London: HarperCollins. Hobson *probably* underestimates capital values.

11. T. Tapper and D. Palfreyman (2000) op. cit., Chapter 7.

12. For the story of similar income generation at the University of Warwick see D. Palfreyman (1989) The Warwick way: a case study of innovation and entrepreneurship within a university context, *Journal of Entrepreneurship and Regional Development,* 1 (2): 207–19 (partially reproduced in Chapters 3 and 4 of CUA (1992) *Universities in the Marketplace.* Manchester: CUA/Touche Ross). See also Chapter 2 of Burton R. Clark (1998) *Creating Entrepreneurial Universities: Organizational Pathways of Transformation.* Oxford: IAU/Pergamon.

13. A.J. Ryan (1999) The American way, *Prospect,* August/September: 24–30; A.J. Ryan in inter alia, the *Independent,* 2 March 2000. See also the report by D. Greenaway and M. Haynes, University of Nottingham School of Economics prepared for the Russell Group on *Funding Universities to Meet National and International Challenges,* July 2000 (available electronically at www.nottingham.ac.uk/economics/funding). This report provides easily accessible UK and OECD data on the funding of HE, student fees, loans, access, etc.

14. J. Newman ([1852] 1965) *The Idea of a University.* London: Dent; S. Rothblatt (1997) An Oxonian 'idea' of a university: J.H. Newman and 'well-being', in M.G. Brock and M.C. Curthoys (eds) *History of the University of Oxford: Volume VI, Nineteenth-Century Oxford, Part I.* Oxford: OUP.

15. Thomas Hughes (1861) *Tom Brown at Oxford.* London: Macmillan; Thomas Hardy, (1895) *Jude the Obscure.* London: Osgood and McIlvane.

16. J. Johnes and J. Taylor (1990) *Performance Indicators in Higher Education.* Buckingham: SRHE/Open University Press.

17. For an intellectually rather more rigorous approach see Franks (1966) *University of Oxford: Report of Commission of Inquiry.* Oxford: OUP; and Chapter 6 of T. Tapper and D. Palfreyman (2000), op. cit., who observe that the only fully articulated defence of the tutorial system dates back to W.G. Moore (1968) *The Tutorial System and its Future.* Oxford: Pergamon Press.

18. See a range of material on the rise of the academic profession and its decline with the 1980s Thatcherite attack upon it: H. Perkin (1989) *The Rise of Professional Society.* London: Routledge; P. Scott (1989) Higher education, in D. Kavanagh and A. Seldon (eds) *The Thatcher Effect.* Oxford: OUP; J. Paxman (1991) *Friends in High Places: Who Runs Britain?* London: Penguin; S.R. Letwin (1992) *The Anatomy of Thatcherism.* London: Fontana; S. Jenkins (1995) *Accountable to None.* London: Penguin.

19. See J.A. Soares, op. cit., pp. 240–8, for an account of the Honorary Degree debacle.

20. For a critical assessment of academic life in the 'modern', 'managed', 'corporatist', and 'McDonald' 'Fordist' UK universities see R.C. Warren (1994) The collegiate ideal and the organisation of the new universities, *Reflections on Higher Education,* 6: 34–55; and A. Ryder (1996) Reform and UK higher education in the enterprise era, *Higher Education Quarterly,* 50 (1): 54–70. See also for a counterview D. Watson (2000) *Managing Strategy.* Buckingham: Open University Press.

21. For further discussion of a collegial approach within organizational structures see Chapter 2 of D. Warner and D. Palfreyman (1996) *Higher Education Management: The Key Elements.* Buckingham: SRHE/Open University Press; also M. Pattison (1868) *Suggestions on Academical Organisation.* Edinburgh: Edmonston and Douglas; J.L. Bess (1988) *Collegiality and Bureaucracy in the Modern University.*

New York, NY: Teachers College Press, Columbia University; R. Birnbaum (1988) *How Colleges Work*. San Francisco, CA: Jossey-Bass; W.H. Berquist (1992) *The Four Cultures of the Academy*. San Francisco, CA: Jossey-Bass; M. Trow (1994) *Managerialism and the Academic Profession: Quality and Control*. London: Open University Quality Support Centre; J. Dearlove (1995a) Collegiality, managerialism and leadership in English universities, *Journal of Tertiary Education and Management*, 1 (2): 161–9; I. McNay (1995) From collegial academy to corporate enterprise: the changing cultures of universities, in T. Schuller (ed.) *The Changing University*. Buckingham: SRHE/Open University Press; C. Hardy (1996) *The Politics of Collegiality: Retrenchment Strategies in Canadian Universities*. Montreal: McGill-Queen's University Press; R. Deem (1998) New managerialism in higher education: the management of performance and cultures, *International Studies in the Sociology of Education*, 8 (1): 47–70; and in terms of governance see J. Dearlove (1995b) *Governance, Leadership, and Change in Universities*. Paris: UNESCO (IIEP); D. Palfreyman and D. Warner (1998; 2nd edn, Jordans, 2001) *Higher Education and the Law: A Guide for Managers*. Buckingham: SRHE/Open University Press; D. Braun and F.X. Merrien (1999) *Towards a New Model of Governance for Universities? A Comparative View*. London: Jessica Kingsley; D. Watson (2000) *Managing Strategy*. Buckingham: Open University Press. See also the classic and deservedly oft-reprinted F.M. Cornford ([1908] 1993) *Microsmographica Academia: Being a Guide for the Young Academic Politician*. Cambridge: Main Sail Press.
22. K. Dover (1994) *Marginal Comment*. London: Duckworth.
23. M. Proctor (1957) *The English University Novel*. Berkeley, CA: University of California Press; I. Carter (1990) *Ancient Cultures of Conceit: British University Fiction in the Post-war Years*. London: Routledge; J. Dougill (1998) *Oxford in English Literature: The Making and Undoing of 'The English Athens'*. Ann Arbor, MI: University of Michigan Press.
24. A. Duke (1996) *Importing Oxbridge: English Residential Colleges and American Universities*. New Haven, CT: Yale University Press.
25. A. Davies (1986) *A Very Peculiar Practice*. London: Coronet; (1988) *A Very Peculiar Practice: The New Frontier*. London: Methuen.
26. C.P. Snow (1951) *The Masters*. London: Macmillan.
27. T. Sharpe (1976) *Porterhouse Blue*. London: Pan; and (1995) *Granchester Grind*. London: André Deutsch/Secker and Warburg.
28. J.I.M. Stewart (1974–78) *A Staircase in Surrey* (a quintet of novels). London: Gollancz.
29. North (1997) *Commission of Inquiry: Report*. Oxford: OUP.
30. T. Tapper and D. Palfreyman (2000) op. cit.
31. A.J. Ryan (1998) *Liberal Anxieties and Liberal Education*. New York, NY: Hill and Wang. (UK edition published 1999 by Profile.)
32. See, for example, the interview with Oxford's newly appointed seven-year Vice-Chancellor in the *Financial Times*, 23 May 2000. But see also John Kay's polemic in *Prospect*, December 2000; and Alan Ryan's riposte in *Prospect*, January 2001; plus Kay in the *Financial Times*, 22 November 2000, *The Times Higher*, 24 November 2000 and the *Guardian*, 28 November 2000.

3

The Big Civics

David Holmes

A little history

It is curious to write about a general category of university in which one no longer works. It is doubly curious when one's own experience of it – in my case at Liverpool for the six years 1982–88 as Academic Secretary and latterly Deputy Registrar, and at Birmingham from 1988–98 as Registrar and Secretary – form a thick sandwich between 12 formative years at Warwick from 1970–82 on the one hand (though I did spend a term at Sheffield on an exchange in 1975) and less than two years as Registrar of Oxford on the other hand. But perhaps one is able to write with some degree of perspective from a short distance.

The 'big civics' one might classically define as the old Joint Matriculation Board universities – mostly emanating from the Victoria University of Manchester (though interestingly at least one, Birmingham, disdained any chartered extension from Manchester, under the influence of Joe Chamberlain, and went straight for its own Charter) towards the end of the nineteenth century. These are Manchester, Birmingham, Leeds, Sheffield and Liverpool, and to these one might add the rather later foundations of Bristol, Newcastle, Nottingham, Southampton and Reading, though the precise provenance of these universities was rather different. Edinburgh, of course, describes itself as the 'oldest of the civics', and that is literally true, but the Scottish context and history put Edinburgh and Glasgow into a rather different category, as do the peculiarly Welsh and Northern Ireland contexts of Cardiff and Queen's, Belfast.

Each of the big civics differs from the others in the details of its foundation, but there is much that they have in common. It would not be appropriate here to go into the history of each of them in turn, but I will look briefly at what led up to the granting of the Royal Charter to the University of Birmingham, as an example with which I am familiar. Similar origins and histories apply to most of the other civics. Vincent and Hinton wrote in 1947,

It should be realised that what had happened in Birmingham was happening at about the same time, and from the same causes, in every industrial centre in England, and that the history of the University of Birmingham is, by and large, the history of any modern university founded by private generosity, continually expanding, and eventually securing a Royal Charter to grant its own degrees, to establish its interests and to contain its students – concentrating the industrial and professional learning of the district under a self-governing body offering the highest obtainable educational opportunities.[1]

Josiah Mason founded his College in Birmingham in 1875 and a few months after it opened it was renamed 'Sir Josiah Mason's Science College'. Despite its name, it offered a wide range of disciplines and in 1892 took over the Medical Faculty from the much older foundation of Queen's College. The potential of Mason Science College to attract students of a high calibre was severely restricted because it did not have the authority to grant degrees, and there were also practical problems because, for example, medical students had, on occasions, to be prepared for the examinations of nine different bodies. Beyond such mundane considerations, idealism – largely, but not entirely, rooted in civic pride – played a most significant role in the move towards obtaining university status. It was mooted in public as early as 1831 that a university might be founded in Birmingham, but discussion only really began – and then in a somewhat desultory fashion – in the late 1880s. Nevertheless, once Joseph Chamberlain became involved in the late 1890s, matters proceeded very rapidly. Mason Science College was established as a university college with effect from 1 January 1898, and gained its Royal Charter as the University of Birmingham early in 1900. However, Chamberlain was not alone in his efforts; this was very much a civic enterprise and a town's meeting was convened by the Lord Mayor in 1898 with a view to gaining support and raising money for the project.

It was never intended that the new civic universities should be modelled too closely on the examples set by Oxford and Cambridge, although there was no reluctance to copy from these institutions in some ways. From the outset it was envisaged that the new universities would have a role to play which was of more direct functional relevance to the regions in which they were sited. Thus, in 1892 Sir Bertram Windle, later to be the first Dean of the Medical School at the University of Birmingham, stated,

> Every new university . . . should be not merely the expression of a local desire for the direction of the best form of education, but should also be informed by the spirit and influenced by the peculiar nature of the pursuits of the district in which it is located; and this is the best of reasons why, when we come to create our university, we should not hesitate to strike out on new lines, if such should seem advisable and beneficial. Our chance of success must rest in the measure of the capacity which we are able to show for assimilating that which is intrinsically good and good also for us in our special circumstances, in the

older foundations, without, at the same time too slavishly adhering to precedent.[2]

Joseph Chamberlain himself was even more eloquent and enthusiastic, and it is easy to understand his success in attracting not only modest donations from the local populace for the new university, but also much more significant sums from benefactors such as Andrew Carnegie and the gift of a 25 acre site at Edgbaston, where the present university now stands, from the Calthorpe family. The link with the City of Birmingham was demonstrated once again when the new buildings on this site were opened in 1909 by King Edward VII and Queen Alexandra, the opening ceremony only taking place after the then Lord Mayor had been knighted.

A benchmark within the system

But what of the present? As far as England is concerned, one is accustomed to hearing the big civics described as the 'backbone of the system', connoting the strong nexus of traditional and solid academic virtue and standards characteristic of this group of universities in the British context. The same image is conjured up by the term 'redbrick' (interestingly the Australian equivalents – Sydney, Melbourne, Alelaide – are referred to as the 'sandstone' universities!). But where do these institutions, largely founded at the zenith of the Victorian and Edwardian heyday, now stand in the very different and diverse world of higher education we see at the start of the twenty-first century, and what are their prospects?

The first truism about the big civics is that they do stand for high academic standards. The school and college examining board they founded and supported had such a reputation, though in a real sense their influence on its successors, the Northern Examinations and Assessment Board and in turn its successor, is a waning one. The second thing to remember is that their foundation owed everything to local civic initiative and aspiration born of the industrial revolution, and nothing to the state and very little to Oxford and Cambridge, though both of the ancient English universities provided in the twentieth century a number of important and senior figures in the big civics, particularly in the fields of science and technology – Chadwick leaving Cambridge for Liverpool, Rutherford for Manchester, Oliphant for Birmingham. The issue of quality and equality is easier in the USA than in the UK, since nobody believes the institutions of higher education in the US are all equal academically or serving the same purposes. In Britain, as the civic universities expanded in the twentieth century, ultimately leading to the erection of the 'plate glass' universities in the 1960s, elaborate precautions were taken to ensure that 'standards' were maintained. A voice might have been heard saying that in such and such a subject a first at Sheffield would only have obtained a II(i) at Cambridge, but until the creation of approximately 50 new universities in 1992, the assertion of intellectual and academic equality had some meaning. While today nobody seriously believes that all UK HEIs are intellectually or academically equal, or are engaged in the same academic purpose, nobody really wants to discuss it, nor what the implications of such a hierarchy might be.

Challenges

Here we reach one of the crucial issues facing the big civics. Their claims to distinctiveness have, arguably, been undermined by the huge expansion during the late 1980s and early 1990s; the relatively generous funding base they enjoyed in the 1960s and 1970s has been undercut by the successive moves to formula funding; their research performance, and their continuing ability to invest in very expensive subjects, have been in some doubt ever since Sir Peter Swinnerton Dyer launched a wave of attacks on the big civics in the wake of the Jarratt efficiency reports in the mid- to late 1980s;[3] and the allegiance to them of the big cities (and their political leadership) whence they sprang has been weakened by the increasing national and international role the civics had come to perform, as well as by the changing political and social ethos and priorities of the big cities themselves. The response of the civics has been to seek to reform themselves, often in radical ways, from within. Birmingham, for example, led the way, as befitted a university with Sir Alex Jarratt as its Chancellor (and the author in the mid-1980s of the influential report on the efficiency of university decision making), in cutting away large swathes of committees, refining its traditional faculty system, and moving swiftly to a business model of devolved management and budgeting. At the same time the civics began to seek to re-establish the civic roots they had been in danger of losing. The pace of regionalism has quickened this political move, together with the realization that the image, quality and economic prosperity and well-being of the big cities of which they are part is as much a factor in successful student and staff recruitment as anything they themselves can do.

Viewed from a second perspective, the big civics are caught squeezed in a pincer movement between the 'golden triangle' of Oxbridge and the leading London colleges (between them and the rest there is a discernible gap opening up in terms of research performance) on the one hand and the rest of the system on the other. The figures in Table 3.1 show that the four research giants – Imperial College, UCL, Oxford and Cambridge – are increasingly in a superleague of their own in terms of research income. The 'golden triangle' universities were the only institutions each managing to attract more than £150 million of research funding in 1997–98, with a £60 million gap separating them from other institutions. Mergers of the larger London medical schools have had a dramatic impact on the position of UCL, Imperial and KCL, while Oxford, Imperial, Cambridge and UCL attracted over a quarter of the external research income for the UK sector, securing

Table 3.1 Total research income 1997–98: the top 20 institutions

Institution	Total research funding £m 1997–98
Oxford	172.3
Imperial	164.7
Cambridge	153.9
UCL	153.5
Edinburgh	90.1
Manchester	83.5
King's, London	81.3
Leeds	78.1
Birmingham	78.0
Glasgow	68.3
Southampton	68.2
Sheffield	68.2
Nottingham	63.8
Bristol	63.3
Newcastle	57.5
Liverpool	53.5
Queen Mary	40.3
Warwick	39.7
Cranfield	38.3
Cardiff	37.5

Source: *Guardian Higher*, 13 July 1999

40 per cent of charitable funds, 30 per cent of research council income and 24 per cent of funding council grants. If anything the Joint Infrastructure Fund outcomes are tending to reinforce this superiority,[4] although the big civics are maintaining a respectable performance in specified areas, and are generally reasonably well represented in Table 3.1.

The sleeping giant awakes

In these circumstances, the civics' strategy has to be to exploit their natural advantages and strengths. First they have to grow bigger, and engage in mergers with their civic partners, as opportunity offers. Size will be important to them if they cannot compete on research quality across the board, and it will give them huge importance and influence regionally and nationally. The big civics already have among the largest student populations in the system, having grown significantly, both at undergraduate level and particularly in the taught master's area at the postgraduate level, over the last decade. See, for example, Table 3.2, which shows the 20 largest universities in terms of student population in 1997–98. Leeds is a good example of a successful growth strategy in a buoyant local economy. If the civics can develop new campuses (as is happening, in different ways, in Birmingham

Table 3.2   FTE student numbers 1997–98: the top 20 institutions

Institution	FTE student numbers 1997–98
Open	57709.6
Manchester Metropolitan	24157.5
Leeds	20980.3
Nottingham Trent	20850.9
Manchester	20357.7
Sheffield	19885.9
De Montfort	19604.5
West of England, Bristol	18876.7
Middlesex	18557.7
Sheffield Hallam	18142.1
Wolverhampton	17656.1
Birmingham	17504.3
Glasgow	17407.9
Central England in Birmingham	17203.2
Plymouth	16946.5
South Bank	16534.8
Liverpool John Moores	16093.1
Edinburgh	15969.9
Oxford	15936.6
Cambridge	15804.0

Source: Higher Education Statistics Agency

and Nottingham), diversify further into part-time and distance delivery and maintain a sizeable range of selected areas of research excellence, their sheer weight and size will provide an effective counterbalance to the golden triangle, where conventional student growth prospects are much more limited. Second, they need to seek institutional mergers. The size and importance of their medical schools gives them an entrée into all kinds of cognate academic fields offered by other institutions in the same city or vicinity. And internationally too, alliances, such as those offered by Universitas 21, will be important to them in their efforts to create a global presence for their offerings.[5]

The civics have shown a great resilience over the last 20 years in adapting to the new circumstances confronting them.[6] Competition from their 1960s neighbours has spurred them to think hard about their mission and place in the system. They are in a position, more than ever before, better enabling them to portray themselves as socially inclusive, high-quality institutions, important in economic terms to their localities and regions, and producing for the nation large numbers of highly employable graduates, particularly in areas such as medicine, law and engineering. Their problem is how to compete in global and international terms, and, on a declining financial base, how to attract the best to themselves. They have certainly become much more efficient, and have become considerably more entrepreneurial

over the last 20 years. But they are very broadly based institutions academically, and will find it increasingly difficult to maintain research quality across
all areas of activity, especially in 'big science' where their traditional aspirations have been high.

An intriguing question is whether they (and others) will be able to follow
the golden triangle institutions if and when the latter go for a differential
fee regime. Over the next ten years this is likely to be a difficult and divisive
issue for the Senates and the Councils of the civic universities, even within
the powerful lay majorities on their governing bodies which often represent
diverse sections of lay opinion. If I am right and the big civics take the path
of merger and diversification, in a sense their traditional distinctiveness will
tend to disappear, and the old groupings will fall away. The Russell Group,
itself a fragile informal coalition which, in truth, does not know if it is a
dining club or something else, may also evolve into a number of different
interest groups.[7] The information age and the wired society will undoubtedly affect the big civics in vitally important and unforeseen ways. But their
strengths will enduringly arise from their big city locations and the large
population base that surrounds them, especially if there is a revival in the
UK of the live-at-home-and-commute student prevalent at the time of the
creation of the big civics. In the end, provided they adapt sensibly and
sensitively, their survival is more sure than that of many in the system.

As many of the big civics celebrate a century of their Royal Charters, they
can undoubtedly be proud of what they have created, a truly rich infrastructure of libraries, art galleries and museums, botanical gardens and well-
found campuses, laboratories and educational outreach facilities, and
governance and management structures which are certainly the envy of
many in the European systems. Their ability to raise new private endowment is, however, very uncertain, although the work they have carried out
with their alumni over the last 20 years or so could turn out to be a vitally
important key to their future financial and, therefore, academic strength in
a fiercely competitive world.

Notes and references

1. E.W. Vincent and P. Hinton (1947) *The University of Birmingham: Its History and Significance.* Birmingham: Cornish Brothers.
2. Ibid.
3. I hasten to add that Sir Peter's onslaught was entirely constructive in its purpose and outcome, and intended to be so: that is to shake the great oil tankers of the system out of their complacency – Indeed he was a great supporter of the civics in reality.
4. The Joint Infrastructure Fund is a fund established in 1998 with additional government funding allocated through the Funding Councils and the Research Councils, together with funding made available by the Wellcome Trust, with the principal intention of upgrading the research infrastructure of the UK universities.

5. Universitas 21 is a loose global association of universities in the UK, USA, Australia, China, New Zealand and Europe, of which some of the UK civic universities are members. Note that Birmingham and Aston seem at present to be edging towards merger, driven by a search for critical mass: the new institution would have 30,000 students and a £300 million turnover.

6. Very little has been written about 'the big civics', or indeed about 'the civics', as a collective, as opposed to individual centennial corporate histories of varying quality – one of the better being T. Kelly (1981) *For Advancement of Learning: The University of Liverpool 1881–1981.* Liverpool: Liverpool University Press, which has a good bibliography. See also its successor volume, Sylvia Harrop (1994) *Decade of Change: The University of Liverpool 1981–1991.* Liverpool: Liverpool University Press. For their origin in a mix of civic pride and vocational, scientific and technological purpose, see D.R. Jones (1988) *The Origins of Civic Universities: Manchester, Leeds and Liverpool.* London: Routledge, D.S.L. Cardwell (1972) *The Organisation of Science in England.* London: Heinemann Educational, and Michael Sanderson's two books (1972) *The Universities and British Industry, 1850–1970.* London: Routledge and (1975) *The Universities and the Nineteenth Century.* London: Routledge. See also E. Ives (2000) *The First Civic University: Birmingham 1880–1980.* Birmingham: University of Birmingham Press.

7. The Russell Group is an informal association of 19 research-led universities, formed in the early 1990s. They are Oxford, Cambridge, Warwick, Southampton, Nottingham, Cardiff, King's College London, University College London, Imperial College, London School of Economics, Manchester, Liverpool, Sheffield, Leeds, Birmingham, Newcastle, Bristol, Edinburgh and Glasgow.

4

Exeter University: Going Back to the Future?

Philip Harvey

Origins and background

The University of Exeter received its Royal Charter in 1955, a decade or so before the establishment of the seven 'new' universities of Sussex, York, Lancaster, Essex, East Anglia, Kent and Warwick, and in doing so became one of only 22 universities in Britain at the time. Unlike the 'magnificent seven' in the 1960s (the first institutions to be permitted to be launched as fully fledged universities in the UK since the creation of London and Durham Universities in the 1830s), Exeter's receipt of its Charter came at a time when institutions aspiring for university status were required to show a lengthy track record in higher education and usually as colleges of an older establishment offering courses for externally validated degrees.

Exeter University was no different in this regard. Its origins date back to the creation of Schools of Art and Science in Exeter in the period immediately following the Great Exhibition in 1851 and the popular growth of extra-mural studies in the late nineteenth century.[1] The Royal Albert Memorial College in Exeter was established in 1900 from these origins and in 1904 its first student to graduate, an Exeter-born woman Janet Algar, took her University of London degree in general science. Far-sighted efforts by a committee chaired by Sir Henry Lopes for Furtherance of University Education in the South West in 1918 failed to persuade government to create a federal university of the South-West based on the Colleges of Exeter, Plymouth, Camborne, Truro and Seale Hayne. B.W. Clapp records that the Minister of the time – H.A.L. Fisher (later Warden of New College, Oxford) – saw little merit in the deputation's case:

> Federal universities had had an unhappy history; the University of Wales was a new experiment, but the earlier federation of Manchester, Leeds and Liverpool had broken up in 1903. Where he asked were the students, the staff and the money to come from? . . . At the time of the deputation in November 1918 the official attitude, reflected in Fisher's

speech, was extremely hostile to the campaign for a university in the South-West: 'To propose at this time of day to form a university out of a second-rate College at Exeter, mainly filled with Training College Students, a newly founded Agricultural College at Newton Abbott, a School of Mines at Camborne and a Technical School at Plymouth is a very tall order.'[2]

Despite the evident scepticism from government, the campaign for a university in Exeter remained undaunted and in 1922 it led to a visitation by the newly established Universities Grants Committee (UGC). The visit was a major turning point and the UGC agreed forthwith to place the College on the list of those institutions to receive grants from the Treasury as the University College of the South-West. In the same year, a major benefaction from Alderman W.H. Reed provided an estate of more than 100 acres about a mile north of the city centre with the imposing nineteenth-century Streatham Hall – later renamed Reed Hall – as its centrepiece. Halls of residence, laboratories and a library were constructed on the Streatham estate in the period leading up to the Second World War and villas in the surrounding countryside were acquired to provide for further student residential accommodation. In the five years following 1945, the College doubled in size and the UGC successively increased its grant. An uninterrupted period of construction of academic, residential and other buildings then followed, notably during the era of expansion of higher education in the 1960s and 1970s launched by the government's accept-ance of the Robbins Committee's call in 1963 for a tripling of student numbers in the period up to 1980/81.[3]

A further application for university status and the power to award degrees was made in 1947 by a federation of colleges in the South-West that this time included St Luke's College, but was rejected outright by the UGC. Eventually, after some 30 years of grant support from the Treasury, in October 1955 the University of Exeter received its Royal Charter of incor-poration. HM the Queen presented the Charter when she visited the Uni-versity in 1956 to unveil the foundation stone of the Queen's Building – possibly the only time a monarch has personally presented a Charter of incorporation to an English university on its own estate.

Since receiving its Charter, the University has continued to expand and elements of the broader vision for higher education for the South-West envisaged in the early years of the twentieth century were realized by two notable mergers. In 1978 St Luke's College – a teacher training college of some 1400 students – was absorbed within the University to become the University's School of Education. In Cornwall the Camborne School of Mines had taught courses in mining engineering and related subjects to those involved in the industry for over a hundred years and had developed an international reputation in the field, and in 1993, a little over 70 years after the failed deputation for establishment of a federal university for the South-West, CSM also merged with the University of Exeter.

The late 1970s and 1980s saw a less rapid period of capital investment in new academic buildings on the estate but during the 1980s and 1990s over £30 million was spent on providing additional student accommodation and upgrading the original residential stock. Benefactions and gifts have continued to play an important part in the development of the University – particularly those arising from the University's close associations with figures prominent in the Arab world and notably from the Gulf States. These have enabled the building of a new library in 1983, a social and study centre for postgraduate students in 1991, and now at the start of the new century the commencement of a building for an Institute of Arab and Islamic Studies. In 2000 the University opened the first phase of the Innovation Centre, in conjunction with Exeter City Council and a private developer. The building will house up to 15 'incubator' units for high-technology small and medium-sized enterprises (SMEs) working in fields such as biotechnology, software engineering, and biomedical applications keen to be based on the University's campus and linked to academic developments taking place in its schools and departments.

The university's present student profile

In 2000/01 full-time undergraduate education and the high quality of the educational experience offered to students by a research active academic staff remain Exeter's core strengths. The indicators of the quality of the undergraduate education offered at Exeter are, principally, the number of well-qualified applicants competing for places, the high retention and progression rates, and the demand for its graduates from employers. The University receives around 20,000 applications each year for the 2000 or so places on its undergraduate degrees it has to offer. In 1999 a survey of the leading 200 companies employing graduates in the UK placed Exeter in the top ten UK universities from which they recruited.

The University has a medium-sized student population of nearly 11,000 – of which 8000 are studying full-time for undergraduate degrees in Exeter, in Camborne and also now in Truro in Cornwall. Over 3000 students are studying for University of Exeter degrees taught in various forms of partnership with other institutions at home and abroad. The University's postgraduate community continues to expand and now comprises 25 per cent of the total student body with over 2000 students taking postgraduate master's degrees and 700 studying for MPhil/PhD. Eight and a half per cent of the total student population come from countries outside the European Union. Part-time students comprise 13 per cent of the University's undergraduates – the majority being drawn from the South-West region. Of the total student body entering Exeter in 1997/98 under the age of 21, 66 per cent were from state schools (against a national average of 82 per cent) and 13 per cent (national average – 25 per cent) came from groups identified by the HEFCE as under-represented in higher education.

The University is committed to retaining essential elements in the under-graduate student experience, such as the operation of the personal tutor system, and adding value to others. It is active in embedding new forms of student-centred learning in the curriculum and has set out a five-year pattern of investment for its Learning and Teaching Support Centre which serves as a focus for module and programme developments using ICT. To maintain its edge with employers, a major initiative exists to locate and accredit key skills within every undergraduate's programme of study and to provide schemes that exploit the student–employer interface. This extends beyond the UK, and use of the European Union's (EU's) LEONARDO vocational training programme work is underway to expand the capacity for transnational work placements for Exeter's students. The University's recent success with the HEFCE's 'reach-out' or 'third-leg' funding will provide employers with a coordinated one-stop shop service offering full-time graduate-level employment, part-time term-time work, project-based activities, vacation opportunities and casual work. Student project officers will be appointed to enhance the business liaison service to be run out of the Innovation Centre. Their role will be to promote the student resource for business and act as a clearing house for requests from business for support with short-term projects.

External factors driving change at the University of Exeter

Like all large and complex organizations, universities require effective man-agement and strong leadership if they are to succeed. The pressures for change from today's society are well known to all students and staff working in higher education although, as Anthony Giddens has recently noted in his 1999 Annual Lecture to the Association of University Administrators, we understand more about the origins of these pressures than their conse-quences.[4] The landmark speech by the Secretary of State for Education and Employment at Greenwich University on 15 February 2000 encapsulates the need for higher education to be at the epicentre of delivery of the global knowledge-based economy, and the speech throws into sharp relief the speed with which change is expected to take place.[5] Recognition of higher education's centrality in the agenda is welcome but such a role lays down significant challenges for institutions like universities and the people who manage them. The breadth of issues contained within the globalization agenda, the predictions for the speed with which society is set to become more fragmented and complex, and the crucial role that knowledge man-agement will play in determining organizational success all contribute to asking universities fundamental questions about their purpose, structures and ability to manage themselves in a world where competitive advantage will remain shortlived and monolithic slow-moving businesses perish. If projections of a global economy containing a billion graduates by 2020 are correct,[6] with many western societies facing demands from an ageing population that outstrip productivity and revenue, then students embarking on their higher education careers in 2001 have the right to raise significant questions about whether their university education will equip them adequately.

The following list of drivers behind change will be familiar territory to those in higher education today. Many of course are equally relevant to other parts of modern society:

- rapidly changing technologies offering flexible and distributed learning;
- demands for consumer-led rather than supplier-driven provision;
- increased competition for diminishing public sector resources for teaching and research;
- increased collaboration with public and private sector organizations within regions;
- pressure for diversifying sources of income;
- calls for improved quality, explicit standards, and 'relevance';
- rapid movement from elite to mass to universal access to higher education;
- demands for flexibility in programme design and delivery as part of a 'lifelong learning' approach to higher education;
- increased regulation, monitoring and demands for transparency.

These external factors, manifest in all their day-to-day variation and involving a wide range of stakeholders, present significant challenges for the modern university. The diversity of objectives and the conflicting priorities demand a *managed* response from institutions. Resource constraints mean that difficult choices have to be made daily and the constant need for monitoring progress against targets and regular reappraisal of the validity of the targets themselves are seen by many to place staff under considerable pressure. An 'accountancy mentality' is in danger of pervading and perverting higher education in the UK to an extent that the broader purpose and values which brought many to work in the sector are under threat. On the other hand, the external context creates for managers an exciting, fast-moving and stimulating work environment that demands organizations have in place effective and efficient structures for communication and decision making, and well-led and highly skilled teams who can aggregate and disaggregate quickly around problems, identify and maximize opportunities and deliver services in new ways.

It is not relevant here to engage in the debate over the role of academics as managers or administrators qua managers (see for example Warner and Palfreyman),[7] or indeed to confront what is pejoratively termed the rise of managerialism in higher education (Trow).[8] Rather, this section's purpose is to set out the University of Exeter's recent response to some of the challenges listed above and in particular its efforts in developing a management structure fit for the purpose of running a university in the year 2001.

Strategy for the twenty-first century

In 1995 the University embarked upon a review of its strategy for the next ten years. Led by the newly appointed Vice-Chancellor, Sir Geoffrey Holland, the review marshalled a series of working groups involving members from inside and outside the University. Sir Geoffrey Holland had previously pursued a career in the civil service and prior to his appointment as Vice-Chancellor was Permanent Secretary at the Department for Employment and therefore was particularly well placed to interpret the political context affecting higher education. He remained close to the centre of the national debate on higher education by being appointed a member of the National Committee of Inquiry into Higher Education which was established with cross-party support in May 1996. The result of the review at Exeter was a document that recognized the next ten years as an era of challenge, change and turbulence.[9] There would continue to be demand for higher education at Exeter from traditional markets but demand would also come from new areas, particularly in continuing professional development and part-time education. There would be greater expectations from students and other customers for improvement in the quality of service and programmes of study. Increasing selectivity in funding for excellence in teaching and research would prompt greater competition for human, financial and capital resources. Moves to merge academic and vocational qualifications were set to continue.

A strategy for managing change

The University recognized that if it were to respond effectively to this agenda it needed to change its management structures – decision making was deemed to be too slow to make the most of the opportunities that presented themselves and insufficient capacity existed for taking advantage of such opportunities. A working group was established. Its priorities were to enable the University to manage more effectively in a worsening financial position; to speed up decision making; to reduce administration for academic staff; to streamline the handling of academic business; to provide an environment which would enable leadership to flourish; to integrate deans of faculties more effectively into the senior management of the institution; and to find structures that would make the most of the multidisciplinary and interdisciplinary opportunities available.

The work of the group on management structures was given added impetus by the results of the University's performance in the 1996 Research Assessment Exercise. Follett's analysis[10] of institutional performance in the four RAEs held since 1986 shows that 22 of the top 40 research universities have not changed their rank order position; eight have improved and 11 weakened. Exeter's performance in the 1992 RAE had placed it fifteenth in tables produced to show the rating of research quality per member of academic staff, but in 1996 the University's position deteriorated dramatically to thirty-sixth. No other research-led university's position changed to such an extent between the RAEs of 1992 and 1996. The comparative under-performance of the institution in 1996 (only 62 per cent of staff rated Grade 4 or 5) was further marked by a lower proportion of the academic workforce returned as research active (81 per cent), and heralded the announcement of an adverse grant settlement from HEFCE in 1997. When it came in March 1997, the University knew that it faced a cut in recurrent budget of £3 million or around 10 per cent of its grant. The Funding Council operated its safety net to protect the real-terms reduction to no more than 2 per cent per annum.

The University had already acted before the announcement of the grant settlement to overhaul its academic profile radically. Plans were produced for consultation by May 1997 to disinvest in areas of activity by sums that exceeded the cuts required in the academic sector of the University's budget (£4.5 million) and reinvest in other areas (£2.1 million). The work being undertaken by the group responsible for producing its report on the new management structures was accelerated and brought together with proposals for the new academic profile in a set of recommendations to the University's Council in July 1997. Within seven months of publication of the RAE results the University approved a restructuring plan that provided for a 9 per cent cut in the academic sector budget over four years; the identification of £6 million from University reserves and departmental resources to provide an attractive early retirement/voluntary severance scheme; the dissolution of over 50 separate budgetary and management units and the creation of 17 new units or schools; the disappearance of the traditional subject-based faculty structure and their 'baron' deans (arts, education, engineering, law, science, and social studies) and the creation of three new functional faculties providing a pan-institutional focus for undergraduate studies, postgraduate studies and programmes delivered through academic partnerships. A new breed of heads of schools and deans were to be appointed with clear job descriptions and responsibilities.

The timetable for managing change was tight. By 1 August 1998, one year after Council's decisions, the 17 schools had been established with integrated plans for teaching, research, finance and staffing. The new Faculty Boards came into force with terms of reference and membership that underpinned their new role – with emphasis especially on providing common approaches to quality assurance; on the harmonization of academic business practices; and on giving a focus or 'champion' to the task of identifying opportunities, setting objectives and implementing change. By the same time, 70 academic staff or 10.5 per cent of the academic workforce had left employment via voluntary means at an average age of 56. Of these, 56 had not been returned as research active in the 1996 RAE and were considered unlikely to do so for the next exercise, or would have reached normal retirement before 2001. In addition, the process of recruiting new staff was well underway. By August 1999 21 new professors and 52 new lecturers had started work at the University, with an average age of 35.

At the end of 1998 the University had substantially strengthened its core management team of academic and non-academic managers through the appointment of new heads of school and new deans of faculty. Improved channels of communication were opened by enlarging and formalizing the role of the executive comprising the vice-chancellor, three deputy vice-chancellors, three deans, registrar, academic secretary and director of finance, and by generating a Senior Management Group meeting monthly outside the formal committee structure and comprising the above plus all heads of schools and heads of administration and academic services (around 30 individuals in all).

Since 1998 proposals have been approved by the Privy Council to bring the University's governance arrangements in line with the recommendations from the Dearing Report and the guidance issued by the Chairmen of University Councils, with the result that the University's governing body will comprise 33 members from 2000. Further steps have been taken to reduce the membership of Senate by two-thirds and to recast the composition of its membership, with around half from those holding executive or management roles and half being elected from the corpus of academic staff. A major exercise to re-examine the committee structure that underpins the new Council and Senate of the University is underway, as well as a re-evaluation of the means by which heads of school are identified, appointed and supported.

Mechanisms for institutional transformation

These emergent structural changes at Exeter are not underpinned by some managerial master plan or blueprint for corporate strategy linked in some artificially linear way to tidy annual operating statements. However, they are indicative of a management that knows it has to develop its architecture to support institutional change and the changes it wishes to make. In this context, Burton Clark's[11] study of five innovative universities in Europe and his resulting identification of the characteristics that these innovative universities are using to become more entrepreneurial is a useful organizational framework within which to assess Exeter's progress. Burton Clark sees the following elements as constituting an 'irreducible minimum' for institutional transformation:

- a strengthened steering core;
- an expanded developmental periphery;
- a diversified funding base;
- a stimulated academic heartland;
- an integrated entrepreneurial culture.

First, Exeter has explicitly recognized that its previous management and decision-making structures have provided a weak basis from which to steer the institution during rapidly changing times. The poor RAE performance in 1996 may in the long run prove to be Exeter's salvation in prompting it finally to reappraise its performance root and branch and to identify the size and shape of the task it faces to maintain the excellence of what it produces. The University's changes in management are ambitious and have been founded on generating greater managerial capacity in central management groups and in academic schools. The 'strengthened steering core' at Exeter recognizes that the tension between managerial values and more traditional academic ones does not have to be destructive. Central to this shared understanding is the belief that only through becoming more entrepreneurial can traditional values and approaches survive.

Second, the new schools structure and the new Faculty of Academic Partnerships is a tangible statement of Exeter's outreach policy that embraces Burton Clark's concept of an expanded developmental periphery. Disciplinary protectionism and subject fragmentation is challenged in Exeter's management model of schools and there are early indications that some multidisciplinary schools are reaping the benefits from an integrated teaching and management structure that looks outwards towards the interdisciplinary opportunities between disciplines, and uses the stronger and broader funding base of the new school to support their exploitation. Exeter's present performance in expanding its periphery is patchy, however. It will be a measure of success when students can readily identify as tangible the benefits of the structure or when putative research centres or other entrepreneurial units embedded within or between schools are able to look back on the present as a period of sustained growth.

Third, Exeter recognizes the demand for greater diversity in its funding base. Central to its strategy for development is the improvement of project funding for research and the expansion of research grants and contracts activity, and the generation of more earned income from what Burton Clark identifies as 'third stream sources': income from contracts and consultancy with targeted sectors of the business community; contracts with public sector bodies; foundations and charities; student and other client fees from post-experience and other short courses; benefactions; alumni; retail and other campus services; conference facilities, etc. Exeter is examining three main strands in its approach to diversifying sources of income: the University's comparative performance against major lines of non-grant income; the organizational structures it needs to bring together disparate strands of earned-income activity and manage the diversity of business more effectively; and the human resource issues that are raised by running a multi-purpose organization with a mixed economy. The latter is probably the most significant. Four working groups exploring recruitment and selection, rewards and recognition, job evaluation, and appraisal is underway to produce a fundamental reappraisal of the way staff are appointed and managed in order that they can succeed in meeting the widely ranging objectives within the institution's diversified economy.

Fourth, Burton Clark identifies the importance for successful transformation of the institution of a 'stimulated academic heartland', and by this he means that the academic departments undertaking the core teaching and research must accept the need for transformation and embrace innovation – each element of the heartland becoming ultimately its own entrepreneurial unit. Participation of their membership in the activities of the central steering core is essential. 'In the entrepreneurial university', Burton Clark asserts, 'the heartland accepts a modified belief system.'[12] It would be fair to say that full acceptance by the heartland at Exeter of such an entrepreneurial ethic is a little way off. But the progress of the University in embracing change has been impressive. An indicator of progress is the recent performance of the University's incentive scheme whereby a proportion of income produced from non-grant sources such as student fee income and overhead recovery on research council grants is fed directly to schools. In 1999/00, provisional earnings through the incentive scheme were 21 per cent higher than forecast and showed an 84 per cent increase on the out-turn for 1998/99. Another indicator is the increasing and welcome upward pressure from schools on senior management for new work practices and supporting infrastructure to assist academic staff in the earned-income task. Like many other universities in the UK, Exeter has responded by investing in administrative and support services geared to the production of new revenue streams – in the areas of international student recruitment; schools and colleges liaison; marketing; research and development services; academic partnerships; and management information and planning.

Fifth, the enterprising university is described by Burton Clark as having an integrated entrepreneurial culture with changes in values and belief systems interacting with changes in structures and procedures cultivating a strong institutional identity and distinctive reputation. Ten formative years at Warwick University gave the present author ample demonstration of how the blend of elements identified above helped to establish an identity, reputation and self-confidence that many have admired and some sought to emulate. Exeter University's present task is, in part, to find its own blend of strong structures and procedures that will facilitate its cultural change and transformation. But at the same time its task is to think further ahead, beyond opportunism and adventurous management, to the kind of university it wants to be in ten or 15 years from now or rather to conceive of the kind of education, research and service to its region that its new-found self-confidence and entrepreneurialism will spawn. In 2001, Exeter's efforts to transform institutional culture alongside the establishment of a new sense of purpose constitutes its principal immediate task.

Conclusion

The title of this chapter offers no regressive desire to cling to a 'golden age' of higher education, if ever one existed, nor to gaze into the crystal ball and see where the University of Exeter is bound. Rather, it is to offer up the aphorism of history repeating itself and, just as in 1918 when a federal university of the South-West was first being proposed, to wonder whether a new regional structure for higher education in the South-West will be part of Exeter's future a hundred or so years after first being proposed by Sir Henry Lopes. The Universities of Exeter and Plymouth have recently successfully submitted a joint bid to establish the Peninsula Medical School – the first entirely new medical school in the UK for 30 years. It will admit its first students in October 2002. Similarly, these universities and Falmouth College of Arts are engaged currently in a major collaborative project to establish a Combined Universities for Cornwall founded on the principle of higher education's role in regional economic regeneration. In the bold anticipation that these and successor initiatives will proceed, higher education in the South-West will turn a corner towards closer integration between institutions, new forms of association and governance, and economies of scale through collaboration.

Whatever the future holds for higher education in the UK, there can be little doubt that the entrepreneurial university of the UK epitomized by Warwick University in the 1980s and 1990s is here to stay. Michael Shattock's response, as the then Registrar at Warwick, to the publication of the Jarratt Report[13] into the Management and Efficiency of British Universities is as fitting today as it was in 1986:

> The world I work in at Warwick is highly competitive. Within the University, departments compete vigorously for funds, sparking off new ideas and going out and raising money (usually not quite enough) to realise them and then turning to the University for assistance in implementation. Externally, the University is in competition with other universities for high quality students, high quality staff, research funds and recurrent grant, and we are determined to keep our nose in front. Warwick is not a place where we spend much of our time sitting about in carefully constructed Joint Committees of Council and Senate allocating non-existent free money. We are out generating income both to keep the ship afloat and to keep new developments coming on stream.
>
> Jarratt envisages a tidy world where decision-making needs to be better controlled and structured. My world, however, is pretty untidy. It is opportunist in, I hope, the good sense of seeing openings and going for them, of helping academics to raise funds to back good ideas or assisting our hard-pressed local community to improve its flagging economic prospects. It puts a premium on alertness, on moving, at times, very fast indeed, either to attract people or funds or both and on maintaining an effective communication system round the University and outside to get things done.[14]

References

1. B.W. Clapp (1982) *The University of Exeter: A History.* Exeter: University of Exeter Press.
2. Ibid., p. 50.
3. M.L. Shattock (1994) *The UGC and the Management of British Universities.* Buckingham: SRHE/Open University Press.
4. A. Giddens (1999) The future of universities. Second annual lecture of the Association of University Administrators, *Newslink*, Issue 25, December (published by AUA).
5. David Blunkett, Secretary of State for Education and Employment. Speech on higher education, 15 February 2000, University of Greenwich.
6. O. Sparrow (1998) *Open Horizons: Three Scenarios for 2020. The 1998 Report from the Chatham House Forum.* London Royal Institute of International Affairs.
7. D. Warner and D. Palfreyman (eds) (1996) *Higher Education Management: The Key Elements.* Buckingham: SRHE/Open University Press.
8. M. Trow (1994) *Managerialism and the Academic Profession: Quality and Control.* London: Open University Quality Support Centre.
9. University of Exeter (1995) The University of Exeter, into the twenty-first century: a strategy for the next decade, unpublished internal document.
10. B.K. Follett (1997) University research: how should limited funds be deployed? *Technology, Innovation and Society*, 13: 17–19.
11. Burton R. Clark (1998) *Creating Entrepreneurial Universities: Organizational Pathways of Transformation.* New York/Oxford: International Association of Universities and Elsevier Science Ltd, Pergamon.
12. Ibid., p. 7.
13. Jarratt Report (1985) *Report of the Steering Committee for Efficiency Studies in Universities.* London: CVCP.
14. M.L. Shattock (1986) Implementing the Jarratt Report, in *Management and Efficiency in British Universities: The Implications of the Jarratt Report,* Proceedings of a Foundation Seminar, May, Discussion Paper No. 13. London: Public Finance Foundation. See also D. Palfreyman (1989) The Warwick way: a case study of innovation and entrepreneurship within a university context, *Journal of Entrepreneurship and Regional Development,* 1(2): 207–19, and Chapter 2 in Burton R. Clark (1998), op. cit.

5

The 1960s New Universities

Tony Rich

Seven new universities were created in England in the early 1960s: East Anglia (UEA), Essex, Kent, Lancaster, Sussex, Warwick and York. This chapter will focus on the 1960s vision for those institutions and their relative success at the end of the twentieth century, before offering some observations on their possible future development. Inevitably, I will draw heavily on my experience of having worked in three of these universities.

The vision of the 1960s

Seven new universities were conceived in 1958–61, *before* the Robbins Committee reported, as the UK government committed itself to an expansion of higher education which preceded any real debate on the value of higher education (HE). One critical prerequisite was identified – a 200+ acre site, leading to all the 1960s universities being sited on the edges of towns and cities, where land was cheaper and there was room for expansion. The precise location of the new institutions was not predetermined. UEA might have been located at Bury St Edmunds, Essex at Chelmsford, Kent at Folkestone or Margate, Lancaster at Blackpool, and Warwick at Cheltenham, Worcester or Gloucester. Although founded by local initiative, all the 1960s universities aspired to become national and international institutions and, as Michael Beloff remarked, 'as the years pass, the universities, rather than growing towards the towns, will grow away from them'.[1] Albert Sloman, Essex's founding Vice-Chancellor, saw the university's regional role rather differently: 'a great university has a lot to give to the community but in the first years the community will be asked to give a lot to the university'.[2]

The pattern of development differed between institutions: Sussex and Warwick strove from the beginning to cover a full range of disciplines, whereas UEA, Essex and York preferred to concentrate resources on a narrower front. Almost all the 1960s universities, having a bias to the liberal rather than the vocational, failed to respond adequately to the political demand for technologists and applied scientists, with most devoting much resource to arts, social sciences and natural sciences. Some were actively discouraged from pursuing technology, which was seen as the preserve of the colleges of advanced technology – also to become universities in the 1960s. Warwick, for instance, had to press hard for an engineering department. Sussex, which was the first of the 1960s institutions and memorably described in a *Times* editorial as 'Balliol by the sea', became the standard against which 'everything is measured'.[3] Sussex developed a radical academic philosophy, which emphasized the interdependence, rather than the independence, of traditional subjects – resonant also of developments at Essex and UEA. The first eight schools of study at UEA included innovative creations of biological sciences and environmental sciences but 'certain rebels' wanted 'an independent history school'. They got their way, but it took 30 years! York, on the other hand, played it 'traditional rather than modern' and aimed 'not to surprise but to succeed'.[4] Lancaster also developed academic expertise in relatively new fields, notably environmental studies, marketing, operational research, and systems engineering. Three universities, Kent, Lancaster and York, developed a collegiate system, whereas the others opted for different forms of social organization. Warwick, from the very beginning under its domineering Vice-Chancellor Jack Butterworth, was ambitious. It was gifted the largest site – over 400 acres, compared to 200–300 acres for the others – and its appeal was the most successful, raising some £4 million. It developed links with local business and industry, which even at this early stage 'opened up the prospect of a relative independence from government financial control'.[5] Warwick's early connections with business and industry earned it the displeasure of Marxist historian E.P. Thompson in a polemic entitled *Warwick University Limited*, in which Warwick was described as a 'typical capitalist university'.[6]

Most strikingly, many of the founding principles of the 1960s universities are still strongly in evidence in those institutions today – and not only at Warwick. At Essex, the Promotion Committee, comprising representatives not only from Essex County Council, but also Southend-on-Sea, East Ham and West Ham Borough Councils, gave three main reasons for establishing the University of Essex:

1. the post-war development which gave Essex one of the largest populations of any county – a 'modern university . . . would be of inestimable benefit to the community';
2. unsatisfied demand for university places – participation in HE by young Essex people (8.6 per cent in 1957/58) was below the national average (9.82 per cent), so the 'presence of a university in Essex, even though it would and should be national in character, would do much to make up the present deficiencies' in the supply of local graduates; and
3. the needs of industry for skilled manpower – the Committee noted in its submission to the University Grants Committee (UGC) in 1960 that 'many industries in Essex have a direct interest in an expansion of university

places, and there is little doubt that the presence of a university in the county would encourage them to support, for example, postgraduate study by selected members of their staff'.[7]

These principles were most clearly enunciated by Albert Sloman who gave the Reith Lectures in 1963. Sloman declared that the Essex curriculum would be restricted to three fields of study: physical sciences, social studies and comparative studies, noting that serious omissions included biology, some branches of humanities and all the professional schools. He placed great importance on creating big departments (in 1961/62 the average size of a UK department was seven members of staff and even for science departments was only ten), which would be able to meet growing research costs, attract first-class staff, provide opportunities for international exchange, provide sufficient staffing to support study leave, and build up library support for a small number of subjects. Essex's growth was to be organic, trying 'to do a few things well'. In choosing subjects, Essex first took into account 'national need' and was advised by the UGC not to pursue the professional subjects (defined as medicine, dentistry, agriculture and veterinary science); second, the special features of the region; and third, the balance of subjects within the University itself. Sloman advocated that universities 'should work much more closely both with industry and research institutions'. Essex's three schools were to provide a base for the study of electronics and other branches of engineering, which were the leading industries in the county. Future plans included the development of a separate school of engineering, of education and of management studies. In the school of comparative studies, Essex adopted a more contemporary and more international approach than was common at that time, focusing on Russia, North America and Latin America. Essex, in common with several of its peers, aimed for a broader curriculum in the first year and argued that the peak of specialization should be achieved in graduate study, not at undergraduate level. Sloman's vision of the growth of the university coincided with the anticipated growth of Colchester and Wivenhoe, since 'it is only a matter of time before the university town, at present standing alone, joins hands with both'.

Sloman recognized that the lead given by the Academic Planning Board 'will determine the direction which the university takes for very many years'. The first report of the Academic Planning Board to the Promotion Committee in February 1962 declared that it wished 'to establish in the first place a few strong and large departments rather than numerous small departments', intended that the University become 'noted for certain fields of study', and determined that it should be 'distinct from other new universities'. The Board noted that Sussex, York and UEA were covering the traditional arts subjects, but argued that 'there is a place for a university which will have chief regard to the study of modern society'.[8] Thus one of the UK's best social science universities was born.

Sloman planned for a large number of graduate students, setting a target of one in three or four, compared to the one in seven ratio of the time. He also called on the University to meet the needs of adult education, part-timers and women returners. Moreover, he wished to establish a 'tradition that good teaching really matters', but he was already aware of the need to make teaching more efficient – noting that the Robbins Report had revealed that half of all lectures were attended by less than 20 students. Turning to the administration, Sloman stated that Essex intended 'to follow the lead of one or two of the biggest universities in this country and build up under the registrar a strong secretariat'. With 'its variety of interest, its responsibility and its scope for promotion, university administration is a career . . . which will rapidly increase in importance'.[9] One of Sloman's models was Manchester and, although few senior administrators move from Essex to become registrars elsewhere, three incumbents of that post at Essex have moved away to become registrar/secretary at Nottingham, Manchester and The Open University. Warwick developed its administration under Mike Shattock with a similar ethos and has performed in more recent times a similar role to that played by Manchester in the 1960s.

Plate-glass achievements

At the end of the century, the seven new universities of the 1960s have established themselves as among the most successful research institutions in the country and some are challenging the pre-eminence of the golden triangle (Oxbridge and London), having already shaken the complacency of the big civic universities. *The Higher's* analysis of the 1996 Research Assessment Exercise ranked five of the seven universities in the top 12 research institutions: Warwick, Lancaster, York, Essex and Sussex being placed eighth to twelfth respectively.[10] League tables which take account of other factors, such as teaching quality, admissions scores, facilities, etc. have the effect of depressing the positions of the 1960s universities to some extent: the leading 1960s universities Warwick and York were placed seventh and twelfth in the *Times* (23 April 1999); eighth and ninth in the *Financial Times* (1 April 1999); and seventh and sixth respectively in the *Sunday Times* (19 September 1999). York was described as second only to Cambridge for the quality of its teaching (*Sunday Times*, 19 September 1999). UEA attracts proportionally more mature students than any of its peers; Essex and Warwick both attract large numbers of non-EU students; all except Kent have 20 per cent or more postgraduates among their student body (with Warwick at 32 per cent). All the other 1960s universities feature prominently in these league tables, with the exception of Kent which does appear noticeably less successful than its peers. Moreover, Kent is the only 1960s university which is not a member of the 1994 Group of research-intensive, small and medium-sized universities.

Beloff noted in 1969 that an orientation towards research excellence was everywhere discernible among the new universities.[11] Most of the 1960s universities have since established reputations as being among the best institutions nationally and internationally for their research in particular disciplines: UEA for environmental sciences and creative writing; Essex for the social sciences; Lancaster and Warwick for business studies, and the latter also for mathematics and manufacturing systems engineering; and York for biosciences, computer science and psychology.

All the 1960s universities have grown substantially, with Warwick having more than 16,000 students registered (12,600 FTEs) in 1997/98, and all the others between 7200 and 8900 FTEs, with only Essex having a significantly smaller total (5500 FTEs). Warwick, unsurprisingly, is the most attractive to potential students of the 1960s universities, drawing 27,000 applications for undergraduate places; York and Lancaster some 15,000 to 16,000 applications; UEA, Kent and Sussex some 10,000 to 12,000 applications; and Essex 6,500 for entry in autumn 1999. York and Warwick are among the ten most popular universities in the UK, attracting over nine applications per place. Even a young royal was reported in 1999 to be considering study at UEA, rather than its older East Anglian rival.

Financially, Warwick is in a separate league to its 1960s peers, with an income in 1997/98 of £149 million, more than double that received by UEA, Essex, Kent and Lancaster. Warwick's industrial links and its burgeoning conference empire, benefiting from being at the heart of the British road and rail network and close to an international airport, have played a large part in raising its income levels close to some big civic universities such as Newcastle, Bristol and Liverpool. Both Warwick and York earn more than £20 million from research grants and contracts, but Warwick earns almost a further £40 million from 'other general operating income', £15 million of which comes from residential and catering operations.

Several institutions have developed their own science parks with Warwick, at the heart of industrial regeneration in the West Midlands, being most successful. Warwick opened the Barclays' Venture Centre in 1984 and now boasts an impressive 44-acre site and two satellite units in Coventry and Warwickshire. UEA developed close working relationships with the John Innes Centre, the Institute for Food Research and other institutes based at Colney adjacent to the university campus. These organizations formed a loose alliance known as the Norwich Research Park, which now also includes the local acute hospital trust, whose new hospital is sited alongside the Research Park. Kent established a Science Park in 1986 and, coinciding with the redevelopment of east Colchester, Essex is currently planning to launch a Research Park in the next couple of years, earlier efforts having foundered.

Mergers and acquisitions have played their part in supplementing organic growth. Although government policy frustrated Warwick's efforts to link up with the Lanchester College of Technology (now Coventry University) in the 1960s, Warwick (as did UEA) added a local college of education to its portfolio in the late 1970s. Innovation has continued to play an important role in the development of the 1960s universities. UEA took a long-term strategic decision in the 1980s to develop its health studies portfolio, beginning with the creation of the country's first joint school of occupational therapy and physiotherapy in 1991, establishing a health policy and practice unit before taking over the Norfolk College of Nursing and Midwifery in 1995. Critical roles in these developments were undertaken by a chemist Pro-Vice-Chancellor (PVC) (Richard Jones) and a highly innovative founding Professor of Environmental Sciences (Keith Clayton). On the basis of this foundation, a joint UEA/NHS (National Health Service) team led by Shirley Pearce (Professor of Health Psychology) and David Scott (Consultant Rheumatologist) put forward an imaginative proposal for the founding of a new medical school in Norwich, working in partnership with a powerful chief executive of the local NHS Trust, and taking advantage of a new district general hospital being built less than a mile from the University. Although the proposal did not win first-round approval, on 16 June 2000, the HEFCE announced that this would be one of the new medical schools to be established, with an intake of 110 students a year. Beloff had scoffed in 1969 that only Warwick could 'even speculate about a medical school'. Norfolk, apparently, lacked any interesting diseases.[12] Warwick, too, bid successfully in 1999 for a new medical school development in partnership with Leicester, having failed twice with earlier bids in the 1970s.

However, the growth of the 1960s universities has not been a tale of unqualified success. All the 1960s universities have too small a science base. Both UEA and Essex have in the late 1990s closed physics departments due to poor undergraduate recruitment, despite both departments being rated 4 in the 1996 RAE. Essex has integrated a weak chemistry department into biological sciences, thus leaving the natural sciences looking a little sparse. UEA in 1995 and 1999 reconfigured its cumbersome and increasingly inefficient arts schools, creating a single school of history from among three other schools and radically reshaping European studies.

A different future?

Do the 1960s universities face a different future from that predicted by the founders of those institutions? Or will the future emerge organically from the developments over the past four decades? It is striking that the regional role of universities, which was once apparently derided by many of the 1960s universities – but not Warwick – as they attempted to carve out national and international reputations for themselves, is now very much in the ascendant. Warwick has from its inception been very effective at developing relationships with West Midlands industry and has worked closely with local colleges from the early 1980s. UEA, which was noted for its lack of interest in its region for many years, developed a regional policy in the early 1990s under Vice-Chancellor Derek Burke (ex-Warwick), largely in response to the growing influence of the then Anglia Polytechnic which had signed deals under UEA's nose with two local colleges in Norwich, making them regional colleges of Anglia. A powerful East Anglian axis across Norfolk and Suffolk was created in 1996 between UEA and Suffolk College when the latter became an accredited college and, for a brief time, a university college of UEA. Essex, which for a long time after the 'student troubles' of the late 1960s and early 1970s could do nothing right in the eyes of the local landed gentry, in 1996 entered a validating relationship with Writtle College (of agriculture and horticulture), is currently contemplating merger with a small acting school in North London, and is joining with South East Essex College in an ambitious partnership to offer 1500 HE places in Southend – one of the worst cold spots of HE provision in the country. This policy, which has caused some eyebrow raising at Essex and at HEFCE, has the strong support of the Chair of the East of England Regional Development Agency, Vincent Watts – who is also UEA's Vice-Chancellor.

Size remains a critical question for the 1960s institutions. What is the optimum size for each of the seven universities? Warwick, UEA and Essex all started with bold plans of becoming large institutions. Warwick, the largest of the 1960s universities, is well on the way to meeting this objective, especially now that it has a medical school. Essex, the smallest, but which had initial aspirations of growing to some 10,000 students, remains at little more than half that number. Kenneth Capon, the architect of the Wivenhoe campus, drew up plans capable of providing for a student body of 20,000 – many of whom would reside in 28 (14-storey) towers, yet only six were ever built. Multidisciplinary universities of Essex's current size will not survive far into the twenty-first century as successful, research-intensive institutions. This has been recognized and plans are in place for a significant growth in student numbers over a five-year period – HEFCE willing. UEA, now the second largest of the 1960s universities, looks to a medical school and health studies more broadly for continued growth. York and Lancaster remain important regional centres and ought to build on strong research reputations, growing research grant and contract income, and local goodwill, provided that they avoid financial crises such as that which beset Lancaster in the 1990s. Sussex appears to have lost its way in recent years. Brighton remains an attractive location for potential students, but the University's byzantine academic structure and complex degree programmes look a little dated. With a weaker research reputation, Kent appears more vulnerable than any of its peers, but again its geographical location will offer it powerful political protection.

One opportunity for self-preservation and for creating the critical mass necessary to challenge in the global education market place of the twenty-first century would be for institutions to merge or federate with their neighbours. An example in the East of England might see UEA joining Essex and possibly Anglia Polytechnic University, in a federal university of East Anglia, with research and teaching campuses in Norwich and Colchester, teaching campuses in Cambridge and Chelmsford, and FE/HE (community) colleges in Norwich (City College and the Norwich School of Art and Design), Ipswich (Suffolk College), Writtle and Southend (South-East Essex College). The management challenge of running a single institution over several sites would be huge. Would the benefits justify such a development?[13]

Another major issue facing institutions in early middle age is renewal. Where do the new ideas and the willingness to experiment and to challenge come from? How can UEA's motto, derived from an old Norfolk expression 'Do different', be sustained in a climate of increasing conformity driven by rigid funding models, growing accountability and inflexible quality assurance procedures? Beloff warned that 'yesterday's experiment will become tomorrow's tradition', with the 'new map of learning' beginning to 'curl and fray at the edges'.[14] Administrators and academic entrepreneurs have a critical role to play in the process of renewal. Warwick has managed this process very successfully during the Mike Shattock era, but will Warwick find a Bob Paisley to follow its Bill Shankly? Not all 1960s universities have been fortunate to have such a creative manager at the helm, although Michael Paulson-Ellis has exercised a profound influence at UEA over two decades. However, managing universities, despite the long shadows of founding vice-chancellors and powerful registrars, remains a team game. Academic managers, particularly at PVC level and also as heads of department, play a critical role. All the 1960s universities have had their boldly imaginative Keith Claytons or their inspirational Ian Gibsons (ex-professional footballer, Dean of the School of Biological Sciences at UEA and currently Labour MP for Norwich North). Our challenge is to find the next generation of leaders, managers and entrepreneurs and enable them to have sufficient scope to take the risks – which means allowing room for the failures – which will lead to the continuing growth of the 1960s universities over the next century.

References

1. M. Beloff (1969) *The Plateglass Universities*, p. 37. London: Secker and Warburg.
2. A.E. Sloman (1963) *A University in the Making: The Reith Lectures 1963*, p. 15. London: BBC.
3. M. Beloff (1969) op. cit., p. 81.
4. Ibid., pp. 95–102.
5. Ibid., p. 147.
6. E.P. Thompson (ed.) (1970) *Warwick University Limited*, p. 147. Harmondsworth: Penguin.
7. Promotion Committee (1960) *Proposal for a University of Essex*, submitted by the Promotion Committee for consideration by the University Grants Committee, pp. 4–8.
8. University of Essex (1962) *First Report of the Academic Planning Board to the Promotion Committee*, p. 4.
9. A.E. Sloman (1963) op. cit., pp. 23–87.
10. *The Higher*, 20 December 1996.
11. M. Beloff (1969) op. cit., p. 120.
12. M. Beloff (1969) op. cit., p. 39.
13. See D. Palfreyman, H. Thomas and D. Warner (1998) *How to Manage a Merger . . . or Avoid One*. Leeds: Heist.
14. M. Beloff (1969) op. cit., p. 182.

6

Old and New: Durham and Stockton

John Hogan

A traditional collegiate university and widening participation

The development of the University of Durham's Stockton campus is an important tale about academic management in the 1990s. How and why did a very traditional university undertake an innovative development which challenged its previously successful, if somewhat cloistered, image? The tale combines issues of institutional collaboration, widening participation and academic standards with those of academic leadership. There are a number of lessons for the development of higher education in the first part of the twenty-first century.

The University of Durham is the third oldest in England. It was founded in 1832 and modelled itself on Oxford and Cambridge by establishing a residential or 'collegiate' system. From 1852, when the medical school at Newcastle became part of the University, until 1963, the University was based in both Durham and Newcastle and a federal structure was developed, although Durham and Newcastle operated as largely autonomous divisions. The Durham division was known as the Durham Colleges. From the 1920s onwards there was considerable duplication in teaching between the two divisions. This, together with the then comparatively rapid expansion of both divisions after 1959, led to a major reorganization with the creation of the new and separate University of Newcastle upon Tyne by Act of Parliament in 1963. The Durham Colleges continued as the University of Durham.[1]

Durham's range of academic subjects and historic setting helped to confirm an image of a highly respectable, conservative institution. The collegiate structure remains an important and distinctive feature. The University has 14 colleges or societies and all full-time students must be members of one of the colleges or societies. Colleges, in collaboration with departments, are responsible for the admission of students, their general welfare and progress. However, unlike Oxford and Cambridge, the Durham colleges are not teaching bodies. Colleges in Durham help to develop a sense of identity and belonging. They provide a framework for participation in sporting, cultural, religious, social and community care activities. They are increasingly playing a role in the provision of key skills training for students as well as providing academic support facilities, including libraries and IT equipment. The colleges provide full-board accommodation for two years for undergraduate students and the normal expectation is that students will live in for their first and final years, while retaining full college membership and access to college facilities when non-resident. The colleges generate a great deal of loyalty from their students for providing an environment and support which is distinctive and valuable. The University has one of the lowest drop-out rates in the UK. The University believes that a major reason for this is the college system and the high level of pastoral support.

In 1990 Durham had approximately 5500 full-time students, 990 part-time postgraduates and no part-time undergraduates.[2] Eighty per cent of its undergraduates were accommodated in college accommodation. Fewer than 10 per cent were mature students on entry (defined as over 21). Durham is a university which attracts very highly qualified undergraduates. It recruited students from all parts of the country; undergraduates from the North and Yorkshire formed some 25 per cent of the undergraduate population; those from the South and South-East 21 per cent. Thirty-seven per cent of its undergraduates came from private/independent schools. The University was widely regarded as being in the region but not of the region.

The University was not, however, strikingly different from other pre-1992 universities. For entry in October 1990 only 14 per cent of the home applications processed by the Universities Central Council on Admissions (UCCA) came from mature applicants.[3] Only 8 per cent of the home applicants to universities came from the two lowest socio-economic groups as defined by the parental occupation (partly skilled and unskilled occupations). Some 24 per cent of the home applicants admitted came from the independent school sector. The seven universities in the Northern and Yorkshire region (Bradford, Durham, Hull, Leeds, Newcastle, Sheffield and York) accepted 26 per cent of their students from the region.[4]

Throughout the first half of the 1980s there was comparatively little growth in universities. In Durham there were local circumstances which made the University cautious about any growth in student numbers. The full-time student population hovered around about the 5500 mark throughout the 1980s. There was a widespread view that this student population represented a realistic maximum given the small size of Durham City. Durham had, and still has, the highest proportion of full-time students to local residents of any English university. In 1987 the government White Paper *Higher Education Meeting the Challenge* called for a significant increase in higher education and pointed out the need to widen access to under-represented sections of society.[5] The government's policy to expand full-time undergraduate education and widen participation therefore posed a particular challenge to the University. Between 1989 and 1994 higher education grew at a remarkable rate: the age participation index increased from 17 per cent of 18-/19-year-olds entering higher education to 31 per cent.[6]

Teesside

In 1988 a group of northern Conservative MPs urged the Education Secretary, Kenneth Baker, to establish a third university in the North-East. The Teesside Development Corporation approached the Durham Vice-Chancellor, Professor Holliday, with a request that the University should establish a campus on Teesside.[7] The Teesside Development Corporation had been established to address the serious need for urban regeneration of the Teesside industrial conurbation. Teesside had all the classic symptoms of a sick urban economy: high unemployment, poor housing, poor social facilities, low expectations and aspirations. Moreover, it had one of the lowest age participation rates of higher education in the country and one of the poorest business start-up rates. Professor Holliday reacted positively to the proposal. He believed that the Teesside development would give the University access to a major urban conurbation and open up a whole range of possibilities for research and development with industry. Crucially, it offered a way of increasing student numbers and taking non-traditional students, thereby addressing the issues set out in the government's White Paper.

Once news of the approach from the Teesside Development Corporation became public, the then Teesside Polytechnic expressed concerns about the implications of the University of Durham moving into its own area. From the start the University recognized that the Polytechnic would need to be consulted about the project. However, Teesside Polytechnic made it clear that it could only support the proposal if the project was taken forward in equal partnership. After a series of negotiations it was eventually agreed to proceed with plans for 'The Joint University College of Teesside' on the basis of an equal partnership. This was an innovative example of cross-binary institutional cooperation. It avoided any turf wars and ensured that the project would help to increase the range of higher education programmes available to students from the Teesside area without merely duplicating existing provision. There were, however, significant disadvantages to the partnership arrangement. The partnership approach added greatly to the complexity of the arrangements. The new college had to be created as a joint entity which could not adopt, in their entirety, the academic or administrative systems operated by either parent body. Instead there was a range of compromises, new systems or agreed demarcation of responsibilities for particular functions. Durham arranged for its Statutes to be changed to allow it to award degrees jointly with Teesside Polytechnic. It was envisaged that the college would act as a faculty for both Teesside Polytechnic and the University of Durham. The planning effort was considerable for both institutions. In Durham for a 12-month period between 1991 and 1992 it was estimated that approximately £300,000 of staff time was spent in the planning process. Certain service functions were allocated to the parent institutions so Durham became responsible for the provision of careers advice and Teesside responsible for library services, for example. A number of the teaching systems agreed were closer in style to those more typically found in the post-1992 university sector. These included a semesterized academic year and a modular degree structure whereas at that stage Durham was neither modularized nor semesterized.

The reaction within the University of Durham to these developments was mixed. Senate, in February 1990, was asked to support the establishment of the joint college. The arguments were clearly presented on both sides. The development would allow the University to expand at a rate far faster than could be achieved in Durham alone. However, the main argument in favour of the development was not primarily about student growth. Rather it was about the nature of the University and specifically its mission within the North-East region. From its initial inception the project was regarded as a way in which the University could make a significant contribution to a deprived part of the UK. Although not articulated in the public debate, senior officers also recognized that the development would challenge many of the University's traditional, almost stereotypical, assumptions about the nature of undergraduate students, their backgrounds and futures. The project was a piece of social and institutional engineering. It was regarded as a mechanism for change within the University as a whole. The college was to be established with a particular mission to attract local students who would not otherwise have considered entering higher education, certainly not a university with Durham's sort of reputation.

Against the proposal many feared that the Stockton initiative would dilute the University's mission, be very difficult to operate in practice given the geographic distance between the two sites, and be expensive to run which would take resources away from the Durham campus. There was particular concern about the involvement of Teesside Polytechnic. Eventually the matter was put to a vote and carried by the narrowest of margins.[8]

The development of University College, Stockton

It was agreed that the two institutions would establish the new College as a company limited by guarantee. When the College was launched it had its own separate legal identity. Applicants applied via UCCA to the new institution which had its own prospectus. A site was agreed on reclaimed brownfield land on the south bank of the River Tees, and the name 'University College, Stockton' was adopted. The Teesside Development Corporation provided the capital for a £7 million building.

Throughout the planning process the Universities Funding Council and the Polytechnics and Colleges Funding Council had been kept informed of developments and approached for support. Initial student numbers were provided by these two higher education funding agencies and the first students admitted in 1992.

University College, Stockton was established during a period of very rapid growth in student numbers in the early 1990s. The final planning strategy prior to the admission of the first students aimed for 1600 full-time students by 1996. However, in November 1993 the government decided that higher education had been too successful too quickly at expansion and introduced a cap on further growth for a three-year period from 1994/95.[9] In 1994 a revised academic plan cut planned expansion at Stockton to 1500 by the year 2000. This left the two parent institutions with a major problem over the development of the College. Just before the first students had been admitted in 1992, Teesside had become a university with its own degree awarding powers. To some extent this undermined one of the original premises for the partnership arrangement.

By 1994 it had become clear that the cost of establishing a new college which had to develop its own systems, including its own quality assurance procedures, was substantial. The income from the Higher Education Funding Council for England (HEFCE) and student fees was not sufficient to meet the operating costs given the slower rate of growth forced on the universities from 1993 onwards. There was a further series of negotiations between Durham and Teesside. This resulted in an amicable arrangement for Durham to take over responsibility for all aspects of administration at the Stockton college, although some courses were still to be delivered by Teesside staff and the degrees were still to be awarded jointly. At that stage Durham's Registrar and Secretary, John Hayward, also became Principal of the college.[10] This was, in part, an indication of the extent to which the Stockton development was absorbing senior management time within Durham. The difficulties of managing a satellite operation which operated on separate systems to the rest of the University were substantial. In 1996 it was finally agreed that the University of Durham should take full responsibility for all aspects of quality assurance and academic standards. Some staff previously employed by Teesside University became members of the University of Durham and all students graduating from 1998 onwards have been awarded University of Durham degrees. The University, therefore, became fully responsible for an institution which had been developed in equal partnership and the College was finally established on the basis which had been originally envisaged. In 1998 the University took the next logical step of designating the development, 'University of Durham, Stockton campus', with the Principal's title being changed to Provost.

There is no doubt that the management of the campus by a single institution has greatly eased some of the operating difficulties previously experienced. Mr Hayward's energy and ability to persuade external agencies to enter into a series of partnerships with the campus produced a rapid improvement in the financial position. By 1997 the position at Stockton had improved to such an extent that the University agreed to a £15 million development programme for a new academic teaching building and student residences based on projected income from Stockton. Three million pounds of this expenditure was provided by external agencies. In October 1998 the full-time student numbers broke the 1000 mark. The University had been helped in this respect by the government's decision to allow a resumption of modest expansion in higher education numbers. For entry in October 1998 and 1999 Durham bid successfully for 399 full-time undergraduate numbers and 360 part-time numbers at its Stockton campus. These bids were made on the basis of high quality and widening participation. Without the Stockton initiative it would have been almost impossible for a university of Durham's type to have made a credible bid for extra student numbers to support widening participation. The current plans are to break the 2000 student mark by 2001/02 and eventually to reach 3000 students.

Academic development

From its inception, the Stockton campus had a specific focus on developing professional, vocational and transferable skills. Innovation in the curriculum was encouraged and a heavy investment was made in computer-aided learning and multimedia techniques. Competencies and transferable skills were explicitly articulated within the curriculum. The campus did not attempt to duplicate programmes taught at either Teesside or Durham universities but developed complementary programmes with a strong inter-disciplinary bias. Anthropology in Durham was transformed into human sciences at Stockton, biological sciences into biomedical sciences, biology and geography into environmental sciences and so on. This policy avoided the campus appearing to compete with either of its parent institutions and it also provided a clear rationale for the development of new pro-grammes. However, there have been important disadvantages. The develop-ment of coherent interdisciplinary programmes is, arguably, more difficult to achieve than traditional single honours degrees. The amount of manage-ment, planning and coordination is significantly greater. The nature of the teaching arrangements at Stockton has placed a heavy load on staff involved in teaching. The interdisciplinary programmes have not always helped under-graduate student recruitment. While demand in Durham runs at approxim-ately ten applicants to every place, Stockton still enters Clearing to fill its academic programmes. The recruitment position at Stockton, however, improved significantly with the new constitutional status as the University of Durham, Stockton campus.

The crucial issue for the University in the campus development has been the maintenance of academic standards. The issue of academic standards has dominated higher education throughout the 1990s. While many have criticized the bureaucratization associated with quality assurance, and the arbitrariness of numerical grades used in subject reviews organized by the Quality Assurance Agency (QAA) and its predecessors, there can be no doubt that all higher education institutions have had to pay far more attention to the explicit articulation of academic standards, particularly as part of any new development. The Stockton campus, with its emphasis on widening participation, interdisciplinary programmes and physical distance, has therefore come under careful scrutiny both within Durham and externally.

Within Durham the average A level points score for all academic programmes is in the region of 26. At Stockton, where a significant proportion of the students are admitted without reference to their A level points, the average score is 18. How is it possible for the University to ensure that the academic standards are the same for graduates from both campuses when the starting point is different? Between 1995 and 1999 five academic programmes at Stockton were involved in QAA subject reviews. In three cases the provision was rated as 'excellent' and in the fourth and fifth, using the QAA's numerical system, scores of 23 out of a maximum of 24 were achieved. Durham underwent the QAA's continuation audit process in May 1998. The University decided to take advantage of the audit process to ask the auditors to examine specifically the systems in place at Stockton and to offer a view as to whether they were appropriate for ensuring the safeguard of academic standards. The report, published in January 1999, had considerable praise for the Stockton development, commending the University's boldness of vision and fully endorsing the quality assurance mechanisms.[11]

At its inception it was agreed that the Stockton campus would offer programmes by using staff drawn from the two parent universities and not hire its own staff. Since 1996 all the teaching has been delivered by Durham staff working within Durham departments. There are a number of significant features which follow from this. Most of the academic staff who contribute to the teaching make the 47-mile return journey from Durham once or twice a week during each semester. The timetable has been structured to deliver two- or three-hour teaching blocks and this in turn has led to a style of teaching which is different from the traditional lectures/seminars. A greater burden of academic support has fallen on the shoulders of the professional staff who are based for most of their time at Stockton. The campus now has a full-time provost and four vice-provosts. It has developed the equivalent of a faculty administration. It has staff who have been specifically appointed to provide welfare and academic advice and thereby has made available the sort of support provided by the Durham colleges. A significant burden falls on the shoulders of the course leaders and, to a much greater extent than in Durham, the academic programmes are managed by the course leaders. Administrative work, which falls on a department within Durham, is often performed by the 'central' administration at Stockton. As a result the central overheads at Stockton are higher than those in Durham. However, the high level of service has supported the development of successful academic programmes and this would not have been achieved by the adoption of the traditional administrative structures in place in Durham. To a significant extent the success of the Stockton campus has been a management success.

The style of teaching is different. The use of short fat modules, as opposed to the long thin ones used in Durham, is generally regarded by the staff who teach at Stockton as an advantage for the Stockton students. The academic teaching year at Stockton is longer, with a 30-week academic year as opposed to Durham's 28. Students at the Stockton campus are required to take a study skills module. The wastage rate, as might be expected, is higher than elsewhere in Durham at 10.7 per cent compared with 4.8 per cent for the rest of the University, with financial hardship being identified as the single largest problem. The overall degree results show a slightly lower proportion of II(i)s and a higher proportion of II(ii)s awarded than in the rest of Durham. The University's view is that, given the general intake profile, this is in line with the University's expectations.

Since the University of Durham became responsible for all aspects of management and administration at the Stockton site, considerable attention has been paid to the issue of the extent to which Stockton should adopt the same administrative systems as those operated in Durham. The debate about 'Durhamization' occurs repeatedly over a wide range of issues; everything from the length of the academic year through to the organization of degree ceremonies (which are held in Stockton for graduates of the Stockton campus). Inevitably, given the historic development, there are many issues which remain to be determined but the campus has been developing at such a rapid rate that any attempt to overprescribe could be immensely damaging.

Stockton challenges the way in which the University has traditionally operated. It is something of an experimental hot-house. It allows the University to try new things and bring those that work back to the University.

Widening participation

The key mission for the Stockton campus was to widen participation in higher education and, specifically, to make a major contribution to the region by attracting local students. In December 1998, of the campus population of just over 1000 full-time students, 45 per cent came from the North-East and 27 per cent of the students admitted were mature. These figures compare with 13 per cent of students at the Durham campus from the North-East and only 6 per cent mature. There is clear evidence that Stockton has succeeded in making a significant contribution to widening participation. Confirmation of the University's success in achieving its widening participation objective came from HEFCE's announcement that it would support the joint bid made by Newcastle and Durham for the introduction of 70 medical training undergraduate places to be offered at the Stockton campus from 2001.[12] The reintroduction of medical training at the University of Durham has been achieved because the University was able to demonstrate that it had a clear commitment to widening participation.

There are difficulties associated with this success. As the campus becomes better known and is regarded as an integral part of the University, steps will need to be taken to preserve the original intention of widening participation and avoid the campus being swamped with students who might have chosen to study at University of Durham's main campus.

It is arguable that Durham has created a widening participation ghetto with students who do not have the normal academic qualifications to be admitted to Durham degrees being admitted to programmes taught at Stockton. Further, it could be argued that the Stockton project means that the rest of the University will not take on board the widening participation challenge. The two arguments are easily countered. The level of investment at Stockton dispels any suggestion of ghettoization. The facilities, particularly the teaching accommodation, are the equal of anything else within the University. The lessons learned from the Stockton development, particularly with regard to widening participation, are being brought back into the main University campus and have heavily influenced the University's widening participation strategy required by the HEFCE.

The position nationally with regard to the admission of local and mature students has been transformed by the post-1992 universities. For entry in October 1998, 22 per cent of the home applications processed by the Universities and Colleges Admissions Service (UCAS) came from mature applicants. The five universities in the North-East (Durham, Newcastle, Northumbria, Sunderland and Teesside) accepted 45 per cent of applicants from the North-East region. It is widely recognized that progress towards widening participation has been modest. Only 11 per cent of the home applicants to universities came from the two lowest social economic groups.[13] Most of the limited success in widening participation has been achieved by the new university sector. However, the pre-1992 universities have tried to develop a more inclusive admissions policy. The approach adopted by the University of Durham, via the Stockton campus, has been unique and remains an important experiment for the system as a whole.

Conclusions

In a number of respects the University has paid a major price for the Stockton development. It has added an additional level of administrative complexity to the University's operations. The development of a satellite base at a significant distance from the main campus is, and will always remain, a major issue. The development has diluted the institutional image, but many people would regard this as an advantage. Nevertheless, it is somewhat galling to see the University's average A level grade points used as one of the many so-called performance indicators by newspapers and others showing Durham slipping in this particular category as the proportion of students entering our Stockton campus increases.

From its original establishment many have suspected that at some point Stockton will develop into an independent higher education institution and split from the University in a manner similar to the division of Newcastle and Durham in 1963. An alternative view, which is sometimes expressed, is that Stockton and Teesside University will merge. Neither development is probable within the foreseeable future. The structures now in place make it difficult to separate the campus from the host institution. Durham has invested a great deal of time, effort and money into the Stockton project: it is too important to lose.

Notes and References

1. I.E. Graham (1978) *A Brief Note on the History of the University of Durham*, pp. 1–3. Durham: University of Durham.
2. All figures and statistics concerning Durham and Stockton students are taken from the annual *Student Statistics Book* produced by the University.
3. UCCA (1992) *Twenty-ninth Report 1990–91*, p. 9. Cheltenham: UCCA.
4. UCCA (1991) *Statistical Supplement to the Twenty-eighth Report 1989–90*, pp. 17, 30. Cheltenham: UCCA.
5. Department of Education and Science and Welsh Office (1987) *Higher Education Meeting the Challenge*. London: HMSO.
6. D. Robertson and J. Hillman (1997) Report 6. Widening participation in higher education for students from lower social economic families and students with disabilities, in National Committee of Inquiry into Higher Education (1997) *Higher Education in the Learning Society (Dearing Report)*, p. 37. London: HMSO.
7. Professor F.G.T. Holliday was Vice-Chancellor and Warden from 1980. He was succeeded by Professor E.A.V. Ebsworth in 1990 and Professor Sir Kenneth Calman in 1998.
8. University of Durham Senate minutes, February 1990.
9. HEFCE (1994) *Maximum Aggregate Student Number Allocation 1994–95*. Bristol: HEFCE.
10. Mr J.C.F. Hayward succeeded Professor R.T. Parfitt as Principal.
11. Quality Assurance Agency for Higher Education (1999) *Quality Audit Report, University of Durham*. Gloucester: QAA.
12. HEFCE (1999) *Increasing Medical Student Numbers in England*. Bristol: HEFCE.
13. UCAS (1999) *Statistical Summary 1998*, pp. 35, 36 and 38. Cheltenham: UCAS.

7

Higher Education in Scotland: Diversity, Distinctiveness and Devolution

David Caldwell

A diverse sector

For a country with a population of only around five million, Scotland has a remarkably diverse system of higher education (HE). At the time of writing, it consists of 13 universities, one university college, and five other institutions. In addition, The Open University has a significant presence in Scotland, and two other institutions are currently seeking designation as higher education institutions (HEIs).

As in the United Kingdom as a whole, universities in Scotland are often divided into two categories, those which have had university title since before 1992 and those which were granted university title in 1992 or later. For many purposes this simple classification is useful, but in the Scottish case it fails to emphasize sufficiently the diversity which exists, particularly within the first of the two groups. At one extreme, pre-1992 can mean a university founded early in the fifteenth century (St Andrews), while at the other it can mean a foundation as recent as 1966 (Stirling). A helpful subclassification is to divide this group into four 'ancient' and four 1960s universities.

The 'ancients' were all established by the end of the sixteenth century, and as a result for a period of over 200 years Scotland had four universities while England had only two. Even within this subgroup there are differences. The earliest three (St Andrews, Glasgow and Aberdeen, all founded in the fifteenth century) were created by Papal Bull. Edinburgh, the youngest of the ancients, was founded in 1583 as a civic university. Nonetheless, there is a coherence about this group, largely because for nearly 400 years they constituted the entirety of the Scottish university system and parliamentary legislation dealt with them as a group.

The group of four 1960s universities is itself varied. Three had a prior history, two of them (Strathclyde and Heriot-Watt) as Scottish Central Institutions (see below), and one (Dundee) as an integral part of the University of St Andrews. Only Stirling was an entirely new foundation. What they have in common is that their establishment as universities was a consequence of the then government's decision to accept the advocacy of the Robbins Committee for a substantial expansion of higher education. In addition, they are the only Scottish universities which have Royal Charters as their governing instruments.

A significant development during the twentieth century was the growth of a group of higher education institutions outside the university sector. These were the Scottish Central Institutions (CIs) and Colleges of Education (CEs) which were funded and controlled directly by government through the Scottish Office. What the CIs and CEs shared was a vocational mission, but within this group there was also much diversity. A number were polytechnic in character, offering a wide subject range, while others were monotechnic. The larger and more broadly based CIs secured university title – Strathclyde and Heriot-Watt in the 1960s, as already mentioned, and five others (Napier, Glasgow Caledonian, Robert Gordon in Aberdeen, Paisley and Abertay Dundee) in the 1990s. These five constitute the newest group of Scottish universities and because of their shared history have a good deal in common, including the fact that their governing instruments are Orders of Council.

The changing shape of the sector

The 13 universities now represent well over 90 per cent of the HE sector in Scotland. The largest has over 20,000 students, and the smallest over 4000. The combined student numbers of the six non-university institutions are equivalent to those of one of the medium-sized universities. Of the six, Queen Margaret University College in Edinburgh is the largest and embraces the widest subject range. The others are two art colleges (Glasgow School of Art and Edinburgh College of Art), Northern College of Education, the Royal Scottish Academy of Music and Drama, and the Scottish Agricultural College. Several monotechnics have already merged with universities, and merger negotiations currently in progress are likely to lead to the disappearance as separate institutions of both Northern College and Edinburgh College of Art.

The trend in Scotland over the past ten years has been for the number of HEIs – but not the number of universities – to reduce. In 1990, there were eight universities and 18 other HEIs. Now, at the start of the new millennium, there are 13 universities and six other HEIs, with the expectation that this will soon reduce to 13 and four respectively. We will have fewer – but larger – institutions, and (with a few exceptions) monotechnics will disappear and almost all higher education provision in Scotland will be within universities.

This rationalization is one factor contributing to greater coherence of the sector. However, other changes in the early 1990s were even more significant. Until 1992 there were two sectors which interacted to only a limited degree. There was the university sector, consisting of the four ancient and four 1960s universities, receiving funding through an agency with a UK-wide remit, the Universities Funding Council (UFC); and there was the CI/CE sector, consisting of 18 institutions, funded and controlled by the Scottish Office. Each sector had a separate representative body – the Committee of Scottish University Principals (CSUP) for the universities, and the Conference of Centrally Funded Colleges (CSCFC) for the CIs and CEs. This situation was transformed by a series of linked changes: the elimination throughout the UK of the binary line; the designation as universities of the polytechnics and five largest Scottish CIs; and the creation of territorially based funding bodies. In Scotland, this had the effect not just of establishing a single sector but of repatriating the eight existing universities and thus reinforcing the Scottish aspect of their identity. It also led quickly to the establishment of a representative body able to speak for the whole of Scottish HE, the Committee of Scottish Higher Education Principals (COSHEP).

The trend towards fewer and larger institutions has to be subject to the qualification that there is also the potential for additional institutions. Bell College in Hamilton and the University of the Highlands and Islands project (UHI) recently applied for designation as HEIs. They are interesting cases, since both highlight issues concerning the relationship between further and higher education. Some higher education provision is located in further education (FE) colleges. The courses involved are mainly Higher National Certificate (HNC) and Higher National Diploma (HND) programmes, but a few degree courses are also offered, as a result of colleges making collaborative arrangements with universities to validate or franchise specific courses. Many further education colleges thus now offer some advanced courses in addition to non-advanced work. In the case of Bell College, it considered that the proportion of advanced work has reached a level which justified its designation as an HEI. Its case has now been accepted by the Scottish Executive, and it is expected to become an HEI early in 2001.

The case of UHI is different. Many people in the Highlands and Islands have long aspired to have a university located within their region. This dates back at least as far as the 1960s, when Inverness was a candidate in the competition for the site of Scotland's new university, in which competition Stirling was the eventual winner. Interest revived strongly in the 1990s, and advocates of the project secured support in principle from the (then Conservative) government. However, this time the approach that has been adopted is not to create a brand new greenfield institution, but rather to build on and develop the HE work already being undertaken by FE colleges located in the region. It is deliberate that provision is very widely distributed, from Perth in the south to Shetland in the north and Stornoway in the west: it reflects the desire to serve a vast area with a small and scattered population. It will be some years, however, before the Highlands and

Islands have their university. UHI may succeed in obtaining designation as an HEI, but it will probably take another eight years or so before it can hope to satisfy the current criteria for the award of university title. The project continues to enjoy government support, but this support does not extend to allowing any short cuts.

The cases of Bell College and UHI do not, I believe, invalidate the argument that the trend is towards fewer and larger institutions. What it does signal is that there is significant movement on the HE/FE interface, that development and change can take place not just within sectors but across them, and that the sector boundaries are not absolute. It would not be difficult for the extensive collaboration which already exists between FE colleges and HEIs to grow into more permanent alliances, or even lead to mergers. The establishment in 1999 of a Scottish Further Education Funding Council (SFEFC), mirroring the existing Scottish Higher Education Funding Council (SHEFC), is a significant facilitating factor. The two Councils are separate bodies – so far – but they share the same Executive.

Distinctive features

Notwithstanding the diversity in the origins and missions of the institutions, the Scottish system is fairly cohesive. In part, this is related to the fact that Scotland has a small population, and that it has a near neighbour with a population ten times as large. Such a circumstance always tends to reinforce the sense of national identity. However, even more significant is that the Scottish system does have some important features which distinguish it, and which have roots extending beyond the HE sector itself.

The most fundamental is that, even during the period between the political union of Scotland with England in 1707 and the re-establishment of a Scottish Parliament in 1999, Scotland retained its own cultural identity. One consequence of this is that its education system, at both school and university levels, has developed in different ways. Critically, the examination system in the upper stages of secondary schooling, the Scottish Highers, the results of which are the basis for progression into Scottish HEIs for the great majority of applicants, differ substantially from the A level system that prevails in the rest of the UK. Typically, Scottish pupils sit their Highers at age 17, approximately one year earlier than A level candidates take their examinations. Nor is this the only difference. The Scottish curriculum is more broadly based, with candidates being examined in up to six subjects at Higher grade. Although Advanced Highers (which bear a closer resemblance to A levels) are now being introduced, the Higher seems likely to remain the dominant currency for HE entry for the foreseeable future. Many students still enter HE immediately after completing the Higher year at school, but the trend (likely to become more marked as a result of the introduction of Advanced Highers) is for the majority to undertake a further year of study before entering HE.

These differences in the school examination system explain in part the distinctive features of the Scottish undergraduate awards structure. The most widely used awards are a three-year, full-time ordinary degree and a four-year, full-time honours degree. Ordinary degree courses, and years one and two of honours degree courses, usually involve the study of a slightly wider range of subjects than applies in other parts of the UK. Although the majority of students now study for an honours degree, a significant number continue to choose the ordinary degree, which enjoys general recognition and respect as a qualification in its own right. Scotland thus has a more flexible system of undergraduate awards capable of meeting a wider range of student requirements.

The Scottish honours degree has much in common with the honours degree elsewhere in the UK, but there are important differences. The extra year is not to be explained simply in terms of Scottish students entering HE on average a year younger than their English counterparts. The longer duration of Scottish honours courses allows the students to develop their specialities to at least as high a level as honours graduates anywhere in the UK, but to secure this on a more fully developed and broader base. The longer courses are also a closer match to international practice, and articulate better with it.

A further important characteristic of the Scottish system is that the number of HE students in relation to the population is substantially higher than for the UK as a whole. There are two reasons for this: first, the age participation rate (APR) among Scots is higher; and second, Scotland is a net importer of students.

The differences in APR in different parts of the UK are marked. Currently approximately 50 per cent of the 18-year-old cohort enter HE in Scotland, compared with approximately 40 per cent elsewhere in the UK. This reflects the fact that, although very large discrepancies remain in the APRs between different social groups, Scottish institutions have had some success in widening access. Performance indicators for 1997/98 show that Scottish HEIs have slightly better participation rates from low-participation neighbourhoods. However, participation rates from social groups IIIM, IV and V remain low, and are very similar to the rest of the UK.[1]

Scotland's strength as an importer of students is illustrated by figures published by the Universities and Colleges Admissions Service (UCAS) for new full-time undergraduate entrants in 1999. These indicate that over 6100 students from other parts of the UK took up places in Scottish institutions, as compared with approximately 2250 Scots choosing to study in England, Wales or Northern Ireland. The difference between the two figures is equivalent to over 13 per cent of the total figure for full-time undergraduates admitted to Scottish HEIs for the first time in 1999.[2] This pattern of recruiting from outside Scotland – and of course substantial numbers also come from overseas – is important not just for Scottish HE but also for the Scottish economy: it has been calculated that in 1993/94 the expenditures in Scotland of students from other parts of the UK contributed approximately £215 million to the Scottish economy.[3]

Devolution

Although the whole of the 1990s was a period of change for Scottish HE, the change which may well prove to be the most significant of all occurred only at the end of the decade with the devolution of power over a very wide range of matters, including HE, to the first Scottish Parliament to sit since 1707. In some ways the ground had been well prepared by the repatriation of the pre-1992 universities and the establishment of SHEFC as a separate funding body for Scottish HEIs. Moreover, since 1992 public funding for the entire sector had come from the Scottish block grant, and it was Scottish Office ministers who determined what funds should be allocated to SHEFC, and what guidance should be given to SHEFC regarding the distribution of these funds. However, as the senior minister concerned, the Secretary of State for Scotland, was a member of a British Cabinet bound by the conventions of collective responsibility, it remained unlikely that arrangements in Scotland would be very different from those in the rest of the UK. This can be illustrated by reference to an example I shall return to shortly in order to demonstrate the difference that devolution has made: when the new arrangements for tuition fees were introduced pre-devolution in 1998, the same regime applied both north and south of the Border, with the exception of a small concession in relation to year four of the Scottish honours degree.

In a devolved Scotland we need to work on new assumptions: local arrangements can be different, and sometimes they will be. Indeed, if that were not the case, one would have to ask what was the point of devolution. In the event there is already ample evidence to indicate that devolution will make a difference.

One compelling reason why this is bound to be the case is that political control will be in different hands. Even if the same party enjoyed overall majorities both at Westminster and in Edinburgh, the British Cabinet and the Scottish Executive would be distinct bodies. In any case, the introduction of a proportionality factor makes it unlikely that any party will achieve an overall majority in the Scottish Parliament. Even in 1999, when Labour so dominated first-past-the-post constituency voting that it won 53 seats out of 73, it failed to achieve an overall majority because the proportionality factor awarded all but three of the 56 top-up seats to other parties. It is significant too that Scotland enjoys the most far-reaching of the devolution options: it has a Parliament, not an Assembly, and that Parliament will enact primary legislation.

However, what is especially significant is that those matters which are devolved will receive much closer attention from ministers and parliamentarians than was possible prior to devolution. Scottish HE forms a much larger part of the portfolio of the minister and deputy minister in the Scottish Executive responsible for the Enterprise and Lifelong Learning Department than was the case before devolution, when one Scottish Office minister was responsible for all of Scottish education and usually at least one other equally large area. Parliamentary scrutiny will also be greater, both because there is an Enterprise and Lifelong Learning Committee which sees HE issues as representing a large part of its business, and because it is a declared aim of the Parliament that its committees should have a particularly prominent role which may sometimes involve even the initiation of legislation.

These various factors all contribute towards HE issues having a higher public and political profile than before. No more telling example can be cited in support than the controversy over tuition fees which has been one of the major themes of political debate in Scotland since the 1999 election campaign.

Education is one of the most important of the areas which have been devolved. It follows that all levels of education can be expected to feature much more strongly in Scottish parliamentary elections than in those for the UK Parliament where the reserved, that is non-devolved, matters also command attention. It should not have been a surprise, therefore, that tuition fees became one of the issues in the 1999 campaign, nor (since fees had been a policy initiative of the majority Labour administration in Westminster, which had been resisted by the other parties) that all the parties in opposition at UK level should make abolition of tuition fees one of their electoral pledges in the Scottish parliamentary campaign. What was perhaps a surprise – and may have been regretted after the event, at least by some of the Liberal Democrat politicians who became part of the Scottish Executive – was that the issue achieved such a high profile and that their pledges were so unequivocal as to leave them little room for manoeuvre.

This first stage of the debate points up both advantages and disadvantages of devolution. The obvious advantage is that devolved matters attract greater interest than before. There is an opportunity to ensure that politicians have a better and deeper understanding of them. As regards HE, this is reinforced by a factor unrelated to devolution, namely the huge increase we have seen in the APR during the last 40 years. In Scotland in particular, with an APR of around 50 per cent, most families have a stake in HE. The fact that a high proportion of the electorate now has an interest in the subject means that it will become more prominent in election campaigns, particularly in elections to bodies where (as in the case of the Scottish Parliament) education is one of the principal areas of responsibility.

The disadvantage of this higher profile is that the party political cut and thrust of the electoral contest can result in oversimplification of issues which are fairly complex. This was certainly the case with the tuition fees debate in Scotland. However, I am convinced that advantages considerably outweigh disadvantages. It is better that politicians take a genuine interest in HE than that they ignore it. It is up to the stakeholders to ensure that the politicians are well briefed.

In any case, the second stage is one from which some encouragement can be drawn. When it became clear that there was serious political difficulty within the Scottish Executive – Labour wanted to retain tuition fees, and its Liberal Democratic coalition partners wanted to abolish them – it was decided that the way forward was to conduct a thorough investigation focusing not just on the narrow question of tuition fees but the broader issues of student support. A committee was established under the chairmanship of a well-respected lawyer, Andrew Cubie, with a membership well equipped with relevant experience and knowledge.

The Cubie Committee raised the debate to a higher level, dealing with tuition fees in the context of a larger discussion about what systems of student support would best serve the needs of potential students and their families, would best support wider access and social inclusion, would provide institutions with the funding necessary to ensure high-quality provision, and would represent the best value for the public money which was invested.[4] Cubie presented a well-integrated package of measures which won widespread support from students, staff, HEIs and the general public.

The third stage was for the Scottish Executive and the political parties to decide where they stood on the Cubie recommendations. It would have been unfortunate if a well-thought-out and coherent package had been deconstructed. In the event, the Scottish Executive has decided to retain most of the framework recommended by the Cubie Committee, but has made significant changes in the detailed provisions. Although the outcome justifies only a qualified welcome, we should be encouraged by the fact that there has been a serious and well-informed debate on an important issue, which has engaged not just the immediate stakeholders but also the political class, press and media commentators and the general public. It is doubtful whether, without devolution, this particular debate would have happened. On the grounds that, while debating issues thoroughly does not necessarily guarantee a good outcome, failure to debate usually guarantees the reverse, that must be regarded positively.

Scotland, the UK and the world

Having devoted so much space to devolution, it is important that I should avoid leaving the impression that Scottish HE is insular and inward-looking. The opposite is the case. Scottish HE is well integrated into the UK system, and also has a strong international profile. For different institutions there will be a different balance between the Scottish, UK and international foci, but none would see its role as solely Scottish. It is true that service to Scotland is central: Scottish HE has a unique contribution to make to the culture and society of Scotland, but above all to its economic success. However, a crucial part of the mission lies beyond the borders of Scotland itself. It is to do with enhancing the country's international reputation and its economic competitiveness. This requires Scottish HE to aim to be world-class, both in learning and teaching and in research.

These are exceptionally challenging targets, particularly when the sector has undergone a period of fundamental and rapid change. There is no scope for complacency and, as has been observed by the Principal of the University of Edinburgh, Professor Sir Stewart Sutherland, in the wake of this change Scottish HE needs 'to define its corporate and several individual identities'.[5] Nonetheless, there are many positive features, notably the high participation rate and success in attracting students from outside Scotland. The Scottish respect for learning is sometimes exaggerated, but it is not without substance. Devolution offers an opportunity to build on this. My hope is that during the twenty-first century in Scotland lifelong learning will become more than a slogan, more than simply words in the title of a Scottish Executive Department. The target should be to create Scotland, the learning nation.

References

1. Higher Education Funding Council for England (HEFCE), Higher Education Funding Council for Wales (HEFCW), Department of Education Northern Ireland, Scottish Higher Education Funding Council (SHEFC) (1999) *Performance Indicators in Higher Education 1996–97, 1997–98.* London: HEFCE.
2. UCAS (2000) New student numbers rise by 5000. News Release, 12 January.
3. I. McNicoll (1995) *The Impact of the Scottish Higher Education Sector on the Economy of Scotland.* Glasgow: COSHEP.
4. Independent Committee of Inquiry into Student Finance (1999) *Student Finance: Fairness for the Future.* Edinburgh: Independent Committee of Inquiry into Student Finance.
5. S. Sutherland (1999) Current priorities in higher education, in T.G.K. Bryce and W.M. Humes (eds) *Scottish Education.* Edinburgh: Edinburgh University Press.

8

Higher Education in Wales

David Warner

Introduction

This chapter resembles Caesar's description of Gaul in that it is divided into three parts, albeit somewhat unequal ones. The first looks at Welsh Higher Education as a whole and, in particular, examines its key characteristics within the context of some aspects of Welsh culture. This will be undertaken through the eyes of a relatively recent incomer – and one from England at that! I trust that this impertinence will be excused, both by the value of having an outsider comment on the situation and by the fact that I have sought and plundered the views of many of my fellow principals of Welsh HEIs. In the last analysis, however, everything in this chapter – both good and bad, both easily acceptable and provocative – can be attributed only to me.

So let me start with a paradox. The classic English perception of Wales is that it is a region of the UK and a fairly insignificant one at that. This is a true perception, but it involves a false belief. Wales is a nation and one which is growing in national pride and strength as every year passes. Nevertheless, notwithstanding this important difference, a major argument of this chapter is that there are certain aspects of the current Welsh situation which might well provide pointers for the future of the remainder of the UK HE system. These aspects would include the probability of future structural and constitutional changes, the concept of the community university, the current and expected impact of HE on the Welsh economy, the role of the National Assembly as a harbinger of the role of regional councils, the future of the Welsh Funding Councils and the newly agreed participation of all Welsh HEIs in the Committee of Vice-Chancellors and Principals (CVCP). These issues will be dealt with in more detail as the chapter progresses.

The second part of the chapter will examine those Welsh HEIs which are neither constituent colleges of the University of Wales nor universities in their own right. This is a tortuous way of defining that ragbag group of HEIs which in England (at least at the time of writing) is eligible for membership of the Standing Conference of Principals (SCoP). These HEIs are included here both because of my own personal passion for their contribution and because otherwise this whole book would have passed over them in silence; a fate which is not uncommon in the mainstream of debate about HE in the UK.

The final part will be an attempt to look through the glass darkly at the future of Welsh HE. To do this I will construct a series of alternative structural models and examine some of their strengths and weaknesses. Such flights of fancy are commonplace in Wales since the Higher Education Funding Council for Wales (HEFCW)[1] published its report to the National Assembly in September 1999.[2] At the time of writing, I genuinely do not know which model is likely to predominate, but then a similar problem affects each of my co-authors in this book. The future is another place, but perhaps the current Welsh situation can provide some sort of street map.

Structure of Welsh HE

The University of Glamorgan

There are 13 HEIs in Wales,[3] plus a growing amount of HE work taught in further education colleges, and yet there are only two universities: the University of Wales and the University of Glamorgan. The latter was reconstituted as a 'modern' university in 1992, having followed the classic metamorphosis of many similar institutions in England. Originally established in 1913 as the South Wales and Monmouthshire School of Mines, it became Glamorgan Technical College in 1949, a regional college of technology in 1958, Glamorgan Polytechnic in 1970, and was renamed 'The Polytechnic of Wales' in 1975. In 1998/99 Glamorgan had more than 17,000 enrolled students, which would appear to make it by far the largest single institution in Wales. However, a significant percentage of these students are franchised out and taught primarily at Welsh FE institutions. Glamorgan therefore lies at the heart of a national network and acts as a major counterbalance to the otherwise all-embracing University of Wales.

The University of Wales[4]

Over the last 11 decades the Federal University of Wales has slowly grown to encompass, or at least significantly affect, all of the other Welsh HEIs. It was founded by Royal Charter in November 1893, bringing together three existing colleges, which had previously prepared students for external degrees of the University of London: the University College of Wales Aberystwyth (opened in 1872), the University College of South Wales and Monmouthshire (opened in 1883) and the University College of North Wales in Bangor (opened in 1884). In 1920 part of the former Swansea

Technical College was incorporated as the University's fourth constituent college, followed (after a complex genesis) by the Welsh National School of Medicine in 1931, and then in 1967 by the University of Wales Institute of Science and Technology (which was later to merge with University College, Cardiff, and form what is now correctly known as University of Wales, Cardiff). Finally in 1971, St David's College, Lampeter, which had been founded in 1826 and already held its own degree awarding powers, which are now suspended, joined the University.

The new 'university colleges'

The above institutions are now known as the 'constituent colleges' in order to distinguish them from two new university colleges, namely the University of Wales Institute, Cardiff and the University of Wales College, Newport, both of which joined the University in 1996. These university colleges currently have what could be described as a second division status within the University, despite being able to trace their roots in both cases back to the nineteenth century. Nevertheless, they represent the division which some of the 'non-leaguers' described in the next paragraph are striving to attain.

The Welsh HEIs

There are four other HEIs in Wales: North East Wales Institute of Higher Education (NEWI), Swansea Institute of Higher Education (SIHE), Trinity College Carmarthen,[5] and the Welsh College of Music and Drama (WCMD). The first two of these are actively seeking to join the University of Wales as university colleges and both have been accepted in principle, subject to meeting certain conditions which include the attainment of taught degree awarding powers. It is ironic that when such powers have been gained, the institutions immediately have to promise not to use them! The other two currently wish to remain independent, although Trinity may in the near future enter into a constitutional relationship with another institution. However, the most important feature for students is that the degrees of all four institutions are awarded by the University of Wales.

Higher education in further education

One of the most significant growth areas of HE in Wales during the last decade or so has been through courses offered by further education colleges. The rationale for this has been to increase geographical opportunities and to widen participation. The majority of such courses have hitherto been franchised from the University of Glamorgan, which was given an unofficial remit to develop this work. In recent years, however, the other Welsh HEIs have begun to franchise courses and, in addition, a small amount of HE in FE is directly funded. These courses are therefore not franchised but validated. If, in due course, Wales follows the English lead of directly funding most HE in FE, then the existing arrangements may change dramatically with a significant impact on the franchising institutions.

Higher education statistics and location

Table 8.1 sets out the key statistics for HE students in HEIs in Wales. In addition, there are 2801 HE students in Welsh FE institutions and 5177 Open University students domiciled in Wales. The grant figures are the allocations for 1999/2000. The two maps show the geographical spread of higher and further education institutions respectively and are particularly relevant for the third section of this chapter.

Higher Education Funding Council for Wales and the National Assembly

The Higher Education Funding Council for Wales (HEFCW) shares the same building and the same chief executive as that for further education. This model has recently also been adopted in Scotland which hitherto had no funding council for FE. HEFCW operates within the framework of UK governmental policy on HE, but is entirely independent of England. Indeed, during the last few years it has seemed to be perversely proud of fostering different special initiatives or the same initiatives with a twist to its English counterpart.

The Government of Wales Act 1998, which created the Welsh Assembly, places FE firmly into the hands of that body but says little about HEFCW, which is only mentioned twice. In law, the Welsh Assembly can only enhance the functions of HEFCW and can neither diminish them nor abolish the Funding Council. In practice, as early as January 1999, the Welsh Office was instructing HEFCW to produce a series of reports to the National Assembly including the one on mergers mentioned earlier. It is therefore widely expected that the Assembly will take 'democratic control'[6] of HEFCW and emphasize the unending search for value-for-money. Certain Assembly Members were already upset that they could not formally influence the appointment of the new chief executive (who has an expanded role in also managing the organization which will replace the TECs in Wales) in May 2000, but they will definitely have a say in the appointment of future Council members. In due course, new legislation could be introduced to further this process.

The Welsh way of life

HE in Wales has functioned as a guardian of the national culture in a way which has no parallel in England. For example, until the creation of the

Table 8.1 Key statistics for HE students in HEIs in Wales, 1997/98

	Full-time undergraduate and equivalent students	Part-time undergraduate	Full-time postgraduate	Part-time postgraduate	Total students	Total grant allocations 1999/2000 £
University of Glamorgan	9,995	3,162	393	1,598	15,148	32,603,242
University of Wales, Aberystwyth	5,862	1,898	1,356	627	9,743	23,977,794
University of Wales, Cardiff	11,704	3,782	3,047	1,761	20,294	56,183,661
University of Wales, Bangor	5,721	1,481	1,235	1,580	10,017	24,427,869
University of Wales, Swansea	8,009	1,905	1,283	1,888	13,085	32,128,525
University of Wales, College of Medicine	2,165	39	167	837	3,208	13,975,661
University of Wales, Lampeter	1,542	313	105	353	2,313	5,074,334
University of Wales Institute, Cardiff	5,211	1,471	516	655	7,853	19,677,645
University of Wales College, Newport	2,756	4,004	233	764	7,757	13,740,334
North East Wales Institute of Higher Education	2,642	1,861	33	416	4,952	10,322,321
Swansea Institute of Higher Education	2,889	880	38	465	4,272	9,728,697
Trinity College Carmarthen	1,347	0	154	89	1,590	4,707,558
Welsh College of Music and Drama	532	40	10	17	599	2,737,587

Source: Higher Education Statistics Agency (1999) *Students in Higher Education Institutions*, Student Record.

Figure 8.1 Higher education institutions in Wales

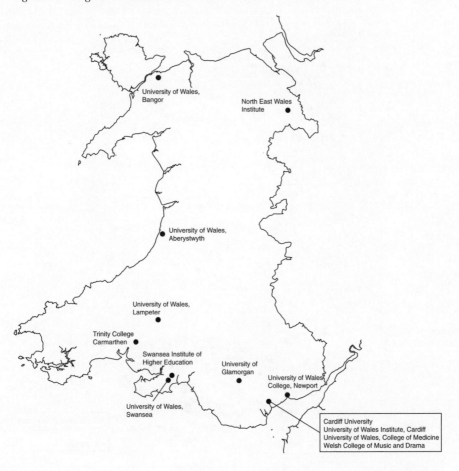

National Assembly, the Court of the University of Wales was for about one hundred years the only truly pan-Welsh body and it acted accordingly. Moreover, education has always been regarded as the only certain way out of the cycle of hard, dirty, physical jobs which typified the Welsh economy. Wales is famous for its production of teachers and preachers, as well as miners and metal producers. As a result, HE in Wales has more public support and respect than in England and this is particularly noticeable to an incomer.

What are the other characteristics of Welsh life which provide the context for HE? From a purely subjective standpoint the following seem to be of most significance:

- Although one nation, Wales is still paradoxically riven by divisions and factionalism. The key splits, which overlay each other, are between the

Figure 8.2 Further education institutions in Wales

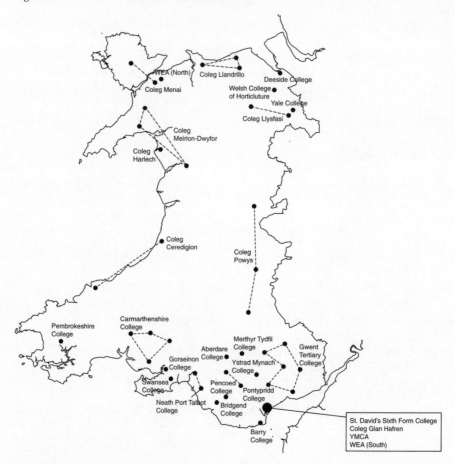

North and South, between the rural and urban areas and between everyone else and the success of the South-East, typified by Cardiff. The lack of
good internal communication links exacerbates this situation.
* Bilingualism is also a growing opportunity or threat, depending upon
one's perspective. Although a significant majority of those living in Wales
do not speak Welsh, nevertheless bilingualism is underpinned (at considerable cost) by legislation and is becoming very fashionable, particularly
among the middle classes who are never slow to spot an economic advantage. Table 8.2 sets out the proportion of Welsh speakers in West Wales
and the Valleys; the percentage of young people is particularly interesting.
* Welsh life is still almost completely male-dominated.[7] The key social institutions are the rugby club, the pub, the political party and such male
bastions as the Rotary Club and the Freemasons. Until recently, it would
have been possible to write 'Labour Party' for 'political party', but the

Table 8.2 Proportion of Welsh speakers in West Wales and the Valleys (in percentages)

County	Age structure				Total
	3–15	*16–44*	*45–64*	*65+*	
Gwynedd	90.9	75.6	65.6	68.4	74.3
Anglesey	78.1	62.5	57.4	55.9	62.6
Ceredigion	76.8	57.8	53.9	62.7	60.9
Carmarthenshire	56.5	46.0	53.0	65.3	53.5
Conwy	45.6	35.7	30.2	34.2	35.8
Denbighshire	35.3	27.4	28.7	29.4	29.6
Pembrokeshire	28.3	15.7	20.0	22.2	20.4
Neath Port Talbot	21.7	14.1	19.5	26.0	19.1
Swansea	16.0	8.5	15.1	21.8	14.0
Bridgend	19.3	8.8	5.4	10.5	10.1
Rhondda Cynon Taff	17.0	8.1	4.6	10.9	9.5
Torfaen	29.2	3.8	3.3	3.1	8.3
Merthyr Tydfil	3.7	6.6	4.8	9.5	8.1
Caerphilly	17.4	6.1	3.3	4.5	7.4
Blaenau Gwent	22.6	3.4	2.7	2.6	6.4

Source: Welsh Household Interview Survey

upsurge of nationalism has taken Plaid Cymru with it. Not surprisingly, there is no female principal of a Welsh HE institution.

Higher education in detail

Welsh HE displays a number of characteristics of which the following are the most important:

- Table 8.1 shows that each Welsh HEI is typically smaller than its English counterpart and, as a matter of fact, receives fewer full-time student applications. Of the top 60 (by size) UK HEIs only two are in Wales. The reasons for this are both historical and geographical in that several Welsh HEIs are based in rural areas with small local populations. It has, therefore, been argued by HEFCW that too many Welsh HEIs fail to achieve the critical mass necessary for success and efficiency.
- The small size of the Welsh HE system as a whole has two major consequences. First, it entails an intimate relationship between HEFCW and its institutions. Almost all key staff know each other by their first names and the Funding Council becomes a spectre (albeit benign) perching on the shoulder of every Welsh principal. Second, the pan-Wales organizations really do work most of the time. The best example is that of the meeting of Heads of Higher Education in Wales (HHEW). Although of relatively recent creation, HHEW is a superb information exchange, provides an open forum for testing ideas, reaches collective decisions which

are (usually) adhered to, is recognized as *the* representative body in Wales and is therefore consulted by all appropriate bodies and is becoming more adept at lobbying.

During the summer of 1999, HHEW metamorphosed into CVCP (Wales) and the four HEIs described on page 78 were offered associate member status of CVCP. Similar arrangements were made in Scotland and, in due course, it seems possible that this regional, all-embracing approach will be adopted in England also and, as a consequence, SCoP will disappear.[8] There will then be a single representative body for HE in the UK which is long overdue.

- Although the Welsh HEI system is small when compared with England, it is large when compared with the total population of Wales. In 1997/98, Wales had 68,945 full-time students and a population of approximately 2,933,000. England had 943,963 full-time students and a population of 49,284,200, and Scotland had 128,337 full-time students and a population of 5,122,500. These figures give ratios of 1:42.5; 1:53 and 1:40 respectively. Not surprisingly, Wales imports 56 per cent of its full-time students and its student import/export balance is very positive. If the introduction of tuition fees and the abolition of student grants result in more students going to their local HEIs, then this could prove ruinous for several Welsh HEIs.

- The student profile in Wales is very similar to that in the UK as a whole. There are more female students than male, both at undergraduate and postgraduate levels; the number of mature students is growing, but slowly (and this phenomenon may be reversed by the new funding arrangements), and there is an almost complete range of subjects available with the exception of veterinary science and certain minor languages. However, on all three key indices revealing the participation of under-represented groups in HE (i.e. the percentage of students from state schools/colleges, the percentage from social classes IIIM to V inclusive, and the percentage from low-participation neighbourhoods) Wales scores higher than the UK averages.[9] Moreover, when the disaggregated data become available, the author expects that those Welsh students who choose to remain in Wales to study will be significantly from under-represented groups.

- The Welsh HEIs consistently argue that they are underfunded per student when compared with their English and Scottish counterparts. Certainly, despite a significant improvement in the 1996 Research Assessment Exercise,[10] they consistently fail to secure their fair share of research council grants. This lack of successful research bidding is one of the main drivers behind HEFCW's proposals for reorganization discussed below.

- In late 1997, the HEIs in North Wales set up a collaborative network with the FE colleges in that region, which has gradually become known as the 'Community University of North Wales'. Unwilling to pass over such an interesting concept, Swansea Institute and the University of Wales Swansea floated a few months later the idea of a similar community university in South-West Wales. This idea proved to be so attractive that the HEIs at Lampeter and Aberystwyth asked to join the arrangement

Figure 8.3 West Wales and the Valleys Objective 1

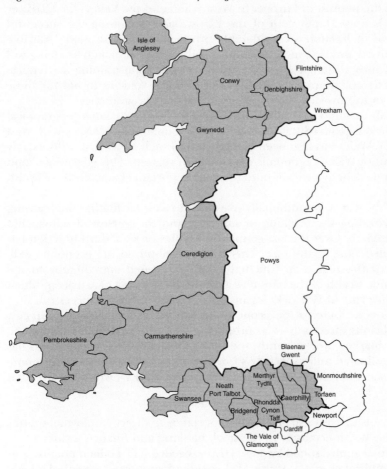

and, with pump-priming support from HEFCW, this is now functioning as the 'Community University of West and Mid-Wales'.

The initial objectives of this latter community university have been to establish a high-level regional forum to discuss issues of mutual interest; to identify progression routes (primarily from FE to HE, but at all levels throughout the network); to identify gaps in provision and to seek to fill them on a planned basis which thereby might foster more HE level work being offered by FE institutions; and, above all, to stimulate increased demand for further and higher education (FHE) by throwing down the perceived barriers of fragmentation and unwarranted competition.

All of the institutions which comprise the Community University of West and Mid-Wales lie within the area recently designated by the European Union as having Objective 1 status (see Figure 8.3). To gain such a status is in fact an admission of failure because it means that the area is one of the poorest in Europe. In West Wales and the Valleys the GDP per capita is only 71 per cent of the EU average. Following the successful example of Ireland, a considerable proportion of these newly available Objective 1 funds (which, of course, still have to be match-funded!) will be put into a human resource strategy based upon training and education. The community universities will be ideal vehicles to bid for these funds and to provide the necessary articulated programmes.

Collaboration between HE and FE institutions in the same geographical area makes good educational sense. The Community University of West and Mid-Wales has also been constructed in such a way that it fits exactly with two of Wales's economic development regions. This educational and economic coherence leads onto the next important characteristic of Welsh HE.

- HE in the UK has traditionally played two roles: facilitating the learning and providing the teaching of students, and the pursuit of scholarship and research. Over the last couple of decades or so, a third function has gradually come to the fore. This is to contribute to the economic well-being of the region in which the HEI is located and thereby to the economic wealth of the nation as a whole. It is an area of activity in which the University of Warwick, for instance, has been hugely successful.

HEIs contribute to the economy in two ways: directly and indirectly. The obvious direct way is by producing well-educated graduates for the labour market. More recently, the actual impact of HEIs as employers has been evaluated and especially so in Wales. In 1997 an important monograph was published,[11] under the auspices of HHEW, which showed that in 1995/96,

- the Welsh HEIs were of similar importance in direct employment terms to the Welsh economy as the steel, banking and finance sectors;
- the total annual spend by these HEIs exceeded half a billion pounds; and
- the multiplier effect of this HEI spending supported a total of 23,200 full-time equivalent jobs throughout Wales.

A year or so later, this general economic impact analysis was supplemented by a specific examination of the export earnings of Welsh HE.[12] This work revealed that no less than 2500 jobs in Wales were supported by a combination of HEI overseas trading and the recruitment of international students to Wales.

Significant incentives are being provided both by HEFCW and the Welsh Development Agency (WDA) (and these will no doubt be enhanced by Objective 1 funding when available) to encourage HEIs to contribute indirectly to the economy. This is achieved in a number of ways which include the provision of consultancies, bespoke training and other services to businesses (and especially SMEs); technology transfer; the attraction of new inward investment into Wales and the establishment of spin-out companies from the work of staff and students. There are hosts of examples of this activity but I will use the privilege of authorship to describe just one.

Swansea Institute is the lead organization in a consortium of five, which has won a European grant to build a Business Innovation Centre (to be known as 'Swansea Technium') on a derelict dock site. This building will house 15 small businesses and provide central services to assist them to grow. Technium is an important project in its own right, but its major value is to act as a turn-key for the development of the whole site, which is already beginning to attract considerable interest. The site comprises up to three large docks which, it is envisaged, will form an Innovation Village, intermingling housing, social facilities and appropriate businesses, especially those concentrating on research and development. Waterfront properties are sexy and sell at a premium and this will probably be the first 'science-park type' venture in the UK by the sea, prospering by the use of the sound bite 'Blue Seas for Blue Skies'. It is important to remember that it is a small HEI which is leading the first phase of what could be the largest economic development in South-West Wales. Only time will tell, but readers of this book in the future will be able to check for themselves whether the venture has succeeded or failed.

• Many parts of Wales are very beautiful (the Gower was the first district in the UK to be designated as an 'Area of Outstanding Natural Beauty' in the 1950s) and all parts engender a loyalty which exceeds anything to be found in England. As a result, many Welsh people prefer to pursue their complete careers in Wales and almost all of those who do leave hanker for the opportunity to return. To some extent, therefore, Welsh HE is inbred. Staff turnover at many institutions is low and new blood is more often than not Welsh either by birth, education or ancestry. This phenomenon has enabled one of my fellow principals to describe a key weakness of Welsh HE as 'the tendency towards fratricide'. There are occasions when this author feels this claim to be almost literal and he is ever-mindful of the fact that most murders occur within the family!

The 'outsiders'

When the Further and Higher Education Act was passed and the then polytechnics were given the option of using the title 'university', it became fashionable to argue that the binary line had been abolished. This, of course, was untrue because the line had merely been shifted and had come to rest between the newly enlarged university sector and the other HEIs (approximately 55 at the time). This bifurcation has been further exacerbated recently by restricting the use of even the title 'university college' to those institutions which have taught degree awarding powers, while simultaneously making the gaining of these powers much more difficult.[13]

It might be thought that life would be very difficult for those institutions which lie on the wrong side of the binary line. They are subject to exactly

the same funding regimes, quality controls and research assessment procedures as the universities, but are generally much smaller and therefore
do not have the infrastructures to mount major promotional campaigns
and even to deal with the endless flow of circulars and reports which
emanate from their respective funding councils. Not necessarily so – for
these HEIs have become adept in identifying the niche markets in which
they can fare well.

These 'outsider' HEIs can be grouped into three distinct categories. First,
there are those institutions which offer courses over a wide range of subject
areas and at all levels. In effect, they are polytechnics in all but name. The
HEIs at Bolton, Northampton and Southampton are good examples of this
category. Second, there are the 'monotechnics' which specialize in a few
closely related subject areas. Such institutions include the conservatoires of
music (except Birmingham School of Music which is a faculty of the University of Central England in Birmingham), and the freestanding institutes of
art and design, for example, London, Kent and Surrey. The author has
chosen an American title for the third category, that of 'liberal arts colleges'. Almost all of these institutions diversified out of teacher education
colleges, initially as a result of the ill-fated White Paper of the early 1970s
entitled *Framework for Expansion*.[14] Many of them still have a religious con-
nection and they include those at Chester, Chichester and York.

The Welsh 'outsiders' have been referred to earlier. The following ex-
tracts from their mission statements illustrate the niches which they are
aiming at:

> *The North-East Wales Institute of Higher Education* provides high-quality,
> career-enhancing higher education . . . It serves the needs of the region
> and beyond by being dynamic, responsive, flexible and accessible.

> *Swansea Institute of Higher Education* is a vocational, comprehensive,
> regionally based, student-centred institute of higher education.

> *Trinity College, Carmarthen* is a church-related institution of higher edu-
> cation, with a Christian ethos [aiming at] a dynamic and active academic
> and administrative partnership with the community.

> *Welsh College of Music and Drama* aims to develop as an innovative Euro-
> pean centre of excellence for professional training and education in
> the performing arts.

NEWI and SIHE are first-category institutions, concentrating on vocational
programmes, aimed primarily at regional students and with an emphasis on
the government's widening participation agenda. WCMD is a monotechnic,
but still essentially vocational, and Trinity is a category 3 institution. All at
the time of writing are recruiting well. Indeed, it appears to be some of the
modern universities throughout the UK which have the worst problems
with student recruitment.

The future structure of Welsh HE

The HEFCW Merger Report referred to earlier, which was produced without any consultation whatsoever with the Welsh HEIs, has been scathingly attacked by HHEW. Nevertheless, it has undoubtedly set the agenda for discussions between institutions about mergers or other forms of close relationship.[15] It would not be wild speculation to suggest that every HEI in Wales is talking to at least one other potential partner at some level, however informally.

There are several hundred possible combinations of 13 institutions, and recent events indicate that none of them can be ruled out, notwithstanding their apparent geographical and constitutional improbability. For instance, despite being several hours' travelling time apart (and seemingly light years away in terms of history and missions) the Council/Board of Governors of the HEIs at Lampeter and Newport have just agreed to begin exploratory discussions about merger. Almost none of the following models is mutually exclusive; indeed some have clear overlaps. However they do provide a focus for the future, although the most likely outcome is some admixture of one or more which has been attained by progressing through a series of dynamic stages.

No change

This model proposes that the current status quo be maintained. It seems very unlikely and, at the least, leaves the four 'outsider' HEIs in a difficult position and Lampeter probably in an impossible one. A slightly more likely variation is for NEWI and SIHE to succeed in their bids to join the University of Wales as constituent colleges, without any other changes. This would still seem, however, to be insufficient to meet the current mood for change.

One all-Wales university

This model proposes that all of the HEIs in Wales join the University of Wales on some basis or other. This would probably not cause a major problem for the 'outsider' HEIs, but it is very radical with regard to the University of Glamorgan. This latter institution would have to amend its title, suspend its degree awarding powers and accept the constraints of a federal structure where it would become one among many rather than the 'other university'. Almost certainly under this model the University of Wales would itself require major organizational changes, but some of these may happen in any case. There is a certain marketing attraction in the concept of 'One Nation, One University'.

Reduction to six?

HEFCW's model is not altogether clear because in its Merger Report it puts forward several somewhat inconsistent arguments. However, its analysis of the problems for the status quo are powerful. HEFCW identifies six 'stimulants for change':

- that governments of whatever hue will continue to seek economies;
- that there will be a continuing tightening of research selectivity;
- that during the next decade there will be major developments in methods of learning and teaching predicated upon technological developments which are already underway;
- that there may be globalization of HE through the Internet and other forms of distance learning – the 'virtual' university;
- that there may be a growth of 'corporate' universities to challenge the current arrangements;
- that there will be significant changes to the composition of the student body, emphasizing different study modes.

On the basis of the above 'the Council believes that there is a case for seeing some five or six, general, multi-mission institutions in Wales as an aim'.[16] HEFCW does not indicate openly which institutions should merge, but makes gnomic comments about WCMD and the College of Medicine as independent institutions and includes a eulogy about the University of Glamorgan which should not join the University of Wales but 'should grow through merger'. HEFCW is silent about the future of the federal university per se.

Mission-based

There are four HEIs in Wales which have very similar missions (NEWI, SIHE, UWIC and Newport) and were once all known by the distinctive title of 'institutes'. This model proposes that this common vocational approach, with a commitment to the widening participation agenda, should be the basis for some sort of relationship. Glamorgan, which has a similar mission, may or may not then join the arrangement. This model is educationally seductive, but has some problems regarding geographical spread, the lack of full degree awarding powers by any of the original four HEIs (but not so Glamorgan!), and the fact that Newport is already in discussion with another institution. The obvious first stage, however, might be some meeting of minds in the South-East of Wales.

HE and FE relationships

Both HEFCW and the Department for Education and Employment are completely against HE and FE mergers 'in the foreseeable future'. This embargo, which has already been broken in England by institutions in Derby and the Leeds area, makes this model particularly attractive. Geographically, there is at least one HEI in Wales which shares a site with an FE college, and another two institutions which are only separated by a few hundred yards. Educationally, there are many who argue for a seamless post-16 education system and such relationships are the logical conclusion of this position. The major argument against such relationships (after putting on one side the official embargo) is that a merger might result in the HEI involved no longer meeting the criteria for HE status. There are few who would be so radical.

Regional groupings

The 'community universities' described earlier could well be the forerunners of real regional universities, either based solely upon HEIs or combining FE and HE institutions. This model fits the educational needs of most of Wales, but runs into trouble in the South-East where there is a major concentration of institutions and no obvious groupings.

Big boys go it alone

For some years it has been rumoured that the University of Wales, Cardiff intends to become a university in its own right. This rumour has been supported by the fact that Cardiff recently gained full degree awarding powers, although it does not use them, and now trades under the title 'Cardiff University' rather than its formal name. The rumour goes on to suggest that if Cardiff secedes from the University of Wales, then it will be quickly followed by University of Wales, Swansea. This latter HEI does not have degree awarding powers, but has been reassured by the QAA that there is a 'fast track' route to gaining them for suitable institutions.

If the two big boys leave the University of Wales, what will happen to the remaining HEIs in Wales? There are several scenarios which include the rapid entry of the 'outsiders' to make up numbers; the succession of all of the constituent institutions to become independent; and the retention of the (valuable) title by the remaining current members.

The University of Wales

The future of the University of Wales is an open question. Like the federal University of London it has been under attack on more than one occasion and survived. The current public position of all of its members is to remain as a federal institution, even though the majority wish for weaker central control. All of the above models, except the last one, will work just as well under the umbrella of the University of Wales as outside it.

Confederacy

There are many forms of institutional relationship other than merger. The Council for Industry and Higher Education (CIHE) has recently published an interesting discussion paper entitled *Partnerships for Excellence*. This paper investigates the issues involved in developing a *confederacy* model of partnership and the implications for (possibly) evolving this into a *holding company model*. The two are described as follows:[17]

> A '*confederacy*' model is one where organisations mutually agree to co-ordinate and even combine some of their functions and services. Individual identities are preserved but economies achieved, the range of products increased and quality improved as resources are pooled and focused on developing the best the partners bring to the group.

> A '*holding company model*' is one where certain functions are formally passed to an umbrella oganisation which carried out those functions for a fee on behalf of all the partners. The economies and other benefits can be greater as those functions are not duplicated; as they cannot easily be restored so the commitment is also greater.

The retention of individual identities while achieving economies seems the panacea for the Welsh situation. It would be interesting to see if such confederacies could operate with the federacy of the University of Wales; certainly holding companies could.

Final thoughts

This has been a particularly difficult chapter to write because it seems that almost every week the ground has shifted significantly. The author believes that there will be change in Wales and that the current Welsh FHE system may be unrecognizable in less than ten years' time. However, the concluding thoughts must go to an unattributed colleague:

> I suppose the starting point [or in this case the finishing point!] might be whether there is in fact a Welsh system at all . . . Neither in recruitment nor in terms of pre-entry qualifications nor degree outcomes is the system 'Welsh'. I don't think therefore, in a full sense, there is a Welsh system in the way that one can speak of a Scottish system. Would it be improper to speak of a Welsh variant of the English system or of a Welsh 'sub-system'?

It is good to end on a provocative point.

Notes and references

1. In Welsh, the letter 'w' may function either as in English or as a vowel and, indeed, it may have both functions in the same word. Hence, the acronym 'HEFCW' for 'Higher Education Funding Council for Wales' is pronounced 'HEFCOO'.
2. HEFCW (1999) *The Scope for Institutional Mergers at the Higher Education Level.* Cardiff: HEFCW.
3. This figure excludes The Open University which operates throughout Wales from a base in Cardiff but is not (at the moment) funded through the Higher Education Funding Council for Wales.
4. The annual Calendar of the University of Wales contains an interesting bibliography of published histories (22 by 1998/99) of the HEIs comprising the University.
5. Trinity College, Carmarthen is the second oldest HEI in Wales, having been established in 1848. Age is not necessarily an indicator of status in Wales because, for example, two of the three colleges which formed Swansea Institute of Higher Education are mid-nineteenth century foundations, and the third (late nineteenth century) spawned what is now the University of Wales, Swansea.
6. A phrase used in an unpublished speech on 6 September 1999 given by Tom Middlehurst, the Assembly Member who chairs the Post-16 Education Committee, at the annual HHEW/HEFCW Conference.
7. The Labour Party made a brave attempt to ameliorate the situation by nominating women as 50 of its candidates for the National Assembly elections. As a result, 15 of the 27 Labour members are female.
8. This absorption will hardly come as a surprise as the CVCP and SCoP already share the same building and the Executive Secretary of the latter is on secondment from the former.
9. Data taken from the HEFCW Circular W99/112HE, dated 24 November 1999. The respective figures for young full-time first degree entrants in 1997/98 are:

	From state schools/colleges %	From social class IIIM to V	From low-participation neighbourhoods
UK	82	25	12
Wales	88	26	15

10. In the 1992 RAE, only seven departments in Wales were rated 5. In 1996, 21 departments gained a rating of 5 (and three were 5*) and the number of departments rated 4 increased by 56 per cent.
11. HHEW (1997) *Impact of the Higher Education Sector on the Welsh Economy: Measurements, Analysis and Enhancement*, commissioned by HHEW with financial support by HEFCW and the Welsh Office.
12. S. Hill, A. Roberts and C. Strong at the Cardiff Business School (1998) *The Export Earnings of Welsh Higher Education and their Impact on the Welsh Economy.* London: British Council.
13. The Quality Assurance Agency which administers the degree awarding powers ('daps') scheme was refused the right to take 'daps' away from 'failing' institutions

which already possessed them. (This would have required new primary legislation.) If this power had been granted, then it is estimated that about 15 institutions, including the Universities of East Anglia and Leeds, would have been in
danger of losing 'daps'.
14. In fact, within two years of the publication of this White Paper, the teacher
education system in the UK had been halved through a ruthless combination of
mergers and closures.
15. The author has written elsewhere about FE and HE mergers (Palfreyman, Thomas
and Warner (1998) *How to Manage a Merger . . . or Avoid One.* Leeds: Heist Publications). This book contains a chapter on various alternative forms of relationship
to merger.
16. HEFCW (1999) op. cit., p. 10.
17. CIHE (1999) *Partnerships for Excellence: A Confederacy Model for HE/FE Partnerships,*
p. 7. London: CIHE.

9

The Modern English Universities

John Gledhill

Conception, birth and naming

It was a difficult, multiple birth. Some of the babies were unsure about being born; others were anxious to greet their new life. But in the end the law made it happen. The 'modern' universities started their existence with a problem: a problem of 'image', and an accompanying debate about market position and educational niche. And yet the practice of creating new universities was not new. New universities had been created from the 'university colleges' of London University about a century before; new universities had again been created in the 1960s expansion and from the colleges of advanced technology; so the idea was not in itself new either. What constituted the difference for the '1992' universities was not so much the destination as the journey. The polytechnics had, over many years, evolved what they regarded as a mission which was distinct from that of the universities: parallel and equal. They developed their own market niche, their own style, their own approach: although often labelled as 'vocational' this was a misnomer, since little could be more vocational than the mainstays of the old universities – law and medicine and, in centuries past, theology.

The former polytechnics[1] were determined to keep their distinctive mission; for this reason the choice of the designation 'modern' was a significant one, since it related to the institutions' approach, not to their age. It was specifically, and imaginatively, invented by the institutions and their consultants in order to counter the overtones of 'immature' and 'unfinished' contained within adjectives such as 'new'.

Teaching and research

The modern universities' great strength lay in teaching and applied research. Although this was sometimes stigmatized by some of the older HEIs as a cover for not doing much 'academic' research, it was actually an accurate representation of the distinctive mission mentioned above. One of the great ironies of the development of the Robbins universities was the denigration of industrial links such as those described by E.P. Thompson as 'Warwick University Limited'[2] in the 1970s, whereas in later decades strong links with industry became encouraged or even required. Yet these sorts of links with industry were at the same time vilified as 'applied research' when carried out by the modern universities, as if in some way not being 'pure' research made it (literally) 'impure'. Of course these policies go in cycles, and are subject to the prevailing whim of the government and the funding agencies, but at least the modern universities stayed constant to their industrial links.

The main dilemma for the modern universities was not the concept of research (whether pure or applied), but their role. To say that good research is encouraged so as to support good teaching completely misses the point, and makes it merely a means to an end. Research in all its forms must surely be intrinsic in the philosophy of any active, inquisitive and enthusiastic lecturer in higher education. What caused more problems for the modern universities was that the multifarious mergers and agglomerations which had themselves led to the polytechnics had left a legacy of staff whose horizons were set at best by 'scholarship' than by 'research' (i.e. the desire to keep up with the latest developments, rather than themselves seeking to be involved in these new developments). Many such staff felt threatened, personally and professionally, by the redesignation from 'polytechnic' to 'university'.

Cynically one might argue that the modern universities merely needed to wait until all these staff had retired, to be replaced by a new generation of research-active staff as found in the older universities. But it was more subtle than that, and more urgent. This approach to research sometimes appeared to give staff an inferiority complex; if the modern universities were to counteract this they needed to find a proper place for pure research, though not at the expense of their applied research strengths. They also had to avoid the temptation to see pure research as inimical to a mission for excellence in teaching, and above all to resist labelling 'excellence in research' as a cover for 'teaching is a secondary consideration', and its converse 'excellence in teaching' as a cover for 'no strengths in research'.

One comfort (albeit limited) for the modern universities was that their strengths in applied research income sometimes led to less anxiety about government manipulation of any 'dual funding' arrangements, since sponsored research could give greater flexibility for true recovery of overheads on contracts. With this came more transparency about cross-subsidies between teaching and research than was sometimes the case with the older universities.

Widened participation, 'access', and increased participation rates

What must surely be among the most politically sensitive areas of difference between the modern universities and the others was that which encompassed 'widened participation', 'access' and 'value added'. The traditional mission of polytechnics was to spread excellence in education among all who could participate and benefit from it; the traditional mission of the preceding universities was to educate the academically best in the country. This different approach manifested itself in a variety of ways: polytechnics saw strengths in the vocational qualifications such as the Higher National Certificates and Diplomas awarded by the Business and Technology Education Council (BTEC) and its predecessors, whereas universities rarely offered these; polytechnics saw ordinary degrees as worthwhile qualifications in their own right (often upgradable to honours by further study), whereas English universities offered almost exclusively honours degrees as the benchmark award. These traditional differences persisted in the varied range of courses offered in modern universities and other institutions, although the 'widened participation' policies which began in the 1990s led to massive growth in honours degree recruitment at the expense of undergraduate certificate and diploma courses.

Politics and money played their part too. Many initiatives on widened access, foundation courses, 'Two Plus Two' degrees, etc. in the older universities looked suspiciously as if they had been inspired largely by government funding changes; this was inevitable for as long as 'education' was a political issue. Although some of the initiatives were driven by a shortage of students in subjects such as engineering, the modern universities tended to see the display of enthusiasm on the part of the others as a cynical funding hunt, and a search for good public relations with the funding councils, whereas their own traditions in these areas were always treated as being worthwhile for their own sake and part of their institutional mission. Such lip-service to widened participation by some of the older universities did great disservice to the ethos of widened access. There were recorded cases of older universities being on the validating body for access courses, but not actually having a good record of admitting any of the students who came through those courses; that did them no credit, and increased the cynicism of some modern universities about the motives of the others.

Even worse than the politics and funding issues was the rise in, and iniquitous misuse of, meaningless league tables. That is not to say that performance measures, whether absolute or relative, are valueless or dangerous, but the use of *inappropriate* measures is noisome; and when manipulated deliberately it is destructive. The value attached to particular measures by those who compile (or conglomerate) league tables betrays a particular model of the world; the outcomes will therefore inevitably reflect the standpoint and value-judgements of the compilers rather than an objective assessment of the achievements or status of the institutions.

The modern universities again felt that the odds are stacked against them in the league tables and associated performance measures; some would say deliberately so. Counts of 'the number of first-class honours', for example, could merely show low standards or extreme generosity, rather than excellence; 'low A level scores' could show strengths in non-standard entrants rather than scraping the barrel to meet targets. It was surely no coincidence that almost without exception the league tables showed the older HEIs in the top half, with the modern universities in the bottom half: that was largely the product of the choice of measures, not of their comparative excellence. This again risked driving a wedge between the older and modern universities, and one to which the latter could not object without sounding merely defensive. Government policies did not help: widened access was encouraged, but lower entry standards and slower progression were penalized.

Widened access had another, more subtle effect on the range of students admitted to modern universities. When participation rates were low and entry targets were restricted by government, the top universities could pick the cream of the entrants but left behind a very large number of excellent students for the other HEIs (whether universities, polytechnics, higher education colleges or others); low intakes meant that there were enough excellent students for all to share in them. The increase in total student numbers, against a relatively static population, not only meant that students with lower qualifications were now in the entry pool, but also that the top universities (with their increased intake figures) now actually sliced off a larger part of the excellent students. So widened participation simultaneously admitted weaker students to the pool and reduced the number of good students for any but the top universities; it therefore led to an increased stratification of the higher education market. As the age participation rates increased further, and the extra numbers were spread among all institutions, this effect became more marked.

Campuses

The amalgamations which created many of the polytechnics that were to become the modern universities showed up in the different types of campus which they occupied. The bulk of the Robbins 'new universities' found themselves on greenfield sites, the 'civic / redbrick' universities received massive investment from proud city councils when they were set up, giving them large 'proud' buildings, but the modern universities inherited a range of buildings of mixed age and style, typically scattered around various sites in a large city; or in some cases dispersed among several different towns. There were only a few modern universities (and they were very fortunate) which could rightly say that they occupied a single campus. This gave a different feel to the modern universities, sometimes one of loose confederation rather than unity, especially compared to the Robbins universities.

It also had another effect: when the university was wedged into a variety of small city-centre sites, the scope for expansion or renewal was very limited; this was in often stark contrast to the large acres of the Robbins universities, or the sometimes massive landholdings of the older and ancient universities. Very often the modern universities found themselves waiting for local industries to go bankrupt so as to release large 'brownfield' sites for acquisition. This could be a severe constraint on development plans not experienced to the same degree by many older 'campus' institutions. Indeed, instead of having to pay as much as half a million pounds per acre for city centre expansion, the greenfield campuses often had broad acres simply waiting to be built on to the extent that the planning regulations would permit.

Quality assurance

The reaction of the modern universities to the rise in the 'quality assurance' industry was very illuminating. The older universities resisted (and in some cases tried to reject) the concept of quality assurance: they knew they were excellent, their external examiners confirmed this, and students flocked to their doors, so what else was needed? The modern universities, with their background in external procedural intervention from the Council for National Academic Awards (CNAA) and Her Majesty's Inspectors, saw these mechanisms as much less threatening; they were familiar with peer review, used to external judgement on course proposals, less anguished about being asked for critical self-evaluation of processes and standards. Conversely, however, the modern universities showed a marked tendency to assume that the CNAA models were intrinsically immutable and unquestionably optimal. Both extremes were wrong: one was arrogant, the other betrayed lack of imagination.

Being cast free, first from local government, and subsequently from the CNAA, was little less than traumatic for some staff in modern universities. Being able to develop policies and plans without external interference led to some conceptual agoraphobia and clinging to traditional ways. This was not universal, of course, but it certainly existed to some extent. When what was actually an unwillingness to adapt was presented in the guise of the preservation of traditional mission, it was a threat to the future of the institution concerned.

Management style

'Management' is a term and concept which presented no threat to the modern universities. The older universities did not have managements; they had 'administrations'. Their management was carried out (to put it rather simplistically) by senior academics and by a mere handful of managerial posts often held by former academics: the registrar, the bursar, the librarian. All else was administration.

One of the most clearly seen differences between modern universities and the older ones was the role and status of the pro-vice-chancellors (PVCs). The traditional model was to fill these posts on a rolling basis by seconding (by whatever arcane selection process) senior academics of recognized sound managerial sense and corporate wisdom, typically for three years. They were then given particular responsibility for one or more areas of business (e.g. planning, finance, estates, research), working with, but neither reporting to nor responsible for, the professionals administering those areas. Then, when their three years ended, they handed their portfolio over to the next batch of senior academics and returned to their scholarship, teaching and research. The only way to underpin this rotation was to have an extremely strong executive in the vice-chancellor and the posts mentioned above; in particular a very strong registrar; this ensured continuity of mission, style, purpose and policy. In many ways it was modelled on the national government: the ministers and secretaries of state come and go, often with staggering frequency, and the stability of the country is guaranteed by the permanent secretariat and civil service. Thus too in the traditional universities: Michael Shattock as Warwick's Sir Humphrey in 'Yes Minister'!

One strength of this model was that if a PVC secondment turned out to be less than successful it was easy to return the person concerned to their original academic activities, without the trauma of disciplinary action, probationary periods, or dismissal. Conversely if a secondment produced a real star as PVC, the secondment rules could be frustrating. It was not unknown for institutions in this position to find ways of getting round the regulations. For example, if a particularly valued PVC was approaching the end of the maximum secondment period, he/she could resign from the post at Easter and be replaced by another for the rest of the year; this of course would mean that the former incumbent, no longer being in post, could be reappointed for a further three-year period as if a new appointment. And so on, for as long as the proprieties could be maintained.

The 'modern universities' on the other hand did not derive their model from central civil service, but from local government, which was strongly managerial. The PVCs were not normally seconded senior academics but permanent managerial posts, recruited by advertisement and competitive interview. They may still have been predominantly drawn from the ranks of senior academics, but they usually left their academic activities largely behind when they took on the PVC post. Although their areas of responsibility and power may have been similar to those of the PVCs in the older universities, they were different in that they usually had line-management responsibility for those areas. The key way in which this manifested itself was that the modern universities did not usually have a 'registrar' as such (though they still, of course, needed an 'academic registrar' to manage the student administration); instead that role was filled in effect by the PVC responsible for student administration. The strong, central, dirigiste 'registrar' of the older universities was absent from most modern universities. An unfortunate side effect of this was that academic registrars of modern universities, seeking career development, had no in-house registrar post to aim for, and either had to move into the traditional universities or try to compete with senior academics moving into the permanent PVC posts.

The interaction between these two models of management, the influence each had on the other, was fascinating to observe.[3]

The combination of the traditional registrar post, and the birth of the Robbins universities, led to a unique, unprecedented, and intriguing outcome. Probably never before in the history of higher education in the United Kingdom (and probably never again) was it possible for a vice-chancellor and registrar, between them (or by competitive power-play) to build a university from scratch, mould it to fit their own vision, and physically build it up to fruition. The modern universities found that their birth was very different: the generous funding of the Robbins age had disappeared, government goodwill and encouragement had been replaced by grudging intervention and bureaucracy. Instead of building for a new start, the modern universities found themselves starved of cash and with a tremendous uphill struggle against the existing sector which, in some cases, resented their creation.

Modern universities: the next generation?

When the CNAA was disbanded and the '1992' universities were set up, several higher education institutions did not meet the prevalent criteria for designation as a 'university'. These were principally the 'colleges of higher education' and their degree powers were transferred to one of the universities for validation. Their role and function was almost identical to that of universities; their activities were very similar except that in most cases they had a smaller corpus of research activity. They received their funding through the same funding agencies, underwent the same procedures for quality visitations, and were subject to the same Research Assessment Exercises. The differences with universities were in scale and focus, not in nature. In the years which followed, because of such factors, these colleges felt that they had a legitimate aspiration towards designation as a university. To this extent they are in a similar position to that in which the polytechnics found themselves in 1992, and the colleges of advanced technology in the pre-Robbins era: they also risked feeling patronized by this relationship with those institutions which had acquired the 'university' title in 1992. Several acquired powers to award their own taught degrees; acquisition of research degree awarding powers was made more difficult by frequent modifications to the criteria specified by the government first for eligibility for the title 'university college' and ultimately for designation as 'university'. As described at the start there have been several waves of 'new' universities; there may yet be more waves to come.

The future for modern universities

The modern universities will probably never become simply the same as all the other universities. The earlier generations of 'new' universities kept much of their common origin and development, and there is no particular reason to think that the modern universities will lose theirs either. Nor should they. Their tradition is distinct, be it in terms of access, breadth, or applied studies, and is very unlikely to be submerged into a common undifferentiated sea of similar institutions. Many 'modern' universities are in fact very old; indeed the earliest of the progenitor colleges of some modern universities started out in the middle of the nineteenth century, about the same time as many of those university colleges which became universities later that century.

The main change in role which challenges the modern universities is that they are, despite the point made in the previous paragraph, now in a single catalogue of universities. Those who were, for example, used to being in the top five of the 'polytechnic league' find themselves instead only halfway up the longer list of over 100 universities. This is partly, indeed probably predominantly, driven by the external choice of parameters for such lists (as described above), but it has to be accepted as a fact.

However, the key lesson from the past is that this position is not immutable. Some of the 'new' universities of the Robbins era have already overtaken many much older institutions; for example some have developed impressive reputations for research from the zero start they had at their birth.

The future of the modern universities is strong. There are emotional and structural hurdles to be overcome, but the traditional mission of the modern universities should not be seen as being under threat. The example of the Robbins 'new' universities, albeit with their financial advantages, should serve as a shining example of how far an institution can go in a relatively short period of time, given determination, strong management, and visionary leadership. The modern universities have those too but need government help to release the potential in the way that the Robbins universities were able to do, and notably Warwick and York.

References

1. J. Pratt (1997) *The Polytechnic Experiment, 1965–1992.* Buckingham: SRHE/Open University Press.
2. E.P. Thompson (ed.) (1970) *Warwick University Limited.* Harmondsworth: Penguin.
3. For more on HEI management styles see Note 21 on p. 27.

Part 2
Outsiders and Insiders

10

The Funding Councils:
Governance and Accountability

Steve Cannon

Introduction

This chapter considers the relationship between the state and the institutions funded by it. It examines the role of the funding councils, with particular reference to the Scottish Higher Education Funding Council (SHEFC) and the role of that body in reconciling institutional autonomy with the pressure for greater accountability in the use of public funds. The chapter examines the framework of accountability within which institutions operate and concludes that in Scotland the relationship between institutions and the Funding Council is in a process of transition and may require to be reassessed.

Greater accountability: the price of autonomy

Over the last decade there has been a rapid and unprecedented expansion of the number of students in higher education in the United Kingdom. During the same period funding for research has become more focused and concentrated. Although this expansion has been funded by a combination of efficiency gains, commercial and industrial support, loan finance and increased parental contributions, a high proportion of the funding continues to be provided, as elsewhere, by the state.

In Britain, as elsewhere in Europe, there has been recognition during the same period that the more autonomous the institution, the more adaptive and responsive it is likely to be in meeting the needs of the economy and society. However, pressures from Parliament and from the public in general are such that increased institutional autonomy implies greater accountability for the use of public funds. The second report of the Nolan Committee agreed that 'the exact counter-balance to autonomy is accountability':

> We do not believe there is an absolute principle that prevents the government, the funding council, or some other public body from

attaching conditions to money given to a university . . . the freedom of action of institutions will be circumscribed by the extent of their dependence on public funds.

(Committee on Standards in Public Life 1996: 36)

Nolan went on to suggest that universities and the funding councils have struck a practical bargain between the benefits of autonomy and the need for accountability.

Framework of accountability

Sizer and Mackie (1995) have argued that universities enjoy considerable freedoms within a broadly based framework of accountability. A reliance on the state for funding, however, means that notions of freedom from that state are little more than illusions, although, within a framework of accountability that defines their relationship with the state, institutions continue to enjoy considerable freedom to manage their own affairs. Thus while institutions have freedom to allocate funds, recruit staff, select students, design and deliver the curriculum, set standards and determine methods of assessment, the reliance of the institutions on state funding and the pressure to demonstrate that they are providing good value for money in the use of these public funds means that the idea that institutions are free from the attention of the state is naïve.

The framework of accountability within which institutions operate places clear and specific duties, responsibilities and obligations on institutions, funding councils and the state. Funds flow downwards from Parliament through government departments and funding councils to institutions while accountability flows upwards from the institution to Parliament (Sizer and Cannon 1999).

The Financial Memorandum between a funding council and an institution is the key mechanism through which the latter is accountable to the former (SHEFC 1998). In Scotland there are 18 identical memoranda: between SHEFC and each institution. In effect the memorandum is an agreement between the Council and an institution which sets out the terms and conditions under which the Council will make payments to institutions out of the funds made available by the Secretary of State.

The memorandum is underpinned by the following definition of accountability.

. . . The duty of those responsible for the development and implementation of policy and/or managing affairs and resources is to demonstrate not only propriety but also how economic, efficient and effective their policies and/or management has been over a period of time.

And this in turn has been elaborated by John Sizer, the Chief Executive of the Scottish Higher Education Funding Council, in terms of economy in the acquisition and use of resources, efficiency in the use of resources and effectiveness in the implementation of strategies, and action plans and achievement of institutional objectives (Sizer 1992).

Scottish Higher Education Funding Council

The Scottish Higher Education Funding Council (SHEFC) was established in 1992 under the Further and Higher Education (Scotland) Act (1992) to provide financial support for teaching, research and associated activities in Scottish higher education institutions. The Council is a non-departmental public body, a 'quango' in earlier terminology, responsible to the Scottish Executive through the Scottish Executive Enterprise and Lifelong Learning Department. Its members are appointed by the First Minister of the Scottish Parliament and have a collective responsibility for the proper conduct of the Council's affairs. They are not appointed as representatives of individual organizations and are expected to use the experience gained in their own careers when taking decisions on the Council's behalf.

The UK funding councils are funding and not planning bodies. They are not Higher Education plcs, holding or parent companies with individual institutions as subsidiary companies controlled by the parent company (Sizer and Cannon 1999). Institutions in receipt of Council funds are autonomous, and many generate significant funds from other sources. However the Council has a clear duty to secure not only value-for-money but best value in the use of those funds.

The Council's stated mission is to support the maintenance and further development of Scotland's world-class higher education system (SHEFC 1999a). It seeks to make effective use of public funds in helping Scottish higher education institutions to increase and communicate knowledge and skills that will enrich society, allow individuals to realize their potential, and make a major contribution to the country's prosperity.

In pursuit of its mission the Council aims to allocate public funds to support teaching and research, develop policies and provide advice to government. It undertakes to help Scottish higher education to address the needs of students, employers and society across local, national and international communities and to work towards equal opportunity of access to high-quality higher education. It seeks to encourage institutions to pursue continuous quality improvement and build on their distinctive strengths in teaching and research, promoting diversity of provision and beneficial collaboration. Finally, the Council aims to achieve value for public money by seeking to make the best use of available resources and securing accountability while recognizing institutional autonomy.

This activity is conducted within a political context and the Council's Corporate Plan is written in the context of guidance received from the Secretary of State which details the overall level of funding available to the Council for distribution in the next academic year. That advice identifies governmental priorities in the medium and often in the short term and the Council's task is to translate these intentions into funding policies – to steer the sector in a given direction. The Council pulls the funding levers that in turn steer the sector in the direction of government policy.

This is achieved in four main ways: the allocation of funds; the assessment of provision; the provision of advice and guidance; and the promotion of good governance within the framework of accountability.

The allocation of funds

Council funds for teaching are distributed by applying the principle that similar activities are funded at similar rates. The teaching funding model is a price-based and not a cost-based model, and it is the Council that sets the price. The Council agrees that it will pay a given price for a given student in a given subject. Moreover, the Council agrees the distribution of funded places – it will fund X number of places in subject Y at the University of Z. In effect the Council operates as a surrogate for the market.

Between 1992 and 1997 the price-based model provided stability, consolidation and support for a government policy for higher education that appeared to be 'Our policy is that we have no policy.' Under a reforming administration that method of funding and surrogate role is under increasing pressure. For example, current funding proposals demonstrate a clear link between funding and the government's agenda on widening access and social inclusion. Furthermore the Council has committed itself to establishing a core-and-margin structure for teaching funding to enable it to target resources in accordance with Council and government policy objectives:

> The core-and-margin system is the means by which the teaching funding method will provide the incentives and resources to promote national policy priorities more effectively. The main bulk of the new teaching funding formula will provide the core of the system and, once the new structure for the core is in place, will provide the continuity of funding for all institutions. The margin – once its size has been determined – will be the identified resources to deliver specific policy objectives.
>
> (SHEFC 2000)

In 1999/2000 the Council allocated over 20 per cent of its resources, about £129 million, in support of research. The Council interprets its responsibility for funding research broadly to include support for:

- the people and infrastructure in existing areas of research;
- the development of new or emerging areas of research activity;
- the dissemination of the outcomes of research and the promotion of their commercialization;
- the promotion of improvements in the management of research and the spread of good practice across the sector in Scotland; and

- participation in UK-wide initiatives that are judged to be of importance to the research base in Scotland.

Four main funding streams support the research programme.

The first and largest is the RAE-based grant that supports people and the infrastructure in areas of research excellence. This stream is a competitive formula-based grant that allocates funds to institutions according to judgements on the quality, and measures of the volume, of research in different subject areas derived from the Research Assessment Exercises.

The Research Development Grant (RDG) is intended to develop the research infrastructure in new or emerging areas of research, particularly in areas that will meet long-term needs and are aligned to the needs of the Scottish economy. Indeed, all applications to the RDG are required to demonstrate how they will contribute to the economy. The grant is allocated on the basis of submissions from institutions, acting singly or as a collaborative group, and is assessed by an expert lay panel. Recent years have seen an increasing emphasis on the funding of research through the RDG. The current year has seen an increase of 20 per cent in the funds allocated through this method and that in turn means that some 10 per cent (£12 million) of all the funds available to support research are allocated by this method.

In addition to the two main sources of research funding, grants are available to support a range of initiatives designed to promote improvements in the management of research and the spread of good practice, and the dissemination of the outcomes of research, including the promotion of their commercialization. Initiative funding has supported a variety of funding schemes including the Contract Research Staff Initiative, the Libraries Research Collections in the Humanities grant and the Professionalization of Commercialization grant. In addition the Council participates in UK-wide initiatives that are judged to be important to the research base in Scotland: a variety of funding schemes including the Joint Research Equipment Initiative and support for the Arts and Humanities Research Board.

The total funding for teaching and research provided by the funding council is allocated to each institution as a block grant. Mike Shattock has rightly pointed to the University Grants Committee's pride in the block grant (Shattock 1994), quoting an exchange between the Chairman of the UGC and the Chairman of the PAC in 1982: 'We give block grants to universities . . . it is for the university itself to decide on a disposition of resource between departments' teaching and research and so on. That is what is meant by university autonomy'. Traditionally institutions have been free to distribute this grant internally at their own discretion, as long as they comply with the conditions set out in their Financial Memorandum with the Council, and the money is used to support teaching, research and related activities. This arrangement gives managers in higher education the freedom to make decisions in the best interests of the institution and its stakeholders, but safeguards the public investment. However these funds are granted in exchange for teaching and research and are conditional on their delivery and, as Sandbach and Thomas (1996) have pointed out, an increasing pressure is being brought to bear on institutions for them to be more accountable for their use. In Scotland the Council has taken an increasing interest in research expenditure, first by requiring an account of how the original development grant was spent, then of how all monies on research were spent, and, most recently, the more detailed transparency review. The principles that underlie the concept of the block grant appear to run counter to those that support activity-based costing and the transparency review.

Quality assessment

The requirement to obtain value-for-money and best value in the use of funds requires the Council to engage in judgement of quality as well as cost. Quality judgements impact on both the teaching and research funding models. The ratings for both research and teaching quality are made publicly available. Good assessment ratings for teaching are believed to have a positive impact on student recruitment, and high marks in the RAE improve the chances of attracting research funds from research councils and other awarding bodies. The reverse is also true.

Information and guidance

The councils produce a range of information by which institutions can assess their own performance, so that they can then target efforts to improve value-for-money. Financial indicators, procurement, estate management and high-quality teaching and research are the areas of benchmarking that are most advanced within the Scottish Council. The councils have collaborated on and produced a range of best practice guides and value-for-money studies. A series of high-profile investigations by the National Audit Office provided further information and guidance.

Governance

Legislation establishing the funding councils and the framework within which the Council interrelates with institutions both assume that the legal bond is with the governing body of an institution. This manifests itself in the Financial Memorandum which exists between SHEFC and each of the institutions and is expressed as follows:

> The Governing Body of the Institution is responsible for ensuring that funds from the Council are used only in accordance with the Further

and Higher Education (Scotland) Act, the Financial Memorandum and any other conditions prescribed by the Council from time to time.

(SHEFC 1998)

The Council emphasizes the key role of the governing body in determining the strategic direction and approving the strategic plans of the institution:

It is for institutions' governing bodies to form their strategic plans, and to ensure that institutions maintain their academic vitality and financial viability. The funding councils' responsibility is to secure the most efficient higher education system possible within the funding provided by Government, but it is individual governing bodies and senior management teams who will drive the strategic management process.

(Sizer and Cannon 1999: 196)

In its evidence to the Committee of Inquiry into Higher Education, SHEFC (1996) emphasized the importance of governance and the role of the governing body and linked governance to institutional autonomy:

The Council is particularly conscious of the fact that HE institutions are autonomous bodies. As such, it should be the role of the governing bodies to form their strategic visions and plans within a broader strategy for higher education as a whole to ensure that institutions maintain their academic vitality and financial viability and meet societal needs. This means that governing bodies will have a much more decisive role to play than that to which some have traditionally been accustomed. It is therefore important for new relationships of trust and partnership to be established between governing bodies and their executives.

(SHEFC 1996: para. 46)

In the Council's view the principal, or chief executive, has responsibility to the governing body for undertaking strategic analysis, for developing strategic plans for approval by the governing body, and for delivering the governing body's strategic vision as well as taking operational responsibility for delivery of approved strategic and operational plans. The strategic survival of the institution is, in the Council's view, unequivocally the responsibility of the governing body, which ultimately has responsibility for ensuring that the management of the institution is identifying its priorities effectively.

The Report of the Steering Committee for Efficiency Studies in Universities (CVCP 1985) had anticipated and encouraged this development. The report sought to establish a new framework of governance appropriate for institutions that it considered were 'first and foremost corporate enterprises', and urged universities to examine their structures and develop plans to meet certain key requirements. Governing bodies were encouraged to assert their responsibilities in governing their institutions notably in respect of strategic plans, which should underpin academic decisions and structures to bring planning, resource allocation and accountability together in one corporate process linking academic, financial and physical aspects.

It is this view of universities as 'first and foremost corporate enterprises' that encouraged SHEFC to look to corporate governance arrangements in the private sector to provide a lead. In England the universities had taken the initiative themselves through the Committee of University Chairmen who in 1998 produced a *Guide for Members of Governing Bodies of Universities and Colleges in England, Wales and Northern Ireland* (Committee of University Chairmen 1998). The Funding Council in Scotland took a different line. *The Guide for Members of Governing Bodies of Scottish Higher Education Institutions and Good Practice Benchmarks* (SHEFC 1999b) goes much further than its English counterpart and promotes and develops a set of good practice guidelines against which individual institutions could benchmark and develop their own specific arrangements. The guide makes a series of recommendations in respect of the roles, responsibilities, size and composition of governing bodies. In addition it discusses the procedures these bodies should follow and makes recommendations in respect of the role of the secretary or clerk, the remit of committees of the governing body and the regulation of the relationship between the institution and its related companies. Finally it invites the governing body to adopt a range of performance measures related to the institution's strategic objectives. As with similar codes that govern practice in the private sector, the objective is not to be prescriptive but rather to define what the Council considers to be good practice and to encourage institutions to adopt it. However institutions are *required* to compare their existing practices with these benchmarks, and indicate in their Annual Reports where and why they consider it to be either inappropriate or impractical to follow them (SHEFC 1999c).

There are a number of flaws in this analysis. Unlike company boards, the governing bodies of HE institutions have on the whole not been designed for strategic management but rather as representative bodies of a wide constituency of interests. Governing bodies, particularly in the older universities, derive from an age when their roles and responsibilities were more symbolic than real, when the 'dignified' as opposed to the 'efficient' elements of governance were emphasized (Bargh *et al.* 1996). A university is primarily defined by its business of teaching and research, and, while it must remain solvent, looks principally not to profits but to the value of its outputs (Committee of University Chairmen 2000). In addition, and uniquely, in many of the older universities the core business – academic matters – lies outside the governing body.

Evidence from recent National Audit Office studies at a number of institutions in the higher education sector (National Audit Office 1997a, b and 1998) supports recent research findings that effective governance is likely to depend more on interpersonal and largely informal relationships than on constitutional or structural arrangements (Bargh *et al.* 1996).

Research undertaken by Bargh *et al.* suggests that, although the majority of governors acknowledge their strategic role in taking responsibility for determining the institution's strategic mission, 'in the complex world of university governance only "knowledgeable actors" can operate effectively';

not all governors are invited to play an 'acting role' and those that are often find themselves in minor roles or bit parts.

They further suggest that within governing bodies a relatively small 'core group' of governors control the governance process to the extent that 'some groups of governors are effectively marginalized from important areas of influence'. Moreover the process appears to be self-perpetuating despite the guidance in both the Cadbury Report (1992) and the *Guide for Members of Governing Bodies* (Committee of University Chairmen 1998). While most, if not all, universities have established a Nominations Committee, the researchers found that in practice the process of seeking new members draws heavily on existing members' informal networks via personal recommendations (Bargh *et al.* 1996).

The ability of independent governors to initiate strategic proposals depends, to a large extent, on their background knowledge of higher educational issues and their degree of self-confidence to express and volunteer ideas in the company of seasoned executive professionals. This disadvantage is compounded by the fact that lay governors are frequently almost entirely dependent on the executive for information. The executive decides what information it thinks the governing body needs rather than the governing body specifying what it requires to fulfil its responsibilities. Under such circumstances governors are likely to become passive and reactive, shunning the proactive behaviour necessary for the effective performance of their strategic function. In both old and new universities the evidence suggests that it is the executive, the senior management team, which takes the 'efficient' or most proactive role in the governance process (Bargh *et al.* 1996).

Conclusion

Recent reports from the National Audit Office and the research findings of Bargh *et al.* threaten to undermine the framework of accountability that governs an increasingly uneasy relationship between the Council and the institutions of higher education. Governing bodies have been afforded primacy within that framework and, if they are willing and able to fulfil the responsibilities allocated to them, the state should be able to respect the autonomy of institutions. If they cannot or will not, then the government and the funding councils might be forced to erode further the autonomy of institutions.

References

Bargh, C., Scott, P. and Smith, D. (1996) *Governing Universities*. Buckingham: SRHE/ Open University Press.
Cadbury Report (1992) *Report of the Committee on the Financial Aspects of Corporate Governance*. London: Stock Exchange.

Committee on Standards in Public Life (Nolan Committee) (1996) *Local Spending Bodies*, Second Report, Cm 3270. London: The Stationery Office.

Committee of University Chairmen (1998) *Guide for Members of Governing Bodies of Universities and Colleges in England, Wales and Northern Ireland.* Bristol: Higher Education Funding Council for England.

Committee of University Chairmen (2000) *Progress Report of the Working Party on Effectiveness of University Governing Bodies.* London: CUC.

CVCP (Committee of Vice-Chancellors and Principals) (1985) *Report of the Steering Committee for Efficiency Studies in Universities* (Jarratt Report). London: Committee of Vice-Chancellors and Principals.

National Audit Office (1997a) *Report of the Comptroller and Auditor General, Governance and Management of Overseas Courses at Swansea Institute of Higher Education*, HC222 Session 1996–97, January. London: The Stationery Office.

National Audit Office (1997b) *Report of the Comptroller and Auditor General, University of Portsmouth*, HC4 Session 1997–98, January. London: The Stationery Office.

National Audit Office (1998) *Report of the Comptroller and Auditor General, Scottish Higher Education Funding Council Investigation of Misconduct and Glasgow Caledonian University*, HC680 Session 1997–98, January. London: The Stationery Office.

Sandbach, J. and Thomas, A. (1996) Sources of funding and resource allocation, in D. Warner and D. Palfreyman (eds) *Higher Education Management.* Buckingham: SRHE/Open University Press.

Shattock, M. (1994) *The UGC and the Management of British Universities.* Buckingham: SRHE/Open University Press.

SHEFC (Scottish Higher Education Funding Council) (1996) *National Committee of Inquiry into Higher Education: Submission of Evidence from the SHEFC.* Edinburgh: SHEFC.

SHEFC (Scottish Higher Education Funding Council) (1998) *Financial Memorandum between the Scottish Higher Education Funding Council and the University of Aberdeen.* Edinburgh: SHEFC.

SHEFC (Scottish Higher Education Funding Council) (1999a) *Corporate Plan 1999–2003.* Edinburgh: SHEFC

SHEFC (Scottish Higher Education Funding Council) (1999b) *The Guide for Members of Governing Bodies of Scottish Higher Education Institutions and Good Practice Benchmarks.* Edinburgh: SHEFC.

SHEFC (Scottish Higher Education Funding Council) (1999c) *Circular Letter HE05/99. Guide for Members of Governing Bodies of Scottish Higher Education Institutions and Good Practice Benchmarks.* Edinburgh: SHEFC.

SHEFC (Scottish Higher Education Funding Council) (2000) *Consultation Paper HEC01/00. Funding for the Future: Stage 2 Consultation Paper on the Funding of Teaching.* Edinburgh: SHEFC.

Sizer, J. (1992) Accountability, in B.R. Clark and G.R. Neave (eds) *The Encyclopaedia of Higher Education. Vol. 2: Analytical Perspectives*, pp. 1305–13. Oxford: Pergamon.

Sizer, J. and Cannon, S. (1999) Autonomy, governance and accountability, in J. Brennan, J. Fedorowitz, M. Huber and T. Shaw (eds) *What Kind of University?* Buckingham: SRHE/Open University Press.

Sizer, J. and Mackie, D. (1995) Greater accountability: the price of autonomy, *Higher Education Management*, 7 (3): 323–32.

11

The Admissions System: Expansion, Inclusion and the Demands of Diversity

Anthony McLaren

Introduction

It was in the spring of 1989 that Mike Shattock called me into his office at Warwick University to explain that I was to become Admissions Officer with effect from Easter that year. I took over the post having been duly prepared by attending that year's Universities Central Council on Admissions (UCCA) Admissions Officers' Conference in Dundee and thus came about my real introduction to the intricacies and politics of the world (albeit a very changed one) to which I returned in 1995 when I joined the Universities and Colleges Admissions Service (UCAS). A decade on, the differences between the world then and now were understandably much in my mind as I gave the closing speech to the 1999 Admissions Officers' Conference, held by coincidence at the University of Warwick, and from which I borrow the inspiration for this chapter.

The way we were

Although graded then at the administrative assistant level, the post of admission officer provided plenty of opportunity to exercise real responsibility, with a direct line of report to the academic registrar, a discrete sphere of activity and a large team of clerical staff to manage. Each admissions cycle provided a set of obstacles, internal and external, which one would have to surmount in order to achieve the goal: filling, with the greatest possible degree of precision, the University's funded undergraduate places. The target setting and careful planning were all tested in that intense period following the publication of the A level results when the staffing of the office would be swollen by temporary enquiries assistants answering a bank of phones which never stopped ringing. Nick St Aubyn

MP recently described the Clearing system as something which 'seems to have more of the characteristics of a frenzied trading room in the City than a robust careful analysis of the student's need'.[1] In fact, Clearing, though unquestionably intense, was never, then or now, quite as frenzied as it must appear to the disinterested observer. Nevertheless, there is no doubt that one sometimes had the impression of playing a particularly complex kind of game in which the prizes were being offered by the University Grants Committee (UGC) and the rules and regulations set by UCCA.

UCCA provided the framework for the activities of the Warwick Admissions Office in 1989, as it had done for the rest of what are now sometimes called the 'old' universities, since its founding in 1961. The Ad Hoc Committee on Procedures for the Admission of Students had been established in February 1958 under the chairmanship of Sir Philip Morris, Vice-Chancellor of the University of Bristol. The Committee's third report recommended the setting up of a central organization for admissions in order to solve some of the problems arising from the increased pressure of applications, which had risen steadily from 1955 onwards. The function of UCCA, as expressed in its Terms of Reference, was 'to enable the business of admission to undergraduate courses in all the constituent United Kingdom universities to be dealt with in an orderly manner and, equally important, in a way which allows each candidate freedom to make a responsible choice and each university freedom to select its own students.'[2]

Although applications to Warwick came through UCCA, its work for the university sector was paralleled (although with some distinct differences of emphasis) by that of the Polytechnics Central Admissions System (PCAS) for the polytechnic sector. PCAS had been established in 1985 to cope with similar pressures to those which had caused the universities to establish UCCA nearly 25 years earlier and, by 1989, the existence of both bodies side by side was part of the entrenched binary line which at that time divided higher education in the UK.

Seventy-three institutions were in membership of UCCA in 1989 and, for entry in the October of that year, they received applications from just over 196,000 candidates. More men than women were applying to, and being accepted for, the universities and over 72 per cent of all UK applicants were offering two or more A levels as their entry qualification. Nearly 96,000 candidates were accepted for UCCA institutions; in the parallel PCAS system, 170,000 applicants resulted in 61,000 acceptances.[3]

Broadly, the underlying direction of the late 1980s/early 1990s was an enormous expansion in student numbers which transformed a hitherto elite system into something approaching mass higher education. The most passionate planning debate each year would often be the one in which the Academic Office would mediate between rival expansionist departments, all of whom wanted a greater slice of the total increase in student numbers which we were planning for that year.

The expansion in student numbers which characterized the period was of course not unconnected with the replacement in 1989 of the UGC by the new Universities Funding Council (UFC). As Mike Shattock commented in *The UGC and the Management of British Universities*, 'the introduction of market-led expansion with little concern for individual subjects . . . marked a very sharp divergence from the UGC. The priority accorded to encouraging the development of mass higher education replaced concern for the development of subjects or for any kind of manpower-specific targets'.[4] As the funding mechanisms by which growth was being stimulated became increasingly transparent, so there was a corresponding growth in the need to plan and to make overall judgements on admissions numbers not simply on criteria of academic strength or balance but with due attention to the impact that changes to the units of resource would have upon overall funding.

As an institution in membership of UCCA we were participants in a national system. This is not to say that Warwick was inactive in the area of stimulating local admissions – one thinks of the work of the Department of Continuing Education, the development of the 'Two Plus Two' degree programmes in partnership with local colleges and the joint establishment with the then Coventry Polytechnic of a validating agency for Access programmes – but there is no doubt that the prime focus of the work of the Admissions Office was national. In Mike Shattock's opinion, UCCA, along with other agencies such as the Standing Conference on University Entrance (SCUE) and the Universities Council for Non-teaching Staff (UCNS), formed a 'network of university-created agencies'[5] that tended to increase the strong homogeneity of the British university system which had emerged in the wake of the Robbins expansion. This homogeneity had many strengths but, in the field of admissions, the very existence of a *national* system had, it could be argued, underpinned that separation between a university and its local population which was then, and to a significant degree still remains, a characteristic feature of English (but not Scottish) higher education.[6]

The homogeneity of the system had of course been placed under tremendous stress by the differential funding cuts of the early 1980s, the general erosion of the unit of resource and the emergence of the culture of audit and assessment, the most public manifestation of which were league tables. The system of which the Warwick Admissions Office was a part would undergo very dramatic changes in the next decade.

'Plus ça change . . . ?'

It would be difficult to argue with the assertion that the most significant structural change in higher education between 1989 and today was the ending of the binary line. The government's White Paper of May 1991, *Higher Education – A New Framework*,[7] made clear its wish to see significant expansion of student numbers, a single sector for higher education and the reorganization of the work of the polytechnics, which were to be permitted to award their own degrees and to take on the title of university if they wished. The White Paper included this statement on admission arrangements

for the next sector: 'Building on the greater collaboration already introduced, the Government will look to the Universities Central Council on
Admissions (UCCA) and the Polytechnics Central Admissions System (PCAS)
to come together as a central agency for admissions.' The Further and
Higher Education Act 1992 gave effect to the ending of the binary line and
by 1993 UCCA and PCAS had merged to form UCAS, a single admissions
system to serve the newly expanded university sector and the colleges of
higher education.

It is, however, often overlooked that UCAS is considerably more, even in
organizational terms, than simply the sum of UCCA and PCAS. The merger
of 1993 also took in the Standing Conference on University Entrance
(SCUE), formerly an agency of the CVCP with responsibility for advising on
the impact of changes in the school and college curriculum on progression
to higher education. At the same time, UCAS took on the work of the
Scottish Universities Committee on Entrance (SUCE) and, indeed, still
maintains a separate Scottish Office.

Just before the ending of the binary line PCAS had, in 1991, absorbed
the work of the Central Register and Clearing House (CRCH) which had
previously acted as the Admissions Clearing House for initial teacher training courses in the public sector. The Graduate Teacher Training Registry
(previously under the management of CRCH) was run jointly by UCCA and
PCAS from 1991 and was transferred to UCAS in 1993. The Social Work
Admissions System (SWAS) has been the responsibility of PCAS and then
UCAS since 1992 and UCAS is now also responsible for the Nursing and
Midwifery Admissions Service (NMAS), which is run under contract to the
NHS Executive. In 1996 UCAS took on the responsibility of managing the
admissions process to those courses and programmes which up until then
had recruited through the former Art and Design Admissions Registry
(ADAR). At the time of writing, UCAS is in discussion with the music
conservatoires about the possibility of providing them with an admissions
service.

In some ways, however, the development with potentially the greatest
significance has been the steady increase in the number of further education institutions (FEIs) in membership of UCAS. This growth has, of course,
mirrored the steady increase in the HE provision offered by FEIs and, by
the end of 1998, over 70 FE colleges were in full membership of UCAS, with
a further 20 or so involved in UCAS admissions through partnership arrangements with universities. During 1999 the position has moved forward
very rapidly, with formal requests being made to the UCAS Board by the
Association of Colleges (AoC) and the Further Education Funding Council
(FEFC) for changes in the criteria for UCAS membership which would
permit institutions teaching at least one full-time HND or HNC to become
full members; until now, the essential criterion has been the provision of at
least one full-time *degree* programme. The Board has agreed to this change
and, in response to the invitation to membership sent to further education
colleges throughout the UK, nearly a hundred FEIs applied for membership

with effect from the admissions cycle for entry in autumn 2001. This remarkable development has clearly been stimulated, at least in part, by the decision, recommended by the Dearing Committee and implemented by the HEFCE, that the latter should become responsible for funding all categories of publicly funded higher education in England, irrespective of the type of institution providing them.[8]

In 1989 I worked within an UCCA system which had 73 institutional members; in 1999 UCAS had over 260 institutional members, with the prospect of that number growing to 360 by 2000.

This enormous growth has of course been paralleled and underpinned by the continuing growth in the overall numbers of students entering higher education which, despite the impact of measures designed to curb the expansion of funded student places under the last government and a certain flattening of demand more recently, have grown very significantly over the last decade. In 1997, the total number of applicants in the main UCAS application scheme reached the record level of 458,781 with over 336,000 of those successful in gaining acceptance.[9]

The UCAS system has proved itself to be remarkably successful in coping with growth, both in institutional and applicant numbers, and in transferring the essence of the system (the reliable exchange of authoritative information for purposes of progression) to other educational areas. I am reminded of some comments which Mike Shattock made at a conference several years ago. Mike was considering the impact of the dramatic development of information and communication technology on the university of the future and his gist on that day was that, contrary to current and accepted wisdom, the element of change, as opposed to continuity, can be greatly exaggerated. (This, bear in mind, from the Registrar of a university which has been seen as pre-eminently comfortable with, and able to respond to, change.) He reminded us of the predictions that had been made that the advent of the electronic office and modern means of information and communications technology would render the traditional workplace redundant; instead, there would be a massive increase in home working, with individuals keeping in touch with their employers and colleagues through fax, email and video conferencing. Similarly, there are now predictions about the rise of the virtual university where students will, in a radical development of distance learning, pick the best modules that the world of higher education can offer: a module in business studies from the USA, a semester in computing delivered electronically from Australia or, indeed, from Microsoft's in-house training programme. As the *Independent* memorably said in an article on the subject, 'Shall I nip down to my local university or should I log on to Harvard?[10] But while no one would deny the impact of these technologies either on the workplace or in higher education, Mike's point was that the elements of continuity are equally, if not more, powerful; by and large people still work in offices because we are social animals and operate more effectively within the dynamics provided by group interaction. His guess was that in higher education we would still see students predominantly wishing to move away from home and gather in social institutions called universities and colleges, listening to lectures given by human beings and meeting with friends and peers in seminar groups and bars.

Likewise, the system which UCAS operates today is still recognizably the one with which I worked in 1989. There is undeniably a continuity, just as there is in the world of HE which UCAS serves. Nevertheless, it can be equally misleading to ignore the very substantial challenges which UCAS has faced in maintaining this continuity because they are undoubtedly pointers to the likely shape of post-compulsory education in the future and because to do so is also to ignore the long list of innovations which UCAS has developed or is developing in response to these challenges.

Responding to change

UCAS was born as a result of structural realignment in British higher education and it continues to develop not only in response to, but in planned anticipation of, the continuing changes – structural, curricular and political – which have arisen throughout the period since its establishment, although perhaps with increasing intensity since the election of the current government in May 1997. There are so many developments in the educational world, and so many which, perhaps to the surprise of some, have an impact on progression and admission to higher education, that it is difficult to be selective. I intend, however, to look at two particular areas which help to explain the changing shape of UCAS as an organization and, more importantly, lest that objective sound too parochial, are important indicators of where the system is going. They are the demands of complexity and the social exclusion agenda.

The relatively simple and indeed homogeneous situation described above in the brief backward look at admissions in 1989 has become immeasurably more complicated in 1999. Of course, complexity is never an intended end in itself but it is nevertheless the cumulative result of many of the changes which I have touched on. Enormous growth in the number of institutions participating in the national admissions system and the proliferation of electronic means of communication, which ten years ago were either in their infancy or as yet undiscovered, have inevitably created a far more complex higher education scene than that of 1989. For an organization whose essence is the exchange of information from institution to applicant and vice versa this complexity becomes a challenge in its own right. UCAS, mindful perhaps of the inheritance brought to it by SCUE, has never taken the view that the perfection of an admissions system lies only in its technical excellence; the most effective computers and most efficient workforce in Cheltenham will still not result in a good system if the decisions made at either end of that transfer of information by applicant and institution are ill-informed. It is vital for the effectiveness of its work that UCAS finds the means to convey accurately both the increasing range of choices available to the potential applicant and the increasing diversity of the backgrounds, both educational and social, that those applicants bring with them to HE.

Many of the developments in UCAS over recent years are a response to its need to provide increasing amounts of information in clear, accessible forms, and they have taken full advantage of the new possibilities offered by technology: the development of an Electronic Application System (EAS), the creation of the UCAS website with its searchable database of all the programmes available at member institutions, the StudyLink CD ROM and the videos made in partnership with the BBC, for example. Perhaps two with particular significance are the reform of the points score system, or Tariff, and the development, in partnership with institutions, of admissions criteria profiles (ACPs). Both these ideas, which were presented to the DfEE in the UCAS report *Making Achievement Count* in March 1998,[11] represent an attempt to re-engineer the admissions system to take account of the diversity and complexity of a higher education sector which is itself increasingly being seen as part of the larger whole of lifelong learning.

The reform of the familiar UCAS A level points score was initially proposed by the DfEE in 1995 because it wished to see a system of points which would encompass all the major routes into higher education, rather than only A level and AS. We have seen that in 1989 over 72 per cent of all home applicants for degrees in the UCCA system were offering two or more A levels. By 1998 this percentage had fallen to 66 per cent[12] and, alongside those with A level or Scottish Highers, were those offering Advanced GNVQ, the International Baccalaureate and a variety of Access and Foundation qualifications. The traditional points score system, however, excludes the achievement of nearly 40 per cent of applicants and renders it invisible in the multiplying number of league tables of school and HEI performance which use A level points scores as their only measure of exit/entry achievement. The new tariff provides a much more flexible points score system, capable of coping not only with the diversity of admissions routes which are now available but also with the significant changes brought about by the reforms in the 16–19 curriculum set out in *Qualifications 16–19: A Guide to the Changes Resulting from the Qualifying for Success Consultation.*[13]

The admissions criteria profiles are a response not only to the increasing complexity of course structures in HEIs, brought about by the widespread adoption of credit-based modular structures, but also to the more general trend, observable and indeed encouraged in many other areas of society, towards transparency of information and the exposure, as far as possible, of hidden criteria. Professor Martin Harris, in his final public address as Chairman of the CVCP, mentioned the 'continuing concern' of teachers and careers advisers that 'the entry requirements [for HE] are insufficiently transparent. This is particularly so for entry to "high-demand" subjects where both academic and non-academic criteria may need to be fulfilled.'[14] ACPs, which are still in the pilot stage, attempt to address this concern by providing a flexible electronic format for the presentation of entry requirements in all major qualification routes together with an indication of the other qualities sought and how such qualities might be evidenced by the applicant. They will be available on the Web, both because that is increasingly where students will expect to find entry information and because the medium of the Web, with its ability to link between many different levels and items of information, is so much more effective than paper for conveying the fuller entry criteria which genuine transparency requires. Martin Harris specifically drew attention to the development of ACPs in his speech, expressing the belief that such a development is 'central to the achievement of transparency and fairness in our national arrangements for admission to higher education'. As their use becomes widespread they may do much to dispel some of the myths which have grown up over many years regarding entry requirements and hidden criteria.

Of course, one response to complexity might be gradually to force conformity to a predetermined pattern, a process not unknown in human affairs and particularly in education. If UCCA could be seen as part of the organizational fabric which had enhanced and sustained the homogeneity of the British university system, might UCAS be seen as the body performing the same function for the much more diverse HE sector of today? Although the attempt to employ existing knowledge in the solution of new problems is in itself not an unworthy endeavour (commonly known as not reinventing the wheel), I think it is more than possible to argue that UCAS, even considered at the level of mechanism and structure, has in recent years exhibited a tendency to respond to, and support, diversity rather than attempting to make everything fit the same pattern. The existence within one organization of separate systems meeting the needs of full-time undergraduates, nurses and midwives, graduate teacher training students and social workers, each with different application dates and operational parameters, is itself evidence of a wish to meet needs as defined by the consumers of the service rather than to impose what is thought to be best for them. More recently, the creation of a new route within the main admissions system to accommodate the need for sequential interviewing and portfolio inspection in some art and design courses has demonstrated a flexibility which has surprised even some UCAS staff. Then there are the long-standing arrangements which permit Oxford and Cambridge to operate an earlier closing date in order to accommodate the need for college interviews. Intense pressure caused by the huge demand for places to study medicine has recently led the Council of Heads of Medical Schools to request a reduction from six choices to four for medical applicants and an earlier closing date of 15 October; veterinary science will shortly follow suit and the Council of Deans of Dental Schools has recently indicated a wish to do likewise. Again, the UCAS system has been able to accommodate such diversity within its overall framework. This might be important if, as many suspect, we are moving towards the point where diversity becomes fragmentation and regional or subject groupings increasingly find the need to operate what will be in effect sub-systems customized to their particular needs.

The second challenge is that of the social exclusion agenda. The existence of a unit bearing that name within the Cabinet Office is some indication of the priority which the UK government is giving to this agenda across its range of responsibilities and there can be no doubt that it is an extremely important strand of higher education policy. The need to admit students from a far wider range of social backgrounds is likely to be the dominant note of the next few years, in the way that the dramatic expansion of higher education numbers characterized the late 1980s and early 1990s; certainly it was the theme that ran strongly through nearly all the questions posed by the Education Sub-Committee when it took evidence from UCAS.[15] The HEFCE, through its Widening Participation initiative and in its allocation of additional student places, has tied financial rewards to the genuine widening, rather than simply increasing, of access and the government has made it clear that the bulk of the renewed growth in HE will take place at the sub-degree level and be delivered through FEIs. The Report *From Elitism to Inclusion: Good Practice in Widening Access to Higher Education*, published jointly by the CVCP, COSHEP, SCoP, the funding councils, and the Council for Industry and Higher Education (CIHE), and based on UCAS data, is evidence at one level of a response to 'growing concern about the persistent social class imbalance in higher education'.[16] The escalating number of enquiries which UCAS receives from institutions anxious to understand in more depth the social background of their applicants and those of other institutions is another. Indeed, it is not only institutions that are turning to UCAS with increasing frequency for statistical information which can be used to inform policy decisions; recent years have seen a growing number of joint projects with the DfEE, the CVCP, SCoP and other organizations such as the Higher Education Statistics Agency (HESA) and the Careers Services Unit (CSU) as attempts are made to understand the complex relationships between social class, educational opportunity, financial pressures and progression to HE. UCAS has responded by opening up in ever greater detail a statistical resource of potentially enormous significance which has arguably been underused in the past (although it should not be forgotten that UCCA and then UCAS were home to the Universities Statistical Record (USR) from 1968 until its replacement by HESA in 1994).

UCAS has responded to the enormous increase in the demand for statistical information from government, agencies and the institutions by developing a range of new services which again take advantage of the developments in information technology and also attempt to deepen the level of analysis which is possible. The Institutional Planning Service, which has been operating for over two years, enables institutions to analyse historic and current data on their applicants by any of the categories, singly or in combination, which UCAS codes as part of the applications process: gender, ethnic origin, social class, area of domicile, etc. A new Applications Postcode Tracking Service, recently launched, permits UCAS and its member institutions, through the use of postcode analysis, to examine the social demographics of applicants in much greater detail than has hitherto been possible using only the five traditional social class categories. The possibility now exists to plan and then to monitor strategies designed to widen access to particular programmes or across the institution. A Forecasting Service has also been developed, offering predictive models to determine eventual numbers of accepted applicants in the current cycle and beyond, and enabling various 'what if' scenarios to be tested. The timeliness of such a development is only underlined by the publication of the funding councils' institutional performance indicators,[17] which include indicators on participation from disadvantaged social classes and low-participation neighbourhoods.

In addition to providing statistical information UCAS itself is, with greater regularity, publishing its own reports on particular aspects of the statistical background to developments in admissions. *The Statistical Bulletin on Widening Participation*,[18] for example, published in 1999, analyses changes in participation patterns between 1994 and 1998 by age, gender, social class, ethnic origin, main qualification and subject group. It is interesting to recall that the introduction of ethnic monitoring information on what was then the UCCA application form was very controversial when it was introduced for the 1990 entry, not least with many staff at UCCA itself. By no means all shared the enthusiasm with which Mike Shattock, as a member of the UCCA Council of Management and its Executive and Statistics committees, promoted the idea. I recall visiting one university where I was informed that all the information on the ethnic origin of its applicants which UCAS had passed to it at the end of the cycle had been thrown in the bin as irrelevant. It is surely now unthinkable that government, the institutions and, indeed, applicants themselves should not wish to be able to access information on the performance of higher education in recruiting students from the main ethnic groups in British society.

Make three wishes . . .

There is a satisfying symmetry about concluding a chapter which has reflected on the last ten years in higher education admissions by looking forward to the next decade. Predictions are hostages to fortune and probably best left to the spoken, rather than the written, word but, more self-indulgently, one can at least express one's wishes for the future without fear of contradiction.

My first wish would be for ever greater 'joined-upness' in the provision of information on learning opportunities. The Education and Employment Committee, in its survey of post-16 participation, has stated that: 'The barrier most frequently cited in our enquiry to effective progression in learning was inadequate information, advice and guidance.'[19] It may reasonably be argued that one of the central achievements of UCAS has been to provide impartial and authoritative information on the opportunities available to students in higher education and that it has done this with a thoroughness and a comprehensiveness that has more than kept pace with the expanding numbers of institutions and programmes. The dangers threatening the provision of information will be competitive forces and incomplete information sources set up only to exploit the HE consumer; equally, efforts to overcome these dangers by the government could lead to the reinvention of wheels in the search for the elusive perfect information network which will provide all the answers. It will be vital that the authoritative sources of information – UCAS, HESA, the funding councils, Learn Direct – work together to ensure seamlessness without imposing uniformity. In the higher education field, we must watch the development of the UK HERO (Higher Education and Research Opportunities) with great interest to see if this delicate balance can be achieved.[20]

Seamless information will be both the product of, and a spur to, the creation of a seamless post-16 education sector. My second wish is for the success of the planned expansion of HE in FE in delivering the social inclusiveness in higher education which has so far proved so much more difficult to deliver than expansion. The introduction of two-year, vocationally orientated associated degrees may take us several significant steps nearer to a genuinely integrated tertiary education system. UCAS, poised to accept nearly a hundred FEI members, is ready to play its part.

Finally, I wish for admissions officers (and there are already many) who act upon the realization that their role is about far more than simply keeping the machinery of an admissions office in good working order, important though that is. Higher education institutions will face formidable challenges as they attempt to respond not only to intense competition and students whose consumerist instincts will be increasingly sharpened by ever greater financial pressures but also to the issues of social disadvantage and inclusion which are now so firmly on the national policy agenda. Technicians who ignore the policy context will, I fear, not see the wood for the trees.

Notes and references

1. Education and Employment Committee (Education Sub-Committee) (1999) *The Work of UCAS. Payment of Student Loans. Minutes of Evidence and Appendices*, p. 9. London: The Stationery Office.
2. R. Kay and P. Oakley (1994) *UCCA: Its Origins and Development 1950–93*, pp. 8–14. Cheltenham: UCCA.
3. See Table 10A in UCCA (1990) *Statistical Supplement to the Twenty-seventh Report 1988–9*, p. 27. Cheltenham: UCCA.
4. M. Shattock (1994) *The UGC and the Management of British Universities*, p. 154. Buckingham: SRHE/Open University Press.
5. Ibid., p. 57.
6. Ibid., p. 146.
7. Department for Education and Employment (1991) *Higher Education – A New Framework*. London: HMSO.

8. HEFCE (1999) *Higher Education in Further Education Colleges: Guidance for Colleges on Funding Options*, para. 8. Bristol: HEFCE.

9. See Table A1 in UCAS (1998) *Annual Report 1997 Entry*, p. 37. Cheltenham: UCAS.

10. This appeared in an article entitled 'Invasion of the Student Snatchers' in the education section of the *Independent*, pp. 2–3, 15 April 1999.

11. UCAS (1998) *Making Achievement Count: A Report to the DfEE presented by Tony Higgins*. Cheltenham: UCAS.

12. A. Cromar and S. Green (1999) *Statistical Bulletin on Widening Participation*, p. 8. Cheltenham: UCAS.

13. Qualifications and Curriculum Authority (1999) *Qualifications 16–19: A Guide to the Changes Resulting from the Qualifying for Success Consultation*. Suffolk: QCA Publications.

14. Professor Harris's speech was given to the Secondary Heads of Association at its conference in the New Connaught Rooms, London, on 2 July 1999. See CVCP Media Release MR117.

15. Education and Employment Committee (Education Sub-Committee) (1999) op. cit.

16. CVCP, HEFCE, SHEFC, SCoP, COSHEP, CIHE (1998) *From Elitism to Inclusion: Good Practice in Widening Access to Higher Education*, p. 3. London: CVCP.

17. HEFCE, HEFCW, DENI, SHEFC (1999) *Performance Indicators in Higher Education in the UK*. Bristol: HEFCE.

18. A. Cromar and S. Green (1999) op. cit.

19. Education and Employment Committee (1999) *Eighth Report: Access for All? A Survey of Post-16 Participation*, vol. 1, pp. xvii–xxi. London: The Stationery Office.

20. UK HERO will be a website intended to provide an international showcase for the diversity and quality of UK higher education and research.

12

The Cuckoo in the Nest?
The Business School in a University

Allan Bolton

Introduction

At a meeting held by the Association of Business Schools (ABS) on 23 April 1999 a straw poll on the question of whether deans and directors would 'like to renegotiate the relationship of their business school with their university' led all 65 present to endorse that view.

Why is it that business schools within universities seem to pursue a separate agenda and some press for more autonomy? The schools themselves are as varied in mission as the sector in general yet tend to share the ability to generate supplementary income which makes them less dependent than other faculties upon the funding councils. However, their paying customers are notable for being a critical, demanding audience for whom higher levels of service and rapid response are required. Collisions are inevitable with those university central services which run on the principle of 'one size fits all'.

The schools are operating in buoyant markets but against strong and increasing competition: for some, the strongest competition comes, significantly, from institutions which are either independent of the state system or which enjoy a high degree of freedom within it.

The challenges for business schools are so great that, in order to succeed for the benefit of their parent institutions, they need incentives and a measure of autonomy to achieve improvements in staffing, services and infrastructure. However, business schools are not unique: similar devolved arrangements may also be appropriate for some other faculties provided that their internal organization is sufficiently well developed.

Internal negotiations tend to illustrate the fear that some vice-chancellors have grasped only one business concept, that of the cash-cow. Frustration in such negotiations has caused directors of schools to resign: Manchester Business School and Oxford[1] are the two best-known cases. The problem of discontinuity of leadership in business schools has worsened: the ABS calculated in February 2000 that in the previous 18 months, 27 of its member schools had experienced a change in the top job and there were nine current vacancies. This amounts to a turnover of one-third among UK business schools. The difficulties of identifying suitable people to lead business schools[2] are magnified when internal politics prevent deans from directing their energies more profitably to external opportunities.

A brief history

The expansion of business and management education in the 1960s and thereafter was an outcome of a widely shared belief that UK companies were underperforming partly because of underinvestment in the development of their managers.

Influential reports[3] urged significant growth – a process which was already occurring. For example, the output of first degrees in business and management in 1985 was 4500 compared with 1500 in 1975. Constable and McCormick advocated an increase to 7000 (6 per cent of all first degrees awarded) by 1995. By 1996/97, 29,400 degrees were awarded in business and management while total enrolments in the subject at first degree level had reached 11.5 per cent of the overall total, making business and management the most popular of all subjects.[4] At Master of Business Administration (MBA) level, Constable and McCormick recommended an annual graduation rate of 10,000 by 1999. Demand and output have not quite reached this target (see Table 12.1).

Whereas Constable and McCormick envisaged that the MBAs would be the product of 30–5 schools, the reality is that by 1998 there were 116 organizations offering MBAs.[5] The inevitable accompanying concerns about quality of provision and about the ability of smaller schools to sustain coverage of the curriculum are reflected in the fact that only approximately one-third of providers are accredited by AMBA. There are just five schools which are both excellent in research, as defined by holding a rating of 5* or 5 in the 1996 Research Assessment Exercise (RAE), and have AMBA accreditation. They are Bath, Lancaster, London Business School, Strathclyde and Warwick.

The expansion has been much more than a happy accident or a response to market demand for vocational programmes. The business schools have

Table 12.1　Graduates of MBA programmes in UK schools

Year	Full-time	Part-time	Distance learning	Total
1990	2100	1760	220	4080
1995	3441	2743	1869	8053
1998	4286	2979	1189	8454

Source: Association of MBAs (AMBA)

earned their success over decades in which they developed a coherent curriculum at first-degree level, largely in the former polytechnics, at master's level in specialisms as well as in MBAs, and in post-experience provision, some of which now reaches a high level of sophistication. Business and management is 'a problem domain',[6] 'a theme subject, rather like geography'.[7] The market has recognized that it combines the learning of specific skills with a general, liberal education and the gaining of knowledge about the nature of management and its environment,[8] the latter normally illuminated by an integral work experience placement.

Business schools have done more than other faculties to meet and stimulate demand for continuing professional development (CPD) at various levels. They have provided a major impetus to lifelong learning. Nevertheless, the confident expansion of the business schools, fuelled by some overblown promotion of the MBA degree, is unconvincing to many observers.

Criticism: shallow?

Critics have claimed that some or all business schools are academically shallow. It is alleged that 'management theory' has become associated with quick-fix solutions to business problems, with advice on personal skills or with autobiographies of successful business people. Hence texts such as *The One Minute Manager*[9] and writings on the latest management ideas and buzzwords are shown to lack conceptual foundation. It is undeniable that there is a stream of output, some of which may have utility value but which cannot be represented as academically serious.[10] The volume of such material serves to illustrate the high level of interest in improving organizational and personal performance but should not distract us from the serious and innovative work which is readily available. The business school professors who have written extremely influential texts, including some who have marketed themselves skilfully and become millionaires, have made genuine contributions to the field based on research and on conceptual insight. As such they, popularly known as 'gurus' of management, are read by students and by business practitioners. Most others, the staff who populate business schools everywhere, cannot or do not wish to follow such a path. They are responsible for generating ideas based upon research which is normally published in learned journals for which the main audience is academic. They, like most of the gurus, are firmly grounded in academic disciplines such as mathematics, economics, psychology and sociology. Academic research in management subjects has advanced greatly on both sides of the Atlantic since the late 1950s when reports[11] drew attention to weakness in this respect. It remains true that the level of academic performance in research as measured by the RAE is somewhat below average: of 90 submitting institutions, only 10 (11 per cent) gained ratings of 5* or 5 in 1996. Ratings in vocational subjects are generally lower than in non-vocational subjects because of the additional pressures on the staff to maintain knowledge of current practice.

Criticism: too academic?

In seeking academic acceptability, university business academics have adopted and aspired towards the standards set in other subject areas. The criteria for personal promotion and for high ratings in the RAE place incentives firmly within the realms of academic research published in refereed journals. Schools themselves have begun to hire some faculty largely for their potential impact in the RAE, the financial outcomes of which appear to make such actions rational. Some effects run counter to the objectives of business schools: the published research may be seen as irrelevant to practitioners, and staff protect their time for academic research by seeking to avoid other commitments, so that activities which are the lifeblood of a business school – including teaching, applied research, consultancy, and championing new ventures – are either neglected or undertaken by staff who work on non-academic contracts outside the mainstream. These effects can be distorting, may adversely affect the 'product' in the eyes of the student/consumer, and may also leave schools with a major problem in the longer term. For example, if the criteria for success in the RAE are changed radically or if the exercise is abandoned, some schools could face the difficulty of redirecting staff effort. Others – those who are independent of the funding councils or who do not aspire to be well-rated – would not be affected.

One can readily defend theoretical research, notably in subjects such as finance, marketing and operations where the cutting-edge of research is close to the cutting-edge of practice.[12] Certainly the charge 'too academic' is not applicable in schools which are not research-led. It has been avoided in many leading schools but only at the price of creating two classes of staff citizens: some students meet only those who are research-inactive.

Criticism: inflexible?

Business schools have been accused by some students, corporate clients and employers, and occasionally by journalists, of being inflexible and backward-looking. For instance, academics are said to favour a view of the world based on their own functional specialisms (for example, accountancy, operations, marketing, human resources) which no longer correspond to reality in organizations. Business schools have been accused of arrogance in adopting a producer-led, rather than a market-led, attitude by pushing predetermined courses at prospective customers. Their preference for case studies has sometimes served as a substitute for reality, insulating staff and students from the constantly gathering pace of change in the world off-campus and encouraging an analytical view of situations which are in fact far more fluid than normal business education suggests. The elite schools have tended to change least rapidly because of their established reputation and desire not to compromise their brand. Other schools, keen to distinguish themselves from a host of competitors, have been more inclined to redesign their curriculum around themes such as the international business environment, or managing change. Such complex topics necessarily draw on the expertise of staff from various disciplines and require them to work together.

Business schools have shown increasing willingness in their post-experience provision to tailor programmes for the specific needs of corporate clients. Even if the extent of such tailoring can be exaggerated, the schools are aware that the attractive financial margins available in this field justify and require them to invest effort in understanding their customers. This strand of work, which has superseded post-experience provision offered on an open (that is, untailored) basis, is now responsible for 65–70 per cent of revenue for some leading schools.[13] This could not be the case if hard-headed, discriminating corporate clients believed the schools to be excessively academic. In fact, what they value from the schools is the academic mode of reflection and analysis rather than injections of the latest facts and figures which they can acquire more readily from consultants or from their own market intelligence.

Business schools and consulting companies, which are often seen as rivals[14] can form complementary resources for the customer. The schools generate the ideas and train the minds of students who join consultancies which then popularize, package and deliver the material. This may become the norm in future.

Criticism: a poor relation?

Many indicators give credence to the view, held by some within all the constituencies, that business education in the UK is a poor relation compared with the USA. This charge not surprisingly enrages UK business academics who point to the variety and innovation which is evident in their own institutions and which arguably exceeds that offered in the USA. And yet it remains true that leading British companies often take up development programmes and even MBAs for their most senior executives at Harvard Business School, the Wharton School at the University of Pennsylvania or other elite US schools. If they choose Europe, they are as likely to opt for the European Institute of Business Administration (INSEAD) or the International Institute for Management Development (IIMD), which are international schools based in France and Switzerland respectively, as for a UK-based provider. Choices of this kind are often determined more according to reputation or networking potential than to the inherent quality of the offerings: many providers, in both Europe and America, are unjustly overlooked.

The facts show that, when a 'ranking' mindset is applied, the advantages held by top schools in the USA are overwhelming.[15] For example, leading schools and their MBA degrees have a long-established place in the history of boardrooms; they have access to large bodies of alumni who expect to make donations; most are part of private universities which charge full-cost tuition fees and even those ranked just below the elite category command endowment funding of $120–140 million;[16] they effectively control the world's leading academic journals; they employ teams of careers and fundraising professionals; they can offer salaries sufficient to attract and retain the leading talent; they are staffed by professors who have experienced what they teach – the MBA degree (this is not the norm in the UK); are seen as first-choice study centres by international students keen to make contacts with a currently flourishing trading bloc, and are associated with ready access to careers both in leading financial institutions and consultancies and in small high-technology firms. Moreover, at least on anecdotal evidence,[17] the standards and tempo evident in the MBA programmes of the elite and next-ranking US business schools – say the top 40 – are matched by only a handful of schools in all Europe including the UK.

With so many disadvantages, the performance of schools in the UK is remarkably good.

The current markets

The schools' success in achieving income from sources outside the funding councils makes them, in the words of ABS, 'pillars of the economy'.[18] Most striking is their ability to attract international students to the UK. In 1998/99, the numbers of non-EU students enrolled for business and management were as shown in Table 12.2.

Threats within current markets arise from an excess of providers at postgraduate level where there are too many small programmes[19] and possibly too many programmes of doubtful quality. Within the last year, at least three full-time MBA programmes have quietly closed. It would not be surprising if other providers do not also decide to rationalize their offerings.

The maturing of the MBA market does not foretell its demise. At the top end of the market, students will become even more discriminating and

Table 12.2   International students in UK business schools

	Students	*Percentage of total non-EU*
First degree	8,617	18.5
Postgraduate taught	10,475	31.9
Postgraduate research	1,415	6.5

Source: HESA (1998)

prepared to move between one continent and another; the mass market will continue to exist, sustaining schools with a strong regional profile and reflecting an increased acceptance of the MBA as a basic requirement for career progression. The MBA remains a minority qualification among older managers: a survey of the *Fortune* top 100 companies in the world in 1998 showed that 19 per cent of the chief executive officers (CEOs) had an MBA, and that the figure had risen to 21 per cent by 1999. However, the average conceals an international difference: only 11 per cent of Europe-based managers held an MBA whereas in the USA the proportion was 42 per cent, or 39 per cent when the size of the survey was doubled in 1999.[20]

The situation among younger managers is very different: even six years ago in the UK, 61 per cent of chairmen, deputy chairmen and CEOs under the age of 50 held an MBA.[21]

Future markets

It is possible that international demand for residential programmes will continue to grow, for instance from largely untapped vast markets such as India and China. However, it is equally likely that the whole situation will be changed by an accelerated uptake in distance learning. At present the position of the universities is protected by their control of accreditation but there are signs that single providers will cease to dominate the market. Changes are occurring most quickly in the post-experience field, which is typically non-accredited, and most slowly in the undergraduate field.

Leading US business schools and the London School of Economics and Political Science (LSE) have formed alliances with technology partners whose expertise is in developing and marketing material for use on the Internet. Those schools are also taking an equity stake in the companies, thus confirming their interest in the for-profit sector of education. It may prove difficult for lesser schools to compete, and their recruiting ground may be threatened by major rivals who have increasing powers of outreach. If a middle manager in the UK can earn an MBA from the Massachusetts Institute of Technology (MIT) on-line, why should he or she opt for the MBA of his or her local provider?[22] The market is expanding to include people whose circumstances prevent them from taking residential programmes – those tied to a business, living in a remote location, the disabled, military personnel and carers.

Nevertheless, it seems certain that demand for face-to-face programmes will continue, whatever levels of quality are attained by convenient, reasonably priced Internet solutions. The nature of management cannot be fully appreciated on-line.

Advances in the technology of learning are already making it possible for students to develop both deeper and broader understanding of the subject. A more ambitious curriculum is becoming possible because of students' ability to harness more powerful technologies. In addition, since business studies has become a mainstream subject, incoming students tend to share a knowledge of certain basic concepts which many of their predecessors lacked.

Underlying technology-driven change is a question about learning styles. Where the traditional teacher-dominated model persists, the learning experience is impoverished because students' prior experience is not fully used.[23] Failure to engage the prior learning of experienced managers would be highly undesirable in an MBA programme and disastrous in executive education. The demands on teachers in such situations are complex and perhaps only a small minority of schools will be able to operate successfully with senior executives: those schools which 'design learning as an integrated intervention, not a course run by faculty for learners (students) with all the dependence this implies.'[24]

The volume of output from the business schools has created a huge pool for continuing professional development. The fact that there is still no normal route within management education means that needs vary greatly: at various ages and stages people need to redirect their knowledge and skills. Such development is reflected in a wide range of qualifications: the MBA is the best known but is not appropriate for all.

Much has been made of the threat to business schools from 'corporate universities'[25] of which there are said to be more than 1600 in the USA and an increasing number created by high-profile companies in the UK. However, to date the evidence is that they continue to buy in expertise from business schools and from consultancies. They seem to seek good relationships with academia, not to replace it with their own resources.[26] In fact the coming of corporate universities may prove to be excellent news for the business schools which are now likely to have more well-informed clients willing to take seriously the development of their managers. Traditionalists in business schools who disapprove of tailored programmes[27] may have to compromise.

Staffing and resources

Business schools in the UK are keen to recruit staff internationally to realize their aspirations to become truly international in curriculum and outlook, but only a minority can succeed. The level of salaries in the USA makes it impossible for UK schools to compete on this dimension, thus worsening the familiar difficulties of filling vacancies in subjects such as accounting, finance, marketing and information systems, in all of which there is a huge disparity with salaries in the commercial world. The influence of the RAE has deepened this crisis: most good schools will no longer consider hiring people with commercial experience who would make good teachers but who would struggle to start up academic research.

Management teaching fellowships were created in the early 1990s when the Economic and Social Research Council (ESRC) part-funded 'apprentice' lectureships and brought 180 new staff into the profession. The expansion of the system, combined with demographic factors such as the ageing of established staff and recruitment difficulties, makes the revival of such a programme an urgent necessity.

An accompanying solution could come through the Doctor of Business Administration (DBA). The growing adoption of this qualification in the UK has potential to bring industry and academia into closer conjunction at a senior level. DBA programmes impart skills necessary to undertake research but require applied work, normally a major consultancy project, rather than the traditional theoretical PhD thesis. Through such a vehicle business schools can upgrade the commercially 'relevant' knowledge possessed by their existing faculty and also identify a stream of students with experience of senior management, some of whom would be potential recruits to the faculty of the business school.

Staff recruitment is partly inhibited by salary scales, although these days universities are more willing to use their freedom to set their own salaries to attract talented people to professorial positions. Many make substantial additional payments to staff who are successful teachers in post-experience programmes which generate significant financial margins. The real question has become whether business schools can sustain the ability to pay: they are rich only in comparison with some other faculties. The power of the North Americans is built upon endowments and fund-raising capabilities which are outside the league of all but one or two European schools. The majority in the UK subsist on tuition income and grants which are wholly inadequate to launch ambitious developments in staffing, infrastructure and facilities. As long as they are unable to charge realistic top-up fees to undergraduates and to reinvest surpluses UK schools will struggle, particularly since PhD, most masters (even MBA) and undergraduate programmes cannot normally be run profitably at current volumes of activity. The real margins lie in executive education but, as we have seen, this is a demanding arena in which only a minority can prosper.

Reputation

A small number, perhaps up to ten, of UK schools have a chance of projecting themselves into the ranks of world leaders suggested by the *Financial Times*.[28] This is a welcome development for them if they can sustain it, for almost all of them lack the resources of their international rivals.

Other UK schools will continue to pursue regional and local distinction often on the basis of a large market in the conurbation on their doorstep; they can also develop international ventures on a 'niche' basis.

All schools are likely to face some hard choices. In order to enrich their curriculum by responding to demand for coverage of subjects such as entrepreneurship and e-commerce, they may have to withdraw from some activities which are no longer profitable for them, and to collaborate with providers in other schools, consultancies, Internet companies and software houses.

Such developments will be presented as educationally desirable but they will also be financially necessary: most schools acting alone cannot afford the investment required to create and maintain a leading technological position. The majority may have to collaborate, even through partial mergers, in order to survive: greater economy of scale and of scope has to be achieved alongside continuous improvement in quality. The business schools are fortunate in that they can generate the income which makes possible such twin objectives. The buoyancy of the market has so far allowed virtually all providers to enjoy some success but ambition, whether to climb the rankings or to gain greater financial security, will force greater concentration on the business realities of provision.

The business schools have continuously debated the subject of their autonomy. The issue last came to general prominence in the early 1990s when the government appeared to be ǫn the brink of privatizing management education, thus effectively forcing universities into different relationships with their business schools. The withdrawal of that threat, or promise, has merely allowed the question of autonomy to rumble on, without satisfactory resolution.

Some schools have won the battle for academic parity of esteem on their campuses; some may never do so. They will all press for more freedom to pursue their business unshackled by procedures and bureaucracy. Their colleagues on campus may find them uncomfortable bedfellows but, to return to the metaphor in the title of this chapter, also the strongest of the litter and most capable of sustaining the whole brood.

Notes and references

1. *Times* (1999a) Modern ideas hit old buffers, 4 October. See references to John Kay's polemic against Oxford listed in Note 32, p. 28.
2. A.R. Bolton (1997) How to succeed in business school leadership by really trying, *Perspectives: Policy and Practice in Higher Education*, 1 (2): 62–5; *Financial Times* (1998) Deans' posts hard to fill, 20 April.
3. J. Constable and R. McCormick (1987) *The Making of British Managers*. London: British Institute of Management with the Confederation of British Industry; C.B. Handy, I. Gow, C. Gordon, C. Randlesome, and M. Moloney (1987) *The Making of Managers*. London: National Economic Development Council with the British Institute of Management and the Manpower Services Commission.
4. Higher Education Statistics Agency (HESA) (1998) *HESA Individualised Student Record 1996/97*. Cheltenham: HESA, July.
5. Unpublished data are from the Association of MBAs (AMBA) secretariat, London.
6. D. Miles (1996) The development of management education, Second De Lissa Lecture, Kingston University, 25 April (unpublished).
7. S.R. Watson (1993) The place for universities in management education, *Journal of General Management*, 19 (2): 14–42.
8. Ibid.
9. K. Blanchard and S. Johnson (1983) *The One Minute Manager*. London: Willow.

10. J. Micklethwait and A. Wooldridge (1996) *The Witch Doctors: What the Management Gurus are Saying, Why it Matters and How to Make Sense of It.* London: Heinemann.
11. R.A. Gordon and J.E. Howell (1959) *Higher Education for Business.* New York, NY: Columbia University Press; F. Pierson (1959) *The Education of American Businessmen.* New York, NY: McGraw-Hill.
12. M.A. Goldman (1996) The case against 'practicality' and 'relevance' as gauges of business schools: responding to challenges posed by criticisms of business school research, *Journal of Management Inquiry*, 5 (4): 336–49.
13. S. Crainer and D. Dearlove (1998) *Gravy Training: Inside the Shadowy World of Business Schools.* Oxford: Capstone.
14. S. Crainer (1997) The concept crisis: too few big ideas to go around? *MBA*, December: 35–9.
15. A.R. Lock (1996) The future of the MBA in the UK, *Higher Education*, 31 (2): 165–85.
16. *The MBA Newsletter* (1999) 8 (2): 1–8 and 8 (4): 7.
17. P. Robinson (1994) *Snapshots from Hell: The Making of an MBA.* London: Nicholas Brealey.
18. Association of Business Schools (1999) *Pillars of the Economy: Developing World Class Management Performance.* London: ABS.
19. *Times* (1999) Boom time for British MBAs, 7 May.
20. G. Bickerstaffe (1998, 1999) *Which MBA? A Critical Guide to the World's Best Programmes*, 10th and 11th editions. London: The Economist Intelligence Unit.
21. *Financial Times* (1994) Initials that stand for Main Board Advance, 20 July.
22. *Financial Times* (2000a) Deans take on dot-com interests, 10 January.
23. D.J.L. Ashton (1988) Are business schools good learning organisations? Institutional values and their effects in management education, *Personnel Review*, 17 (4): 9–14.
24. C.A. Carnall (1999) Executive education. Briefing for ABS Executive, Paper ABS/99/03/07, June (unpublished).
25. T.E. Moore (1997) The corporate university: transforming management education, *Accounting Horizons*, 11 (1): 77–85.
26. *Guardian* (1999) Is it time to tie the corporate knot? 2 March.
27. *Financial Times* (1997) Extending the learning curve, 22 September.
28. *Financial Times* (1999) 'Financial Times' top 50 business schools, 25 January; *Financial Times* (2000) 'Financial Times' MBA 2000, 24 January.

13

The Changing Fortunes of Continuing Education: From Margins to Mainstream to . . . ?

Russell Moseley

To any reasonably clear-sighted observer of the higher education scene in the UK it must appear that the star of continuing education (CE) has been firmly in the ascendant in recent years. The editors of this collection presumably think so since the title they provisionally gave to this piece was 'Continuing Education: the Cinderella in the Nest' (in contrast to those business school cuckoos). And even some prominent figures in the CE community have been confident enough to claim that 'Far from being on the margins, Continuing Education, as articulated through the Lifelong Learning agenda, has become almost a routine part of vice-chancellors' and Funding Council rhetoric'.[1] A spate of publications over the past few years (too familiar to cite yet again) has served to emphasize the centrality of activities traditionally associated with CE to the lifelong learning agenda, to widening participation and to attempts to combat social exclusion. And yet . . . in many ways CE in higher education has a distinct fragility to it. Not only are there important issues around the extent to which the rhetoric is capable of being translated into a real commitment to change 'in culture, curriculum and pedagogy'[2] but there are also questions about the robustness of institutional commitment to and organizational arrangements for CE – and, indeed, debate about what CE (not to mention lifelong learning) actually means.[3] This chapter traces the changing fortunes of CE in recent years and looks at the price that may be attached to its absorption into the higher education mainstream. In an attempt to ward off (probably justified) charges of Anglocentricity in what follows it should be noted that while the focus is primarily on events in England, developments in the rest of the UK have followed a broadly similar pattern.

The move from the margins

The general consensus would seem to be that over the past 15 years CE in the United Kingdom has moved from the margins (indeed, from beyond the walls in the case of the extramural tradition) to the mainstream. If CE is viewed simply as adult or post-compulsory education then the success of the enterprise can hardly be doubted: by the end of the 1990s over 30 per cent of those studying in higher education were over 30. Other indicators of the scale and importance of CE are not hard to find. There cannot be a single HEI mission statement that does not make some reference to CE in one form or another, and at the practitioner level the Universities Association for Continuing Education draws its membership from over one hundred HEIs and supports thriving professional networks in areas as diverse as work-based learning, educational equality, staff development, vocational life-long learning, women and CE, quality, education in rural areas and flexible learning. And on the policy front, with the emergence of lifelong learning as a political priority, CE finds many of its long-championed causes now taking centre stage.

In the mid-1980s all this would have been unthinkable. A relatively small number of universities enjoyed quaintly named Responsible Body status in the eyes of, and funding from, the Department for Education and Science (DES) which enabled them to offer programmes of adult education for the most part rooted in what Harold Wiltshire had characterized as 'the great tradition'. Apart from the odd upstart (like the University of Warwick, which acquired Responsible Body status and territory from the University of Birmingham in 1984) this activity was confined to those institutions which had been active in the provision of liberal adult education for some time. The scale of this was impressive: in the mid-1980s the 36 UK universities offering extramural provision recorded almost 300,000 registrations a year on their programmes.

From a quite different direction there were signs of what would in future become a major component of CE – provision, often in the form of short courses, aimed at those in work and which subsequently came to be identified (among other things) as continuing vocational education (CVE) or continuing professional development (CPD). This work received a major boost in the form of the PICKUP (Professional, Industrial and Commercial Knowledge Updating) scheme introduced by the DES in 1982. Intended to help universities, polytechnics and colleges meet the updating needs of those in work, to increase awareness on the part of employers of the value of this work, and to encourage new approaches to the updating of adults in work, the scheme at first concentrated on seminars, needs analysis and surveying of provision. From 1987, however, bids were invited for funding to support the development of updating courses and training programmes the full cost of which, it was expected, would be met by employers. Boosted by the scheme, CVE activity immediately prior to the creation of a unified higher education sector accounted for almost 300,000 registrations a year in the pre-1992 universities alone.

The polytechnic sector in the mid-1980s shared some similarities but also revealed some significant differences. PICKUP-funded activity helped boost the substantial amount of CVE short course work which was already undertaken as a result of long-standing links with local business and industry, although the polytechnics fared less well than the universities in the allocation of funds through the scheme. While the liberal adult education tradition was absent from the sector there was a significant commitment to part-time provision, not only in the more obviously vocational areas of engineering and business studies but also in the humanities and social sciences, thereby offering local adults a 'second chance' at a higher education.

A belief, first evident in the polytechnics and only later in the universities, that the higher education system had to become more flexible to accommodate the needs of adults and, indeed, a more general non-traditional undergraduate clientele, gave rise to a number of developments which became closely associated with CE. Among the most notable were the introduction of credit accumulation and transfer schemes, modularization, the accreditation of prior (experiential) learning, and access provision intended to provide a third route into higher education alongside A levels and vocational qualifications. If at first these intitiatives often had a post-18 focus, with the mass expansion of higher education they increasingly became part of the mainstream. In this way CE units in the polytechnics often acted as significant agents for institutional change.

CE under review

With the abolition of the binary line in 1992, CE in the new, unified higher education system consisted of a highly disparate collection of activities. CVE work was firmly established in both old and new universities and, although progress in facilitating access had undoubtedly been greater in the latter, some universities had begun to take seriously issues of credit, modularization and part-time degree provision. Liberal adult education, now funded by the Universities Funding Council (UFC) rather than the DES, had continued to flourish and a number of non-Responsible Body institutions (UEA, Essex and Lancaster) had been allowed to join the club. Recognizing that CE departments were engaged in a much wider range of activities than in the past the UFC had required universities to bid for CE student numbers under headings which, besides liberal adult education, included certificated work, access provision and work with disadvantaged groups. This activity was supported by an earmarked sum of £26 million, an allocation which was not reflected in the funding practices of the Polytechnics and Colleges Funding Council (PCFC) and which was the cause not only of some resentment on the part of the former polytechnics but of some difficulty for the new Higher Education Funding Councils when they were established in 1992.

At first the temptation for the new funding bodies was to leave this difficult area well alone and to deal with more pressing matters. The joint UFC/PCFC working group set up to map the transition to a unified sector made some 'preliminary investigation' of CE but confessed in its report that this was 'an extremely complex and ill-defined area of activity'. It concluded that 'it would not be appropriate to attempt to unravel the complexities and to propose funding approaches for continuing education' at the present time, although it recognized that in due course 'the new Council may wish to examine how this bundle of activities should be funded'.[4] In fact the new funding bodies turned their attention to CE sooner than might have been expected. In order to establish a dialogue the Higher Education Funding Councils for England and Wales jointly set up a CE Advisory Group in late 1992 with the brief of 'recommending principles which underlie the distribution of resources for teaching, research and development in continuing education', taking into account its diversity, its 'contribution to the needs of industry, commerce and society' and its access role.[5] The Group was chaired by the HEFCE's Director of Policy and its membership was made up of vice-chancellors from both old and new universities (including The Open University), together with nominees from the Standing Conference of Principals and the Welsh funding council.

The move to the mainstream

The consultation paper which resulted, and which was published jointly by the two funding councils, focused on three areas: non-vocational provision (essentially the non-award bearing work of the old universities), vocational provision and research. As far as the first of these was concerned the choice of future funding approaches was presented as threefold: 'mainstreaming', meaning that only award bearing work would be funded in future, continued earmarked funding, or a mix of these whereby 'a small amount' of non-award bearing CE would still be supported. The continuation of development funding for vocational provision was not presented as particularly problematic and was certainly seen to be preferable to the alternative of rolling existing allocations into core funding for teaching. The former UFC practice of providing special funding for CE research was presented as anomalous (some £1.7 million was allocated to this work in 1992/93) and although the option was presented of continuing this and extending it to all institutions, there was a strong suggestion that it would be preferable to absorb this into the resource distributed for research under the new research funding methodology.

The suggestion that non-award bearing CE work should be mainstreamed was a matter of considerable concern to the pre-1992 universities. There was a scarcely veiled view that this amounted to an assault on a traditional area of work by the new universities which could see no justification for special treatment (as they saw it) and which, in a broader CE context, were unhappy that the CVE funding they received was less than half that provided to the former UFC institutions.[6] Added to this was a belief that the new funding councils were seeking a tidy solution to what they clearly saw as a funding anomaly. As the consultation paper ruefully, and perhaps ominously, confessed: 'In some respects, as far as funding is concerned, the concept of continuing education is an unhelpful one'.[7]

Despite a vigorous campaign of lobbying by the Universities Council for Adult Continuing Education (as it then was) there was a sense that there was only one likely outcome to the consultation process and so it proved with the publication in May 1993 of the new approach to the funding of CE.[8] CVE would be the beneficiary of a continuing programme of support for development work and earmarked research funding for CE would cease with the £1.7 million previously allocated to this work being added to the sum available for research in education. The first of these announcements was broadly welcomed; the second might have been regretted by the small number of institutions in receipt of CE research funding but it was hardly unexpected – indeed, there were many in the CE community who were privately astonished that such earmarked funding had ever been available at all.[9] As expected, the unwelcome news, at least for those involved in the activity, was that non-vocational work would continue to attract funding only if it was mainstreamed and made award bearing. The prospect of some funding for non-award bearing work was held out, the sum available to be determined by the amount left over after mainstreaming, but this was likely to be modest in size and would be allocated through a bidding process open to all institutions. Clearly, the CE landscape would never look quite the same again.

The consequences of mainstreaming

Several years later it is clear that these decisions, especially the mainstreaming of much CE provision, have had significant (and presumably unintended) consequences in two respects. First, the volume and character of the CE provided in the pre-1992 universities has changed substantially, and second, the institutional base and organization of CE have been radically revised in many cases. It is not easy to present quantitative data in support of the proposition that the amount of CE provision has decreased, since mainstreaming has meant that the bulk of this work is now recorded in returns to the Higher Education Statistics Agency simply as part-time provision. (This goes a long way towards explaining the very substantial rise in the number of part-time students recorded nationally in recent years.) However, work carried out for the Universities Association for Continuing Education in 1997[10] which involved surveying the pre-1992 English and Welsh universities concluded, among other things, that the volume of work had declined and that traditional clienteles were being neglected or were discouraged by having to participate in assessment for accreditiation. The spread of accredited CE work also raised in a particularly sharp form the issue of progression – what was the justification for a programme of accredited, part-time work unless there was either more part-time provision at a higher level or a willingness on the part of the university to permit CE students access to its standard undergraduate offerings?

If each university and its CE department eventually reached some form of accommodation on these matters, then the sudden emergence of a bewildering array of CE awards carrying varying amounts of credit[11] suggested that the process of mainstreaming was by no means straightforward. Indeed, in the extreme cases where CE departments developed entire programmes of their own part-time certificates, diplomas and degrees it is difficult to see what 'mainstreaming' actually meant – the operation looked distinctly 'offshore'. But in one crucial technical sense the mainstreaming of CE was real: in the way it was funded. No longer was there an earmarked sum coming into an institution to support CE work. Instead it was possible for university managers to calculate exactly how much they received for this work and compare this to how much it cost. There is little doubt that this financial transparency was a contributory factor to the spate of CE reviews which almost all of the pre-1992 universities have undertaken in recent years. Whether the motive for institutional review was financial, reflected a wish to explore the wider consequences of mainstreaming or was occasioned by the retirement of a long-serving director of CE, the end result in many cases has been a significant restructuring of universities' organization of CE and its staffing.[12] The final outcome of this process of review and reappraisal has yet to be seen, but the evidence so far points to the radical transformation of many of the largest, long-established CE departments and, increasingly, the creation of units or centres with a smaller number of staff and a shifting balance towards administrative and academic-related posts, often established on a short-term or temporary basis, with a brief for such things as quality, guidance, accreditation and a range of administrative functions. Occasionally a review has resulted in mainstreaming being taken to the extremes of dispersing CE staff to subject departments around the university. The memory of the press release accompanying one such exercise, which spoke of the CE department being so successful that it was no longer required, will long remain with those of us whose reviews resulted (for us) in a more satisfactory outcome.

The end of the special CE initiatives

While the pre-1992 universities were grappling with the challenge of mainstreaming, both they and their ex-PCFC counterparts were enjoying a period of unaccustomed tranquillity as far as their vocational CE activities were concerned. The four-year funding period ushered in by the HEFCE review meant that resources for CVE development work were assured (subject to satisfactory performance), enabling appointments to be made and strategic plans to be implemented in a way that had been difficult as long as funding was drip fed on an annual basis. Following the CE review institutions were invited to bid for funding, showing how their plans would meet the lifetime learning needs of those at work; expand the delivery of flexible teaching, learning and accreditation for those at work; and encourage an active involvement in wealth creation and in regional and local development. Ninety-seven bids were funded in all, and allocations were made up to £300,000 a year over the four-year period. The 20 institutions which were unsuccessful in their bids faced a more difficult future: in some of these CVE activity reduced almost to the point of invisibility, although in others it continued in mainstream departments albeit with little, if any, central direction or input from a dedicated CE unit.

The evaluation of the CVE initiative commissioned by the HEFCE at the end of the funding period concluded that there was clear evidence of its success 'in stimulating growth and innovation in CVE'.[13] Although the evaluation looked at organizational arrangements and incentives, it touched only briefly on the issue of institutional commitment as a key underlying component of an effective CVE strategy. A parallel study to the CVE evaluation, on good practice in promoting vocational lifelong learning, identified this as a crucial feature in developing an institutional culture within which CVE could thrive and be effectively promoted.[14] In light of current funding council policies the matter of institutional support for and commitment to vocationally oriented CE is of particular importance. Towards the end of the four-year period of CVE development funding there were clear signs that the HEFCE was not minded to continue the initiative but was inclined rather to see CVE as one part of the much larger picture which mapped out higher education institutions' many interfaces with the world of work in general. In 1999 the HEFCE announced details of its Higher Education Reach-out to Business and the Community fund (HEROBaC)[15] and the prospect of any further earmarked support for CVE finally disappeared. Reference to CVE could still be found, but now as part of a much broader set of activities intended to enhance HEIs' interaction with business leading to wealth creation. With the removal of earmarked funding to support CVE staff, institutional commitment is now being put to the test – those employed in recent years on development funds will not necessarily have the profile or skills needed to contribute to an HEI's HEROBaC activities and there are already signs of non-renewal of contracts and organizational arrangements for CVE being reviewed in light of the new basis for funding. Despite the rhetoric and the references in mission statements, the immediate future for CVE looks far from secure.

As we saw earlier, the third strand of the HEFCE's 1994 strategy to support CE was the establishment of a Non Award-Bearing Continuing Education programme (NABCE) which, as with the CVE development initiative, provided funding for four years to successful bidders. The NABCE programme involved a sum of £4.6 million a year and had two elements: widening participation and liberal adult education with 46 projects being funded in the former category and 20 in the latter. As it turned out, there was considerable overlap between the two strands – the evaluator of the programme found that 'there were no evident distinctions between the liberal adult and widening participation projects. Many of the development strategies adopted were common to both strands, similar pedagogical approaches and target groups were adopted.'[16] One other feature all the projects shared was the finite timescale to their funding, and despite initial assurances from recipients that ways would be found to embed the work into the institutional mainstream and develop continuation strategies, the ending of the income stream inevitably resulted in many projects being scaled down (or wound up) and short-term contracts not being renewed. As with CVE, institutional commitment to this work may be less robust than the rhetoric would indicate.

Does CE have a future?

Where does all this leave CE today? Is it really at the heart of the drive towards lifelong learning and do those working in CE have a key role to play? The answer is linked to issues concerning both the collective institutional structure and organization of CE and its 'academic' identity. In the former case there is clear evidence of organizational fragility across many areas of CE: long-standing departments have been radically restructured (sometimes out of existence) and the ending of the CVE and NABCE initiatives is likely to result in the loss of staff and expertise built up over a long period. Peter Scott believes that as the CE and higher education agendas converge, CE departments will be 'at the heart of organizational change' and that 'There is no conceivable way in which continuing education departments can become marginal organizations'.[17] But his optimism can only be sustained if there is real institutional support for CE and a secure organizational base, appropriately staffed, from which to drive the changes he sees as inevitable. As universities wake up to the lifelong learning agenda and look to their CE operations to provide a lead, their arrangements for CE must have credibility both within and outside the institution – a string of short-term (mostly junior) appointments on 'soft' money from the HEFCE's most recent widening participation initiative is unlikely to suffice.[18]

The issue of CE's identity – what it actually consists of – is linked to matters of structure and organization. The way it is organized (in both pre- and post-1992 universities) reflects its complex origins: 'liberal adult education certainly, but also the experiences of the former polytechnics, further education colleges, the training and enterprise councils, the wider corporate classroom, the learning society in its entireity'.[19] Given that those working in CE are engaged in such disparate activities as access, work-based learning, CVE/CPD, part-time degrees, provision in rural areas, work with minority communities and partnerships with further education (among many others) it is no wonder that any gathering of practitioners finds it all but impossible to agree on a definition of CE – a problem not confined to the UK.[20] This may not matter of course – the movement of CE into the mainstream in the United States took place over 15 years ago, yet it retains a highly visible and professionally discrete existence. It may even be the case that the diversity that characterizes CE is a strength rather than a weakness, allowing it to make an impact on many fronts rather than be confined by too narrow a focus. Certainly the range of those activities is extensive. The agenda for its future work drawn up by the Universities Association for Continuing Education in response to *The Learning Age* included[21]

- creating a qualifications and credit framework;
- encouraging employers to develop lifelong learning;
- developing partnerships at regional level;
- recognizing the important role of part-time teaching staff;
- building upon the quality provision of CVE;
- developing open and distance learning/IT methods of learning;
- creating a comprehensive guidance and support system;
- developing links with lifelong learning initiatives in other EU countries;
- giving a higher profile to research into lifelong learning.[22]

Perhaps CE can best be seen, in David Watson's phrase, as 'a broad coalition of interests'.[23] Just as a university is sometimes defined as a collection of individuals bound together only by their common grievance over car parking, so the various strands of CE have been seen as 'unified only in their antipathy to the mainstream'.[24] Whether this provides a sufficiently firm base on which to build the lifelong learning agenda remains to be seen.

Notes and references

1. R. Taylor (1998) Lifelong learning policy in England, in R. Taylor and D. Watson (eds) *Lifelong Learning Policy in the United Kingdom 1997/98*, Occasional Paper 23, p. 5. Leeds: Universities Association for Continuing Education. Not everyone is convinced of course. Malcolm Tight has pointed out that 'Those working in post-compulsory education and training have been disappointed too often in the past to believe wholeheartedly that their time has come at last' (M. Tight (1998) Education, Education, Education! The vision of lifelong learning in the Kennedy, Dearing and Fryer reports, *Oxford Review of Education*, 24 (4): 482).
2. R. Taylor (1998) op. cit., p. 5.
3. For a spirited discussion of the contested interpretations of lifelong learning see M. Woodrow (1999) The struggle for the soul of lifelong learning, *Widening Participation and Lifelong Learning*, 1 (9): 9–12.
4. UFC and PCFC (1991) *Report of the Joint UFC/PCFC Working Group*, para. 147. London: UFC and PCFC.
5. HEFCE (1992) *Continuing Education Policy Review*, p. 7. Bristol: HEFCE.
6. £5.1 million and £12.4 million for the polytechnics and universities respectively in 1991.
7. HEFCE (1992) op. cit., p. 1.

8. HEFCE (1993) *Continuing Education*, Circular 18/93. Bristol: HEFCE.
9. For an account of the range of CE research generated by this short-lived initiative see C. Duke (1996) *Research in Continuing Education: Summary of Publications Generated by Research Funded by the UFC in the Period 1990 to 1994*, Occasional Paper 19. Leeds: Universities Association for Continuing Education.
10. R. Fieldhouse (1997) *Report on the Process and Progress of Accreditation and Mainstreaming of Continuing Education in the pre-1992 English and Welsh Universities*, unpublished paper. Leeds: Universities Association for Continuing Education.
11. Ibid., para. 4.8.
12. This is the subject of a major survey and analysis undertaken by the author for the Administrators' Network of the Universities Association for Continuing Education, completed in summer 2000.
13. HEFCE (1998) *The Evaluation of the Funding for the Development of Continuing Vocational Education*, Report 98/44, p. 111. Bristol: HEFCE.
14. 'Institutional commitment requires HEIs to avoid short termism which has characterised much [CVE] in the past, and to adopt a more strategic, longer term approach to this work' (J. Field and R. Moseley (1999) *Promoting Vocational Lifelong Learning: A Guide to Good Practice in the HE Sector*, HEFCE 98/46, p. 7. Bristol: HEFCE.)
15. HEFCE (1999) *Higher Education Reach-out to Business and the Community Fund: Funding Proposals*, Consultation 99/16. Bristol: HEFCE.
16. S. McNair (1999) Liberal Adult Education: contemporary definitions and practice, in *Liberal Adult Education: Towards a Contemporary Paradigm*, Occasional Paper 25, pp. 26–7. Leeds: Universities Association for Continuing Education.
17. P. Scott (1996) The future of continuing education, in M. Zukas (ed.) *The Purposes of Continuing Education*. Proceedings of the 1996 UACE Annual Conference, p. 23. Leeds: Universities Association for Continuing Education.
18. This point has also been made by the European Universities CE Network: 'CE activities in universities are best implemented in designated CE centres or departments, which have developed a particular expertise in programming, monitoring and evaluating these activities' (European Universities Continuing Education Network (1998) *Interim Report on the THENUCE Project*, p. 6. Liege: EUCEN).
19. P. Scott (1996) op. cit., p. 24.
20. European Universities Continuing Education Network (1998) op. cit., bemoaned the fact that 'There is currently no clear-cut definition of [university] CE . . . there is a multiplicity of conceptions covering a wide range of practices. It is sometimes difficult even to find a clear and unanimous definition of [university] CE at the national level.'
21. DfEE (1998) *The Learning Age. A Renaissance for a New Britain*, Cm 3790. London: The Stationery Office.
22. R. Taylor (1998) op. cit., pp. 9–10.
23. D. Watson (1997) Conclusion: UACE and the future, in R. Taylor and D. Watson (eds) *From Continuing Education to Lifelong Learning: A review of UACE Strategy and Objectives*, Occasional Paper 20, p. 151. Leeds: Universities Association for Continuing Education.
24. P. Scott (1996) op. cit., p. 31.

14

An Unsuitable Job for a Woman?

Suzanne Alexander

Universities are labour-intensive organizations in which staff costs are the most significant part of recurrent budgets.[1] Effective human resource management and the maximization of human capital must be fundamental to the future of any university. As the report of the Independent Review of Higher Education Pay and Conditions[2] (also known as the 'Bett Report') states:

> From the start of the Review we were at one in recognising, as the Dearing report did, that the continuing success of the UK higher education sector is crucially dependent on its people and on the way they are led, managed and developed. The recruitment, retention and motivation of well-qualified staff of the right quality is essential if the vision of sustaining and improving a world-class system of HE in this country is to be realised.[3]

Yet that same report noted the low priority given to people management issues in higher education, and also highlighted the shortcomings of most higher education institutions in regard to equal opportunities, as illustrated by patterns of employment by gender. The report found evidence that women are being systematically underpaid across all academic, administrative and support grades. Statistics published in the *Independent* (November 1999), based on research by the National Association of Teachers in Higher and Further Education (NATFHE), provide further evidence of the gap between the earnings of male and female academics in universities.[4]

Statistics also demonstrate the under-representation of women at the senior levels of academic life. In May 1999 the *Times Higher Education Supplement* published statistics showing that, while the proportion of women professors is increasing, there is little evidence of any radical change for academic women's career prospects. In 1995 women held 6.7 per cent of all university chairs (a total of 474). By 1998, this had risen to just 9.2 per cent (a total of 907).[5]

Other inequalities have been exposed, most recently in regard to the small number of women who are vice-chancellors or principals of higher education institutions.[6] Not only are they under-represented, but there is evidence that they are paid less than their male counterparts. While it is difficult to make direct comparisons between institutions, it is nonetheless interesting to note that, where a woman has succeeded a man in one of these posts, the appointment has often been made on a salary significantly lower than that of her predecessor.

In the Bett Report data collected on academic-related staff in pre-1992 universities revealed that, although almost half (47 per cent) were women, they were disproportionately employed in the more junior grades, ranging from 62 per cent in Grade 1 to 19 per cent in Grade 6. Overall, just 13 per cent of female staff were on the more senior academic-related Grades 4–6, compared with 31 per cent of men. These differences were further compounded by the fact that female staff earned less than male colleagues on the same grades, so that the overall average salary for female full-time academic-related staff on national pay rates was about £3000 lower than for men.[7] Similar disparities between the grading and salaries of male and female staff were identified in statistics relating to Administrative, Professional, Technical and Clerical (APT&C) staff on national pay rates in post-1992 institutions.[8]

While the proportion of women in higher education has increased, representation at the higher grades remains low, and highlights another characteristic of women in higher education, namely their failure to be promoted through the grades at the same rate as their male counterparts.

This is not a phenomenon confined to universities. The median pay of male civil servants stands at £19,000 compared with £14,000 for women. Out of the top 3000 jobs in the civil service, just 18 per cent are held by women, falling to 13 per cent of the top 600 jobs. Similar patterns can be seen in teaching where women make up 53 per cent of staff on the basic grades in secondary schools, but only 27 per cent of headteachers.[9]

Neither is this a UK phenomenon. Data compiled by the American Association of University Professors show that, regardless of grade, status or institution, women at all levels and in all types of institutions of higher education continue to earn less on average than men.[10] The annual survey of administrative salaries conducted by the College and University Personnel Association shows that, while the average salaries of female staff in some categories are equalling and even exceeding those of men, there is still a considerable disparity in favour of the latter.[11]

Interpreting the statistics

While these statistics state the outcomes, they offer no explanation of how and why this discrimination occurs. Research into what appears to be a record of women's underachievement tends to concentrate on structural factors relating to recruitment, selection and promotion. Much of the research is qualitative and anecdotal in nature, and focuses on aspects of overt or more subtle forms of discrimination which affect women in the workplace. These range from sexual harassment and bullying to less easily defined and more insidious forms of discrimination, and allegations of institutional sexism – the so-called 'chilly climate':

> Gender bias and discrimination against women in academia take many forms, from overt sexual harassment to the much more ubiquitous and insidious problem of subtle and unconscious sexism impacting daily life, work distribution, student evaluations, and promotion and hiring decisions. This confluence of problems has been called the 'chilly climate'.[12]

Freyd[13] points out that systematic research (for example in regard to performance evaluation) does support the empirical reality of the chilly climate, but also notes that much of this work remains outside mainstream awareness.

An unsuitable place for a woman?

Discrimination is not necessarily the result of a conscious sexist ideology. There is a widely expressed belief that while gender bias certainly exists, it is not in our own environment, but elsewhere. In universities this has almost certainly been a major obstacle to the recognition of the operation of discrimination. Whether or not it is deliberate or intentional, discrimination is nonetheless present in universities.

The *Report of the Hansard Society Commission on Women at the Top*[14] analyses a range of organizational contexts (the civil service, judiciary, top management, the media and universities) and notes that discrimination against women is still widespread. Commenting specifically on the situation in UK universities, the report describes them as 'bastions of male power and privilege'. Within academic institutions the report identifies both direct and indirect patterns of discrimination, including selection procedures, 'old boy' networks, age barriers, inflexible structures for work and careers, and a range of discriminatory attitudes and practices.

The description of universities as male-dominated hierarchies runs counter to a perception of the academic community as characterized by equality and academic fairness. Ramanzoglu observes that 'characteristically they are run according to hierarchical systems of organization which are not consistent with the democratic and liberal ethic adopted by these institutions'.[15]

The origins and history of universities are 'man-centred'.[16] Women were excluded from access to university education until the latter part of the nineteenth century. At Cambridge women were not admitted as full members of the University until 1948.[17] Times have changed, and female students now make up more than half of the student body, yet universities remain autocratic, hierarchical and male-dominated.

The 'gentlemen's club' management style has been superseded by a culture of managerialism, with the emphasis on executive decision making by a small inner circle of senior officers, largely as a result of the enormous external pressures from government in the harsh climate of the 1980s, continuing into the 1990s, when universities saw their unit of resource constantly devalued from year to year.

The nature of the role of university administrators has also evolved with this change of culture. The vocabulary of business has infiltrated universities, so that accountability, audit and performance indicators are part of our everyday life. Even in the most traditional of institutions, 'manager' is replacing 'administrator' in job titles, and senior officers are routinely referred to as 'management'.

However, this new managerialism has done little to raise the temperature for women in universities and the chilly climate persists. Publications such as the Hansard Society Commission's report and the Bett Report, as well as articles in the media, have focused attention on the careers and progression of female academic staff, and the difficulties they may encounter in taking on senior academic management roles, especially in regard to alleged bias in selection, promotion and performance evaluation.

Comparatively little attention has been given to women in administrative and academic-related posts, particularly at senior levels. Where are the female registrars, finance officers, estates officers, librarians? Like the professors at the top of the academic career ladder, they are more conspicuous by their absence. Yet university administration is increasingly a female preserve. Any casual observer in a university registry, finance office or other central administrative department would probably be more struck by the absence of men. While women occupy an increasing number of administrative posts in universities, these are still predominantly at the junior levels. In pre-1992 universities Bett reported that 48 per cent were female, and in post-1992 institutions 68 per cent of APT&C staff were female, although concentrated in the lower grades and scales.

Taking as its theme a report that 'Women occupy only 2 per cent of the most senior administrative posts in universities', a 1980s Laurie Taylor column from the *Times Higher Education Supplement* commented on the position of women in university administration. Two (male) administrators are discussing some apparently anomalous estimates received from the Funding Council. They decide that the matter can only be resolved by a meeting of all relevant colleagues. The list of names grows – an exclusively *male* list. They discuss the background papers to be identified, coordinated, sorted and cross-indexed for the meeting, and one of the protagonists agrees that he will see to all this. His way of undertaking this task is summed up in the column's final word: 'Sheila'!

Almost 20 years later, this column still provokes wry smiles of recognition from women in university administration.

Encountering the glass ceiling

Promotion may look like a mysterious upward drift, but in many organizations it is influenced by quite complex processes, often formalised as personnel procedures. The processes are hoops that employees have to jump through to gain access to management jobs ... To reach management, employees have to meet the criteria set by the organization (which may be implicit – 'the face fits') and also understand the nature of the hoops and jump them in just the right way.[18]

The Hansard Society Commission's report identifies significant obstacles which prevent women from reaching the most senior levels in a range of institutional contexts. In academic life, the report highlights two particular problems: generally poor promotion prospects for women and lack of job security. While female administrators experience the same organizational chilly climate as their academic colleagues, their particular barriers to career progression are somewhat different. Promotion is not dependent on lengthy publications lists and unbroken research records, but on more subjective, qualitative judgements regarding suitability for a senior management role.

Job specifications at the most senior levels of universities may be quite vague. Experience will certainly be required, but how much and in what capacity is less easily defined. While for senior specialist posts appropriate professional qualifications and experience may be specified, for other senior management posts, neither a higher degree nor professional or management qualification may be a requirement.[19] It is in appointments to these general, non-specialist senior roles that the suitability of candidates for the post is most susceptible to subjective judgement by selection panels, where members may have a preconceived idea of what a person appointed to this post should be like. It is all too easy to disguise discrimination as expediency.

The 'glass ceiling' is often used as an analogy to describe the subtly transparent barrier which prevents women from gaining access to the more senior roles in their organizations. The concept of a glass ceiling (and also that of a 'glass wall', used to describe thwarted attempts to make a sideways move within or between organizations to act as a springboard for career advancement) has become widely accepted. In 1991 the US Department of Labor even established a Glass Ceiling Commission, defining the term as 'those artificial barriers based on attitudinal and organizational bias that prevent qualified individuals from advancing upward in their organization'.[20]

The Hansard Society Commission's report formally acknowledged the concept:

> For many women there is a glass ceiling blocking their aspirations, allowing them to see where they might go, but stopping them from arriving there. In any given occupation, and in any given public office, the higher the rank, prestige or influence, the smaller the proportion of women.[21]

The experience of women in university administration is no different from that of women in private industry, banking, or the civil service. Overall, women are greatly under-represented in middle and senior management roles. Davidson and Cooper[22] estimated that, in the UK, women held less than 5 per cent of senior management posts, and perhaps some 25 per cent of all managerial-type positions, and this in a situation where women make up more than 40 per cent of the workforce.

Who wants to be a 'token' woman?

While there are many accounts of the frustrated ambitions of those confronted by the glass ceiling, it is more difficult to assess the aspirations of women for senior management posts. Even allowing for the influence of 'headhunters' in identifying candidates for such posts, those applying for senior roles are self-selecting. No one is obliged to apply for any post, or to put themselves forward for promotion, but assessment of the attractiveness of any post (and the chances of a successful outcome) will inevitably be coloured by perceptions of those already occupying these senior positions.

Not every woman would relish the high profile that comes with being regarded as a pioneer or a role model, any more than every man would, if put in a similar position. Being the 'token' or 'statutory' woman has its disadvantages. Davidson and Cooper comment on studies which have found that professional and managerial women in token positions experience particular strains and stresses not felt by dominant members of the same organizational status:

> The disadvantages which have been associated with being the token woman include increased performance pressure, visibility, being a test case for future women, isolation and lack of female role models, exclusion from male groups, and distortion of women's behaviour by others in order to fit them into pre-existing sex stereotypes.[23]

Of course there are always exceptions, but exceptions do not necessarily make good role models. Women who succeed in traditionally male-dominated roles and environments inevitably find themselves at the centre of public attention. The question which all of them are asked is about the significance of being a woman. For example, Hilary Cropper, Chief Executive of the highly successful information technology company FI Group, responded to an interviewer: 'I've really kind of avoided the 'woman' thing. I have always had the view that women were really no different to men in business, and the way to get on is to do it, and be successful, and more would follow from example.'[24]

Sometimes the fiercest critics of women are other women. Women do not always support each other, either out of neglect or even fear of competition, as if this is a zero sum game in which women progress at each other's expense, hence the 'queen bee' syndrome, where the exceptional woman is quite happy to remain exceptional! Also labelled 'company' women, 'safe' women and the 'Aunt Toms of academia'[25] these are women who may claim that they have experienced no discrimination, or that none exists. They have risen to a prominent position on their own merits, and nothing prevents others from doing the same. Staines *et al.* give the following account of the 'queen bee's' attitudes: 'Other women could succeed . . . if they worked as hard as she did. The only way to succeed at executive levels was through individual effort. The queen bee had worked hard to attain her position, and she felt "why should it be easier for others?"'[26]

Being a token woman (defined by Kanter[27] as a situation where women comprise less than 15 per cent of a total category in an organization) not only means having no female peer support, but working in an environment which provides no role models of women in senior positions. Women have not traditionally helped each other by networking, but there has been a growing movement advocating networking for women in the professions. Originating in the US, a number of networks have been established by and for women in higher education. In the UK, the Through the Glass Ceiling Network of Women in Higher Education Management was established in 1990 by a group of senior women in higher education to support the membership, provide role models, and to encourage other women into educational management.[28] In Australia, the National Colloquium of Senior Women Executives in Australian Higher Education was formed in October 1995.[29] The UK's Athena Project, established in February 1999, aims to increase significantly the number of women in top posts in science, engineering and technology.

These kinds of developments are greatly to be welcomed. More networking and mentoring, encouraging women to make and use helpful contacts, could be particularly beneficial for those trying to break into male-dominated 'clubs' and lacking peer support.

Prospects for change: raising the temperature of the chilly climate

The Hansard Society Commission's report made the following recommendations regarding universities in the UK: 'We recommend that all universities should appoint equal opportunities officers and that they should monitor and publish information about women's progress.'[30]

Equal opportunities legislation can have only a limited effect unless there is recognition that a problem exists. The Commission on University Career Opportunity (CUCO), launched by the Committee of Vice-Chancellors and Principals in 1994, has the aim of 'overcoming the barriers to equal opportunities in higher education institutions and ensuring that universities benefit from selecting and developing the best available people from all sections of the community'.[31]

It is too soon to assess the impact on women's pay and status of CUCO's guidelines, which include recommendations that at least one woman should be on appointments panels, that panel members be trained in selection, and that numbers applying and appointed to jobs be monitored. In the US affirmative action campaigns have been subject to adverse publicity and misunderstanding of their purpose, leading to (mostly unfounded) allegations of reverse discrimination.

Suggestions are often made about the actions that organizations can take to achieve greater fairness and a better balance of the sexes in managerial roles. These include such measures as offering opportunities for part-time working, flexible working, job sharing and career breaks; enhancing training programmes for potential managers in such things as leadership and time management (and encouraging women to take part); providing personal development opportunities in the form of secondments or special projects to extend experience in management roles; developing senior management's awareness both of the benefits of more women managers appointed on their merits and the potential loss to the organization if well-qualified women candidates are not appointed to more senior roles.

While some of these are simple, practical measures, others imply considerable change to human resource policies. In their study on the development of women managers, McDougall and Briley[32] suggest that there are increasing external pressures on organizations to reconsider women's roles in the workplace which are giving rise to a number of organizational imperatives likely to benefit women. As well as the more 'family-friendly' policies, which are now being sought by both men *and* women, they note the introduction of flatter organization structures, a greater emphasis on teamworking, and a more participative leadership style.

Again it is difficult to assess the extent to which such cultural changes are taking place within universities but, even if they are, the available statistical evidence suggests that it is unlikely to be a speedy process. However, for universities to fail to exploit the talents and potential of such a significant proportion of their workforce is not a tenable position.

As the Hansard Society Commission's report points out:[33]

> More women at the top has become an economic imperative if British firms are to retain their foothold in an increasingly complex and competitive world. But getting women into top jobs demands strategic planning; it does not just happen through goodwill or good intentions.

Notes and references

1. According to the Higher Education Statistics Agency (HESA), staff pay accounts for 58 per cent of the sector's total expenditure. See HESA (1998) *Resources of Higher Education Institutions 1996/97. HESA.*
2. Universities and Colleges Employers Association (1999) *Report of the Independent Review of Higher Education Pay and Conditions* (Bett Report). London: The Stationery Office.
3. Ibid., p. 25.
4. *Independent* (1999) It's time for women to turn the tables, 11 November.

5. *Times Higher Education Supplement* (1999) 9.2 per cent of professors are women ... , 28 May.
6. *Times Higher Education Supplement* (2000) Female figures that don't add up, 28 January.
7. UCEA (1999) op. cit., Appendix D, Table 8a.
8. Ibid., Appendix D, Table 12a.
9. *Independent* (1999) Women suffering from big pay gap in all sectors, 12 November.
10. *Chronicle of Higher Education* (1997) Average faculty salaries at 1800 institutions, 1996–97. www.chronicle.com
11. *Women in Higher Education* (1999) Gender differences in 1998–99 administrative salaries. www.wihe.com/stats98/htm
12. J.J. Freyd (1998) References on chilly climate for women faculty in academe. An extensive bibliography of 'chilly climate' references, covering bias in student evaluations, bias in hiring and evaluation, balancing academic and personal responsibilities, bias in peer review, pay inequity has been compiled by J.J. Freyd of the Department of Psychology at the University of Oregon, and may be found on her website: www.dynamic.uoregon.edu/~jjf/
13. Ibid.
14. Hansard Society for Parliamentary Government (1990) *Report of the Hansard Society Commission on Women at the Top.* London: The Hansard Society.
15. C. Ramanzoglu (1987) Sex and violence in academic life or you can keep a good woman down, in J. Hanmer and M. Maynard (eds) *Women, Violence and Social Control,* p. 61. London: Macmillan.
16. M. David and D. Woodward (eds) (1998) *Negotiating the Glass Ceiling: Careers of Senior Women in the Academic World,* p. 8. London: The Falmer Press.
17. For a useful summary of the historical position of women in academic life and of the history of academic women in the UK, 1900–90, see A. Brooks (1997) *Academic Women,* Chapter 1. Buckingham: Society for Research into Higher Education/Open University Press.
18. W. Hirsh and C. Jackson (1989) *Women into Management – Issues Influencing the Entry of Women into Managerial Jobs,* Paper No. 158. Brighton: Institute of Manpower Studies, University of Sussex. Quoted by M.J. Davidson and C.L. Cooper (1992) *Shattering the Glass Ceiling: The Woman Manager,* p. 16. London: Paul Chapman Publishing.
19. Examples are given in A. Theodore (1986) *The Campus Troublemakers: Academic Women in Protest,* p. 62. Houston, TX: Cap and Gown Press.
20. Created as part of the Civil Rights Act of 1991, the Commission published its report entitled *A Solid Investment: Making Full Use of the Nation's Capital* in November 1995.
21. Hansard Society for Parliamentary, Government (1990) op. cit., p. 2.
22. M.J. Davidson and C.L. Cooper (1992) op. cit., pp. 11–13.
23. Ibid., pp. 83–4.
24. *Independent* (2000) The IT Woman, 5 January.
25. A. Theodore (1986) op. cit., pp. 201–2.
26. Quoted by M.J. Davidson and C.L. Cooper (1992) op. cit., pp. 109–10.
27. R. Kanter (1977) *Men and Women of the Corporation.* New York, NY: Basic Books.
28. See M. David and D. Woodward (eds) (1998) op. cit. The genesis of this book was a Through the Glass Ceiling Network meeting in which a number of presenters had given accounts of their own career development with a view to identifying the factors that had contributed to their success.

29. The Colloquium consists of all women in Australian universities who are vice-chancellors, deputy vice-chancellors or pro-vice-chancellors or who have equivalent status.
30. Hansard Society for Parliamentary Government (1990) op. cit., p. 11.
31. www.cvcp.ac.uk/Links/LinkedActivities/CUCO/body_cuco.html
32. M. McDougall and S. Briley (1993) *Developing Women Managers*. London: HMSO.
33. Quoted by M.J. Davidson and C.L. Cooper (1992) op. cit., p. 171.

15

A View from the Market Place

Rosemary Stamp

In recent years, the arena of marketing and communications has witnessed a shift in public perceptions of universities and an increased evaluation of the service that those organizations deliver. As Director of Riley Consultancy, I work in partnership with many UK and EU higher education institutions, developing strategic responses to their marketing challenges. For many of our clients recent developments have both altered the way in which educational providers are perceived by their constituencies and extended considerably the depth of stakeholders' expectations of the sector. Such changes spring from an acknowledgement of educational provision as a consumer-focused service, the rise of the competitive market place and the subsequent struggle to achieve marketing advantage through the building of brand personality. This chapter considers these emerging issues and examines future challenges facing the educational institutions.

Market orientation through customer focus

The theory of marketing is based upon the concept of exchange:[1] one party produces goods or services (such as an educational programme or experience) which another wants, and a transaction takes place in which the supplier satisfies the demand of the consumer in need. Marketing advantage emerges when one supplier can enhance its offer to the consumer in some way, and so make it more attractive, useful or better value than that of other competitors within the market place. Marketing philosophy dictates that an organization can only be completely marketing oriented if it understands its markets and the people who decide to buy its products and services.[2] The rise of the customer-led approach in all forms of business has been reflected in the adoption by some organizations of a more overtly market-oriented and customer-focused proposition within the provision of educational services. Within the UK, the pursuit and implementation of techniques to align the process of education delivery more directly towards the service consumer is still a relatively rare approach:[3] a select group of post-1992 institutions have been pioneers in this field. Customer focus, and the desire, ability and vision within an organization to meet the needs and demands of the target consumer better and more effectively than rivals, have now begun to provide an opportunity for competitive advantage within the traditional, service-based environment of education.[4]

The ability of an organization to meet a customer-focused objective can be used increasingly to benchmark universities' market awareness, and continues to be linked closely to images and perceptions of organizations.[5] Today, for many seeking entry to higher education for the first time, recent changes in organizational status or title are not necessarily relevant to their decision-making process; other factors have helped to build perceptions of universities and to create their 'market attraction'. The factors that defined organizational popularity three or five years ago may no longer be as relevant or exclusively attractive to some constituency segments, as the prospective student market becomes more aware of holistic values and value-for-money in the educational experience. To paraphrase Doyle, it is not that some universities are no longer of value, or that they have become 'worse' in some way (for example, in their attractiveness to students) but rather that others have made more effort, and are now perceived to be 'better'.[6] This is especially apparent in the increased emphasis placed by many post-1992 organizations on the stakeholder, added-value service provision and responsiveness to changing market need.

The achievement of market advantage through brand differentiation

For many marketing-aware organizations, such an emphasis has become central to their brand concept. The value of distinctiveness is at the heart of the brand philosophy, and holds within it the ability to manipulate, both positively and negatively, the publicly received impression of an organization's corporate 'personality': some universities have now begun to incorporate customer focus into their developing brands to achieve differentiation. If all organizations, such as universities, and their products or services appear to be the same and equal, there is no perceived value in choosing one as opposed to another. The catalyst for choice is within the innate personality or brand awareness of an organization, however unconsciously developed, and this creates a perception of relative value. Prior to a centralized application system for UK higher education, planned marketing and image management might appear to have played a relatively insignificant part in university selection and choice. However, at this time, differential images of the universities were generated largely on received perceptions of the institution, based on a cocktail of history, anecdotal evidence, illustrious alumni and public success: proactive marketing or strategic communications might appear to have played a relatively small role. Despite this assumption, strong sector 'personalities' existed, rather more by tradition than design, and they, in turn, influenced choice decisions.

After the dissolution of the binary divide some of the former polytechnics sought to compete for student enrolments on a more level playing field, with the possibility, perhaps, of removing elements of the market advantage previously associated with the 'traditional' universities. The former polytechnics had been distinctive, however, for many qualities including their links with industry and business, their approach to teaching and programme portfolios that endeavoured to respond to the needs of a constantly changing macro-environment. In effect, a search for renewed market orientation was readily supported, for some new universities, by an existing and enviable organizational potential for differentiation. Not surprisingly, these differential competencies have become ever more relevant to a rapidly changing market economy and to an increasingly demanding, eclectic and diverse prospective higher education audience with a heightened focus on learning outcomes. This has helped the leading post-1992 universities to continue to develop considerable differentiation from their pre-1992 university counterparts. Any desire for the sector to be composed of institutions of similar style, objective, classification and personality has been subsumed by the recognition that distinctiveness, in a broad-based and crowded market, is of considerable value.

Brand, service quality and responsiveness

'Brand' reaches far beyond the simplistic visual manifestations of logos and style features, and for many traditional universities now reassessing their brand values the concept is increasingly linked to equity, ethos, mission and customer service through market responsiveness. While the imperative for educational organizations to be competitive has its precedent within market developments in the USA,[7] within the UK sector, competitiveness and the scramble for an effective market position is ever more dependent on the management of external perceptions of the organization through brand value. Integral to many winning brands, within the commercial sector and increasingly within education, is the importance of service, consumer satisfaction and adaptation to market needs.[8] Among established universities, there is an emergent market trend to reinforce, underpin and confirm traditional, but nebulous values, such as 'quality' with the articulation of more tangible core competencies, and a number of pre-1992 universities have now built effectively upon the equity of their traditional brand associations.[9] League tables aside, it is no longer enough to be 'good', but equally important to be proactive and effective in the articulation and delivery of differential qualities; generically, to the market place and individually, to all key stakeholders. The concept of service provision is enmeshed within the ability of organizations to provide their potential service users with what they genuinely need, enhanced by competitive and valuable high-level service delivery. The new differentiators for many regional, national and international education brands have become service quality and responsiveness to the needs of the individual and the market: qualities which will become synonymous with their corporate personality.[10]

As service-based operations increase in all areas of the public and private sectors, levels of service and consequent levels of service expectation will rise consistently.[11] Education, together with many other areas, is entering the 'best in class' arena of competitiveness, in which benchmarked customer service is of increasing value: consumers will make direct comparisons between the service (responsiveness, relevance of product portfolio, for example) received from an educational organization, and that which they receive from other sources, such as financial or retail suppliers.[12]

The future

The future holds many opportunities for universities, especially so as the education sector comes to terms with ever more demanding and varied education consumer constituencies. The key challenges may be summarized within the framework of the limited, but useful, 'Four Ps' of the marketing mix: product, place, price and promotion.[13] Issues emerging within the Riley Consultancy client portfolio provide an indication of the main challenges and opportunities for the future.

Product

In terms of 'product', responsiveness, flexibility and continual adjustment will be crucial. It will become more difficult to justify the continuance of some niche market 'traditional academic' programmes, especially at postgraduate level, simply as a matter of course. Increasingly, educational organizations conduct portfolio analysis to give them a better understanding of the needs of the existing market and to predict emergent demands for the future. The traditional approach to programme development is also changing dramatically. Technological change continues to exert an influence on every area of business, and one of the significant results of this has been the compression of traditional planning times and the restriction of traditional product life cycles.[14] In the past, a university may have developed a new programme and expected it to be a long-term addition to its portfolio; this opportunity is continually compromised as, increasingly, market demand requires highly specialized new programmes tailored to a nascent business or industry need. Among universities embracing this approach, there is an explicit understanding that such potential programmes need to be researched, developed and brought to market within much reduced planning times. This awareness is coupled with a realistic acknowledgement that the programme life cycle will be limited, and may possibly be extant for only two to three years: an imperative for an 'index-linked' match between programme provision and the requirements of the economy and the workplace. Inevitably, this approach requires flexibility and foresight of the highest level, plus a market-led commercial focus to seek out and meet potentially profitable market need.

Place

For educational institutions, 'place', in terms of delivery channels, location and physical presence, holds as many opportunities as challenges, but is an issue that is emerging as a major concern. The physical entity of an institution has, traditionally, been integral to public perceptions, awareness and the mode and style of its learning delivery.[15] Technological change now defines such parameters as limited. The emergence of the virtual and e-university concepts, such as UNEXT and the online MBA, the development of strategic alliances between universities across the globe, plus the increased use of, and demand for, new modes of learning delivery have all altered our understanding of what a university is and stretch the limits of what a university might be in the future. If a university can deliver learning via the web and around the globe, the concept of 'place' becomes, to some extent, less relevant. The hope must be that this will deliver greater accessibility to education in the future.[16] If a university commands a presence as a global brand, through its alliances and new media presence, the worth and equity of its brand will change and then opportunities for future development may well outstrip the mission to which it aspired only five years previously. Not surprisingly, the emergence of global brand[17] presence demands that even more attention should be paid to the development and maintenance of regional and national brand identities.[18] How this will affect the end users' experience of their educational service delivers both positive and negative possibilities.

Price

Financial worth and 'price' will inevitably exert influence in higher education in the future. Throughout the last decade, the sector has been encouraged to consider alternative sources of income and to pull away from a dependence on centrally provided funds. The critical issue for students, as a core end user group, has been the relative cost of education. The debate over student fees continues, but increasingly, educational institutions have begun to consider the implications and opportunities for charging differential fees for programme provision. Programme price is subjective, in that it is subject to the influence of additional external factors, such as the relative cost of living, likely future career prospects and unpredictable market factors. However, the crucial issue for those universities that have embarked along the differential fee route is the need to assess and continually evaluate whether they can deliver their service and product effectively and to the level required, when differential fees generate distinctly heightened expectations of product and service quality among the main stakeholder groups. Fees and education price tags have now defined the education consumer as a 'customer' in marketing terms, and the choice of educational provider is inevitably a 'purchase decision', as consumers increasingly demand quality and value-for-money. In an increasingly service-oriented society, consumers will expect the product to deliver as promised and, in the light of their experience, will benchmark the service quality received and will actively seek out those organizations that can deliver above their expectations for the price paid.

Promotion

'Promotion' is a core concern for many higher education organizations. The future challenge lies in the accurate representation of their offerings and services to varied and distinct target markets. Central to such a process is an implicit understanding of the needs of varied stakeholders and a willingness to individualize approaches and communications accordingly. The policy push for incremental, lifelong learning and borderless education creates an unprecedented diversity of target groups with whom an educational organization might expect to communicate. The ability to tailor approaches and communications to widely differing groups, each with widely differing perceptions of 'education' and 'university', will be crucial. The University for Industry opted for the name Learn Direct when research indicated that the term 'university' might prove a barrier to a proportion of their target audience. Linked to effective communication is the need to maintain the humane, holistic and individualistic touch. The student population is destined to rise and many institutions will grow in size and population to meet this demand. In such a situation, remote, distant and on-line learning will become more prevalent, but it can be expected that the potential consumer will still wish to be treated respectfully as an individual. For those institutions that can do this successfully, the ability to promote this distinctive added-value advantage will be integral to future market share. The proliferation of electronic communications has already begun to exert an influence on students' decision-making processes.[19] The increasingly discerning audience (for example, international students or those in employment wishing to engage in continuing professional development programmes) may demand 24-hour information delivery and prefer instant communications and programme information via the Web rather than through the traditional medium of prospectus or published material. In an interactive world, the need to deliver information that is 'smart', responsive and instantly updateable will be a major challenge.

... and People

The basic 'Four Ps' approach has been adapted and supplemented in a great number of marketing studies and it is always possible to suggest additional factors. In consideration of the future of higher education, one fundamental addition to the equation must be 'people': the sector's future success will, of course, depend upon this resource. Those administering and teaching within the higher education sector of the future will need to be multitalented. Academic staff may well become subject more frequently to the vagaries of their marketability. With the academic and research reputations of organizations increasingly linked to the presence of 'stars', the likelihood of individual or team (academic department) 'transfers', as staff move from one institution to another, is likely to increase. Specialist roles within higher education will continue to proliferate and, within administration, there may be a demand for, and influx of, those with commercial management and business skills as the distinctions between the management of educational service provision and the private sector continue to blur. Staff will need to be consumer-oriented; to respond rapidly to changing market demands; to recognize and utilize the competitive advantage of customer service; to be externally focused; and to be fully aware of the market opportunities available as the world grows ever smaller and as educational provision and learning delivery grow ever more complex.[20]

References

1. P. Kotler ([1967] 1994) *Marketing Management*, p. 9. Englewood Cliffs, NJ: Prentice Hall.
2. B.P. Shapiro (1988) What the hell is 'marketing oriented?', *Harvard Business Review*, Nov–Dec: 119–25.
3. A. Parasurman, V.A. Zeithaml and L.L. Barry (1985) A conceptual model of service quality and its implications for future research, *Journal of Marketing*, 49 (Fall): 41–50.
4. T.H. Nilson (1998) *Competitive Branding*, p. 26. Chichester: Wiley.
5. R. Stamp (1996) Marketing orientation in higher education. Unpublished thesis, Nottingham Business School.
6. P. Doyle (1994) *Marketing, Management and Strategy*, p. 49. Hemel Hempstead: Prentice Hall.
7. P. Kotler and K. Fox ([1988] 1994) *Strategic Marketing for Educational Institutions*, p. 5. Englewood Cliffs, NJ: Prentice Hall.
8. D. Gilmore (ed.) (1997) *Brand Warriors*, p. 19. London: Harper Collins.
9. D. Cowell (1984) *The Marketing of Services*, p. 62. Oxford: Butterworth-Heinemann.
10. J.R. Gregory (1998) *Marketing Corporate Image*, p. 21. Chicago, IL: NTC.
11. P. Doyle (1994) op. cit., p. 339.
12. G. Hamel and C.K. Prahalad (1994) *Competing for the Future*, p. 26. Boston, MA: HBS.
13. D. Jobber (1998) *Principles and Practice of Marketing*, p. 14. Maidenhead: McGraw-Hill.

14. G.J. Hooley, J.A. Saunders and N.F. Piercy (1998) *Marketing Strategy and Competitive Positioning*, p. 18. Hemel Hempstead: Prentice Hall.
15. M.J. Bitner (1992) Servicescapes: the impact of physical surroundings on customers and employees, *Journal of Marketing*, 56 (April): 57–71.
16. M. Tight (1996) The Re-location of higher education, *Higher Education Quarterly*, 50 (2): 119–37.
17. R.D. Buzzell, J.A. Quelch and C. Bartlett (1991) *Global Marketing Management*, p. 10. Harvard, MA: Addison Wesley.
18. J-N. Kapferer (1997) *Strategic Brand Management*, p. 339. London: Kogan Page.
19. Riley Research (1999) *Clearing 1999: Benchmarking Advertising and Marketing*, p. 35. Nottingham: Riley Research.
20. For more on the student transforming via the customer into the empowered consumer, and then into the potential litigant, see D. Palfreyman and D. Warner (eds) (1998) *Higher Education and the Law: A Guide for Managers*. Buckingham: Open University Press (2nd edn. due 2001, Bristol: Jordans). On student 'customer-care' see generally J. Gledhill (1996, 1999) and C. Humfrey (1999), with E. Bell (1996) and H. Silver and P. Silver (1997).

Part 3

The Warwick Way

16

Managing Transformation

Jim Rushton

The period since 1980 has seen universities across the world face serious and growing challenges. These include:

- Growth in student numbers. In 1960 it is estimated there were 13 million students worldwide. In 1995 that had grown to 82 million. By 2025 it is expected the number will be 200 million.
- A significant decline in funding per student head.
- A broadening of the kind of student seeking university education. Mature students, short course vocational students, part-time students, distance learning students all contribute to a much diversified student body.
- Employers increasingly demand students who have vocational skills as well as their subject disciplines. Lifelong learning is also increasingly seen as a necessary vocational support and one which universities should provide.
- The growth of knowledge presents an almost insurmountable problem. In the early 1990s, chemistry produced a million research articles in a two-year period, mathematicians are generating over a hundred thousand theorems a year and new business management books come off the presses at the rate of five per day. Other subjects show similar tendencies and new subjects are introduced with a regularity which compounds and intensifies an already impossible situation.
- As if all this were not enough, we see governments demanding greater efforts by universities to make their research and teaching activities more relevant to the economic needs of their region and nation. All of course to be achieved with less state funding but with much increased levels of accountability.
- The IT revolution presents universities with considerable uncertainty about its future impact on teaching and indeed the nature of higher education. In the meantime, what is less uncertain is the ever-escalating cost of maintaining and updating an IT infrastructure sufficient to meet the expectations of staff and students.

In his book *Creating Entrepreneurial Universities*, Professor Burton Clark[1] describes universities as being 'caught in a cross-fire of expectations' and outlines the consequences for university management as follows:

> In the face of increasing overload, universities find themselves limited in response capability. Traditional funding sources limit their provision of university finance: governments indicate they can pay only a decreasing share of present and future costs. 'Underfunding' becomes a constant. Traditional university infrastructure becomes even more of a constraint on the possibilities of response. If left in customary form, central direction ranges between soft and soggy. Elaborated collegial authority leads to sluggish decision-making: 50 to 100 and more central committees have the power to study, delay, and veto. The senate becomes more of a bottleneck than the administration. Evermore complex and specialized, elaborated basic units – faculties, schools, and departments – tend to become separate entities with individual privileges, shaping the university into a federation in which major and minor parts barely relate to one another. Even when new departments can be added to underpin substantive growth and programme changes, the extreme difficulty of terminating established academic tribes or recombining their territories insures that rigidity will dominate. Resources go to maintenance rather than to the inducement and support of change.
>
> As demands race on, and response capability lags, institutional insufficiency results. A deprivation of capability develops to the point where timely and continuous reform becomes exceedingly difficult. Systemic crisis sets in.'[2]

In order to assess how this seemingly impossible state of affairs might best be handled, Clark looked in some detail at five European universities which he felt had handled this situation satisfactorily by becoming, in his words, 'more enterprising, even aggressively entrepreneurial'.[3]

He defined enterprising universities in the European setting as places that actively seek to move away from close governmental regulation and sector standardization. They search for special organizational identities; they risk being different; they take chances in 'the market'. They adhere to the belief that risks of experimental change in the character of universities should be chosen over the risk of simply maintaining traditional forms and practices.[4]

The universities studied by Clark were the Universities of Warwick and Strathclyde in the UK, the University of Twente in Holland, Chalmers University of Technology in Sweden and the University Joensuu in Finland. His study identifies five elements which are common to the experience of all five universities and which he argues are necessary components of transformation. The five elements are as follows.

A strengthened management core

In most universities management tends to be democratic and consensual and where office holders are elected for fixed terms it may well lack continuity. Such a system is not equipped to handle the increasingly specialized and professional nature of university management and deal with the demands of a much more competitive environment. Not surprisingly Clark found that all five of the universities he studied had devised mechanisms to enable them to act more quickly and decisively in the interest of the institution as a whole, and most importantly they had achieved this necessary improvement in managerial capacity without inflicting too much damage on traditional academic values.

Development and expansion at the periphery

All five universities had grown in areas which responded to the need to develop and support external links. This was demonstrated by the establishment of offices for industrial liaison, industrial and commercial research contracts, intellectual property, continuing professional education, alumni activities, public affairs and development. This peripheral growth also included cross-disciplinary developments and a profusion of project-oriented and collaborative research centres. Such centres have more flexibility than large established departments in being easy to establish and terminate. They are often based on new funding sources, bring into the universities new staff and very considerably broaden the range of institutional contacts. Given managerial competence and confidence this kind of activity combines growth with flexibility in a responsive manner hardly possible from the university 'centre'.

An increased and diversified funding base

Each of the five institutions set out to generate additional revenues to compensate for declining government support and to undertake new activities. They were all successful and most noticeably generated funds from the provision of services for local public and private organizations thus making their institutions important contributors to the regional economy.

A stimulated academic heartland

This fourth factor is best expounded by Clark himself:

> When an enterprising university evolves a stronger steering core, *and* develops an outreach structure, *and* diversifies its income streams, its heartland is still found in the traditional academic departments. Whether they accept or oppose a significant transformation is critical. It is here in the many units of the heartland that promoted changes and innovative steps are most likely to fail. If the basic units oppose or ignore

would-be innovations, the life of the institution proceeds largely as before. For change to take hold, one department and faculty after another needs itself to become an entrepreneurial unit, reaching more strongly to the outside with new programmes and relationships and promoting third-stream income. Their members need to participate in central steering groups. They need to accept that individuals as well as collegial groups will have stronger authority in a managerial line that stretches from central officials to heads of departments and research centres.

The heartland is where traditional academic values are most firmly rooted. The required blending of those values with the newer managerial points of view must, for the most part, be worked out at that level. In the entrepreneurial university, the heartland accepts a modified belief system.[5]

An integrated entrepreneurial culture

The fifth element is an entrepreneurial culture. This doesn't occur overnight and sometimes follows and sometimes leads new developments. It doesn't necessarily gain hold across the whole of an institution but in the five institutions studied by Clark there was a clear perception by large numbers of staff that their institution had a special character which involved innovation, risk taking and self-help.

How far did these elements apply to the development of the University of Warwick since 1980? The following account will demonstrate a strong correlation.

First, the *strengthened management core*. This is certainly a most important feature. Warwick has a very tight group at the centre which meets weekly to advise the vice-chancellor, to discuss policy and to take urgent decisions in between meetings of the main statutory committees. This body is called the Steering Committee and consists of the vice-chancellor, three pro-vice-chancellors, three Faculty Board chairmen, the chairman of the Graduate School, the president of the Students' Union and the senior officers (registrar, deputy registrar, academic registrar, finance officer, administrative secretary, estates officer and others as required). There are four points to be made about this arrangement:

1. The vice-chancellor and the officers are permanent appointments while the pro-vice-chancellors and faculty chairs are elected for three- and two-year periods. This gives a good balance between professional and academic concerns, and between continuity and democratic representation.
2. The Steering Committee has strong links into the academic heartland and therefore has the confidence to take quick action when necessary.
3. Warwick has a strong centre and strong departments with little in between. There are no deans and the Faculty Boards are committees with little or no management responsibility. This helps quick and efficient communication and decision making.

4. For many issues of strategic and financial importance, the lay chairs of the Council, Finance Committee and Building Committee will have a considerable involvement. These chairmen are usually widely experienced in business or public service, and there is no doubt that the University benefits enormously from their experience and advice.

Second, the *development and expansion at the periphery* is demonstrated strongly by the Warwick experience. Between 1980 and 1997 the number of research units and centres increased from 3 to 44. These units and centres represent an area of flexible and often responsive activity, very often with links into the community, very often dependent on winning grants or providing services for their survival. The University's three residential management training centres, the Science Park with its 65 companies and 1350 employees and the Arts Centre which has 250,000 visitors per year further exemplify a vigorous presence at the periphery. In addition, all the support functions such as industrial liaison, research contract support, patent and copyright, fund-raising and public affairs were introduced at Warwick after 1980.

The third factor – an *increased and diversified funding base* – is clearly demonstrated by the reduction of government funding as a proportion of total income from 85 per cent in 1980 to the present-day figure of 44 per cent. The earnings which last year totalled £76 million come from 55 different activities, all of which report to the Earned Income Group chaired by the registrar.

The fourth factor – a *vigorous and buoyant academic heartland* – again very much reflects the Warwick experience. This is manifested in the tremendous growth in all subjects, but especially in the Warwick Manufacturing Group, the Warwick Business School and Continuing Education, the development of the Graduate School and growth of graduate student numbers to 40 per cent of the student body, the high scores in the Research Assessment Exercise and Quality Assurance Agency Teaching Assessment, and the recent establishment of a Medical School.

The fifth factor – an *integrated entrepreneurial culture* – has been carefully nurtured at Warwick by the early and transparent use of performance indicators, by means of incentives and rewards for success and by appropriate internal and external publicity. Professional press management and public relations are a vital part of this process.

Clearly the Warwick experience supports Burton Clark's conclusions but there are other factors which contributed to Warwick's ability to transform itself during the 1980s into an innovative and entrepreneurial institution.

First, and arguably the most significant, were the radical higher education policies being implemented by the new Conservative government from 1979 onwards. These included a large reduction in state funding, an increase in the number of students, the intrusion of market forces and competition into the macro and micro management of higher education, and measures to encourage institutions to become more relevant to the social and economic development of the nation. Of these the financial depredations and consequential prospect of serious damage to the quality of academic life created a climate within the University in which previously unthinkable policies could be introduced as dire necessity, but which were subsequently accepted as salvation and eventually embraced with pride as part of 'the Warwick way'. Without the external 'threat' it is most unlikely that Warwick would of its own volition have initiated the radical programme of change and transformation.

The Warwick response was a decade of hyperactivity, of innovation and of growth. It was a decade which saw the University's 'earned income' grow from 15 per cent to 50 per cent of total turnover. Above all it was a decade in which the University came of age as a contributor to the social and economic development of the region. The major contributions came through a rash of new developments outlined below.

A Department of Continuing Education was established and after the transfer of Responsible Body status from the University of Birmingham in 1984 the number of local Open Studies courses and attendees increased tenfold. The Continuing Education Department was also responsible for the introduction of access courses and the innovative Two Plus Two degrees in collaboration with local further education colleges. To further under-line the University's concern for local matters, the Continuing Education Department established an advisory centre in one of Coventry's more deprived areas.

In 1980, Professor S.K. Bhattacharyya established a Department of Manu-facturing Engineering within the School of Engineering Sciences. By addressing regional and national needs through the provision of consultancy, training, research and development services and by working closely with major engin-eering companies and their suppliers, Kumar Bhattacharyya built up one of Europe's largest university centres of manufacturing engineering.

In 1983, Professor George Bain was elected Chairman of the Warwick Business School and proceeded to transform an average department into one of the nation's leaders. This was achieved partly by massive expansion, much of which was based upon the provision of consultancy, training and research services to meet the needs of regional and national, private and public sector organizations.

Local and regional needs were also very much in mind with the establish-ment of the Department of Applied Social Studies and the Department of Postgraduate Medical Education. In both cases the training and updating of professional staff brought the University into a close working relation-ship with an important local service provider.

In response to the very high unemployment in Coventry, the University Science Park was established in 1983 on the University campus in collabora-tion with the Coventry City Council, Warwickshire County Council and the West Midlands Enterprise Board. The Science Park now accommodates 65 companies which employ over 1350 staff.

Other developments introduced during the 1980s which had a strong regional orientation included the building of three residential training

Table 16.1 Growth in activity

	1980	1997
Students (heads)	5,250	15,630
Postgraduates	550	5,769
Overseas students	250	2,474
Self-financing course students	–	3,396
Research Institutes and Centres	3	44
Income	£20m	£1,387m

centres, expansion of the Warwick Arts Centre to generate a quarter of a million visitors per year and efforts by the Sports Centre, Library and Language Centre to make their facilities and services available to organizations and members of the public within the region.

Implicit in the strong regional developments just described was a policy of growth. Growth in student numbers, growth in existing activities and growth of new activities were all pursued vigorously and achieved as shown in Table 16.1.

During the same period the staff–student ratio declined by 50 per cent and state funding per student head in excess of that figure. The growth of the University meant that these cuts could be absorbed less painfully while at the same time expansion created a feeling of excitement, generated new income streams and generally boosted morale in very considerable contrast to the depressed state of the higher education sector as a whole.

A further factor which contributed to Warwick's transformation was the youthfulness of both its staff and structures. There were no departmental 'baronies', no deans defending the indefensible and the decision-making structure had not yet reached the sclerotic state exhibited by many older institutions.

This allowed the development of an important feature of the Warwick model. It is the 'progressive taxation' system under which a sizeable proportion of departmental earnings, where they exist, is redistributed for the benefit of the University as a whole. Youth and related administrative flexibility might also account for the surprising ease with which the Earned Income Group grew from an informal meeting of officers under the chairmanship of the registrar to its current position where it monitors or controls over half the University's total budget in a manner which would not have been possible in many older institutions. A central feature of the Earned Income Group policy has been to appoint high-quality professional managers with relevant business experience and then provide guidance and support to enable them to survive and prosper within what is still a largely uncomprehending and potentially hostile internal environment. In no area is this support more important than in the need for continuous investment for growth and to remain competitive. For example, a costly refurbishment of a perfectly acceptable residential management centre might appear extravagant and even wasteful when put alongside funding needs for 'core' university activities such as teaching and research. However, such refurbishment has to be seen in the context of the competitive imperative of the industry and the fact that a failure to invest would certainly jeopardize future earnings. Warwick has handled this dilemma well partly through the Earned Income Group structure and partly because the very strong centre (vice-chancellor, pro-vice-chancellors, Faculty Board chairs, senior officers and the three senior lay officers) has been able to set a sensible long-term development budget and resist the many and varied short-term pleadings. In contrast, the grim and shabby state of many universities at present bears testimony, not just to shortage of funds, but to weak decision making and a willingness to pass on the consequences of gradual deterioration of plant and buildings to be picked up at some indeterminate point in the future.

In his concluding discussion Burton Clark stresses the incremental and holistic nature of change in universities. He quotes with approval David W. Leslie (1996) who states '... change in colleges and universities comes when it happens in the trenches; what faculty and students do is what the institution becomes. It does not happen because a committee or a president asserts a new idea'.[6]

While the change in universities must embrace the wider community, there is little doubt that the process at Warwick would not have started without the prescient and far-sighted recognition of the need for change by the Vice-Chancellor, Jack Butterworth. He reached this conclusion long before his fellow vice-chancellors and outlined his views eloquently to the University Court in his annual report in 1980. He said:

> I began by drawing your attention to the three functions of a university: teaching, research and service to the community. A university which is doing its job in teaching, research and service to the community will inevitably find that it is an agent of change. Universities are frequently criticised for being ivory towers, often by those who have only an imperfect knowledge of what a university is doing. In most university work there is an element of the cloister, and indeed of dedication and retreat, in order that the highest standards can be achieved, whether in research or teaching, but the days of the ivory tower as such are long since over. A new dispensation is now being differently received in different institutions. Some adopt the new order willingly, some, like the University of Warwick, enthusiastically, some cautiously and a few reluctantly, but all admit that universities must come to terms with the community which we serve. For the reasons which I have tried to explain, community service has now gone far beyond extra-mural work. If I may put it shortly, it is a philosophy, a point of view which affects the whole operation and structure of the university. It may be that the old structure has had its day and that those universities will be successful which do not wait for a new model or precedent but are already moving towards a new and different approach.[7]

Jack Butterworth recognized very clearly that the elitist university system could not last and that movement to a mass system of higher education would inevitably lead to a continuation of the cuts introduced by Mrs Thatcher in 1980. For Warwick to maintain the standard of academic life to which it had been accustomed, it would be imperative to replace the lost government funding. The course was set by the Vice-Chancellor but it required the prodigious energy, imagination and high-level management skills of the Registrar, Michael Shattock, to enrol the active support of the wider University community and to ensure that the pace of change and development did not slacken. Michael Shattock's achievements over a long period at Warwick are numerous and varied and extend to all parts of the institution. In particular, he was largely responsible for the successful establishment of the University's Science Park, the Department of Continuing Education (which he chaired in its first year), the Graduate School and the Earned Income Group. In addition Michael Shattock built up, shaped and inspired an administration at Warwick, many of whose members are now disproportionately represented at senior levels in higher educational institutions throughout the land.

It may be concluded that while Warwick's growth and development since 1980 most certainly incorporated the five elements of transformation identified by Professor Burton Clark, these were not in themselves a sufficient condition of change. Several other factors were important but without the external stimulus of government policy and the far-sighted and dynamic leadership of Jack Butterworth and Michael Shattock, it is most unlikely that Warwick would have become what Lucy Hodges described as '. . . the success story of the university world'.[8]

References

1. Burton R. Clark (1998) *Creating Entrepreneurial Universities: Organizational Pathways of Transformation.* Oxford: Pergamon Press. See also B.R. Clark (1998) The entrepreneurial university: demand and response, *Tertiary Education and Management,* 4 (1): 5–16; B. Sporn (1999) *Adaptive University Structures: An Analysis of Adaptation to Socioeconomic Environments of US and European Universities.* London: Jessica Kingsley; and M.L. Shattock (2000) Strategic management in European universities in an age of increasing institutional self-reliance, *Tertiary Education and Management,* 6 (2): 93–104.
2. Ibid., pp. 131, 132. See also Notes 2, 3 and 21, pp. 26–8.
3. Ibid., p. xiv.
4. Ibid., p. xiv.
5. Ibid., p. 7.
6. D.W. Leslie (1996) Strategic governance: the wrong questions? *The Review of Higher Education,* 20 (1): 101–12.
7. J.B. Butterworth (1981) *Annual Report,* 1980–81. Coventry: University of Warwick.
8. Lucy Hodges (2000) Fear not . . . the Professor has a cunning plan, *Independent,* Education Section, p. 2, 2 March. See also D. Palfreyman (1989) on 'The Warwick Way'; and more generally, H. Gray (1999), and S. Slaughter and L. Leslie (1997).

17

Academic Development

Robert Burgess

In the last 35 years much has been written about the University of Warwick by journalists and by researchers. The University has attracted considerable interest given some of the key features of its academic development. The Warwick 'story' of a university that was developed 'from scratch' on a greenfield site is one of the key successes in British higher education in the latter part of the twentieth century. The University that was criticized for its involvement with industry in the late 1960s is now championed as a classic example of the way in which academic and industrial development can complement each other in a very effective way. Among the themes and topics that have been developed in the literature over the years have been the origins of the University,[1] its involvement with industry,[2] and the development of an entrepreneurial culture.[3] In all these different ways there has been an interest in the developing culture of a university that has been summarized inside Warwick by the phrase 'the Warwick way' – a phrase that identifies a style of working based on a responsive culture which relies on short lines of communication between the centre of the University and the departments. However, this still prompts the question: how does it work in practice? Indeed, a key question that is often posed by researchers, journalists, academics and other commentators is what makes for Warwick's success?

Some clues to the working practices of members of the University and factors contributing to Warwick's success are provided in a comment from Michael Shattock in the volume *Making a University: A Celebration of Warwick's First Twenty Five Years*[4] when he writes:

> Universities are made by people – by scholars, by students, by administrators and by staff generally. Warwick's development, more than most universities, has been determined by positive initiatives, by its first Vice-Chancellor, Jack Butterworth, by its first professors and their successors, by generations of lively and critical students, by energetic administrators and by the interaction of personalities and the ideas

they generated. The University's atmosphere has encouraged people to be active.

But we might ask: in what ways have people been encouraged to be active? In what ways have staff established reputations? How have staff developed their subjects, built teams and changed the structure of the University? In order to address some of these questions I will present two examples which will involve writing in a quasi-autobiographical way – a genre that I developed in social research during my time at Warwick.[5]

A key feature in the University's academic development has been the opportunity for teams of people to work together to promote research through new academic structures that have been brought into existence through active collaboration between academics and administrators. In short, the University has a 'can do' culture. Much of this work has been aided by individual academics having the freedom to develop particular areas of research and academic development: the key attribute established by Jack Butterworth, the first Vice-Chancellor (recruited from New College, Oxford, where he was Bursar and a Law don), in the early years when founding professors were 'given their head' to develop their subject areas in whatever ways they found appropriate. It is this feature that runs deeply through Warwick's history and through many academic developments. As a consequence some academic departments, research centres and research groups have a very sharp focus which has resulted in particular aspects of an academic field being developed rather than the shallow development of a whole subject area. It has also been part of 'the Warwick way' to concentrate resources by establishing strong specialisms in many academic departments. Indeed, during the years that I was at Warwick I found this was a feature on which it was possible to build many academic developments. In examining the patterns and processes associated with the development of the academic culture at Warwick I will focus on two areas. First, my involvement in establishing a research centre; second, my involvement in establishing a University-wide Graduate School.

Developing a research centre

In the 25 years that I spent working at Warwick, I was a member of the Department of Sociology that was located in the Faculty of Social Studies. However, my interests spanned education as well as sociology, but education was located in another faculty (having been developed from the former Coventry College of Education that merged with Warwick in 1978). In the mid-1980s I was asked if I would like to explore the possibility of establishing a new research centre that would bring together the work of two subject areas: sociology and education. It was a classic case of Warwick giving an individual the opportunity to take a research development and shape it in the way in which he or she wished.

I was seconded for half my time to establish this new Centre, physically located in the Faculty of Education, but intellectually located on the inter-face of social science and education. The opportunity was considerable and allowed me to bring together some of my key interests. First, the Centre focused on basic and applied research. Second, its research focus was linked to undergraduate and postgraduate teaching as well as educational development that was disseminated through short courses. Finally, the research brought academic staff together with practitioners – all themes that I had worked on in earlier years. In short, the Centre focused on theory, methodology, policy and practice examined in the context of schooling and higher education.

As I have indicated elsewhere,[6] my involvement in developing the Centre for Educational Development Appraisal and Research (acronym CEDAR) was used to bring together the key elements: research, educational develop-ment and policy-focused activity as represented by appraisal (which was high on the policy agenda when the Centre was established). The areas of activity were summarized in the Centre's Constitution that stated:

The Centre conducts basic and applied research in the field of education and training. The activities of the Centre, therefore, include:
• work on issues and problems that confront schools, colleges and educa-tion personnel;
• policy questions; and
• basic research on theories and methods of research and evaluation.
  Such a range of research work involves CEDAR staff in a variety of activities including:
  (a) studies of appraisal, assessment and evaluation which link
       to theory, policy and practice;
  (b) inservice and development work with headteachers, teachers, advisers,
       inspectors, trainers and staff in further and higher education;
  (c) theoretical and methodological studies that are appropriate for the
       analysis of educational settings.
Research is central to all CEDAR's activities and is related to policy and practice.

It was this research agenda that was worked on by the research staff with support from other academic and administrative staff. However, there was also the question of financial support.

While many universities have developed research centres that have been supported by internal funding, I knew this would not be the case at War-wick. After an initial pump priming grant of £10,000 for two years from the University's research and innovations fund, it was down to me to make the Centre work and obtain external support. In this respect, the University gave me the freedom to develop an area of academic endeavour intellec-tually. However, with that freedom came the expectation that the Centre would be self-financing. Accordingly, the process of developing a research team involved not only bringing together researchers who could work on individual projects, but also developing links with a range of potential sponsors and grant-giving bodies. In this respect CEDAR was an element of the entrepreneurial culture of the University of Warwick, first, through the freedom to develop an academic area and a research agenda and second, through the need to raise grant and contract income from the research councils, from charities, from local education authorities and other organizations. Indeed, fund-raising, from a whole range of sources, resulted in CEDAR being able to establish a staff that grew from two in 1987 to a maximum of 22 in 1994. All the funds that were raised for project work supported staff salaries and related activities. Indeed, it was always my understanding that CEDAR was expected to raise sufficient income in order that it could develop as a research centre rather than becoming dependent upon the University to engage in its activities. As a consequence, the academic staff also developed the habit of searching for funding, writing grant proposals and seeking sponsors for their academic activities.

These were the hallmarks associated with developing a particular research centre in Warwick. However, many of the key features associated with CEDAR's development were a reflection of the broader Warwick culture. Here, it was not sufficient to focus merely on the intellectual concerns of the Centre or to develop staff and staff careers; it was also essential to understand research sponsorship and the way in which funding could be used to shape academic development and facilitate further investment in areas that were ripe for academic and research development. In this way research funding did not merely determine the academic agenda but could be used to develop a set of research themes that were established across a series of projects over a decade.[7] It was some of these features of academic development that were also reflected in the development of the University-wide Graduate School that I was invited to establish in the early 1990s.

Developing a Graduate School

By the early 1990s Warwick had established itself as a relatively strong research-based University. It had been well placed in the Research Assessment Exercises that had been conducted in 1986 and 1989 and a logic of this was to see how it could reflect this major research emphasis in its student base. Accordingly in the late 1980s a decision was taken to establish a working group that would look at the feasibility of developing graduate education. Various models were examined and in the end the working party (of which I was a member) advocated that the University should set up a University-wide Graduate School. It was this development that I was asked by Mike Shattock, as Registrar, to develop in the coming years. Once again, its development reflected 'the Warwick way'. First, an area had been identified and a framework developed but the opportunity was given to an academic to decide how a graduate school (based on a North American model) might be developed in a UK university. This was not a situation whereby the University expected a North American model to be taken and super-imposed upon a UK university, but rather how a graduate school could be developed alongside other aspects of the academic culture which was already firmly established at Warwick. In particular, Faculty Boards had formerly held responsibility for postgraduate work and in turn a Higher Degrees Committee had looked after aspects of student administration. But this was not enough if graduate education was to be developed in a strong form. However, there were no UK models that could be followed. A model that would be appropriate for a UK university needed to be devised.

The task of chairing the Graduate School was summarized by Mike Shattock when he said it would be my job 'to get up the noses of as many people as possible in the University about graduate education'. In this respect, graduate education and training needed to permeate the whole structure of the University. Creating a Graduate School involved developing the Warwick culture in terms of teaching and research. However, it also involved the challenge of developing a new organizational structure in an established system. The Graduate School was designed to enhance the research culture and build upon it through new master's programmes and doctoral training. This involved developments in the teaching programme and growth in student numbers that demanded new ways of working in order to refocus the institution's activities with students. Accordingly the Graduate School was concerned with every aspect of the University including: postgraduate admissions, the provision of graduate accommodation and student facili-ties, the planning and development of graduate residences, the promotion of new programmes, and the development of employment prospects for postgraduates. In short, developing a Graduate School allowed me to think about ways in which graduate education would change the culture of the University which had been predominantly based upon undergraduate teaching.

The way in which the Warwick Graduate School developed was not through a building programme specifically identified with graduate education. Instead, the University encouraged a team of academics and administrators to work together to develop the concept. In the first instance I worked with John Hogan (now Registrar of the University of Durham and a fellow con-tributor to this book) and subsequently with Lee Saunders (now Academic Registrar at the University of Warwick). The Graduate School developed over a four-year period so that by the mid-1990s graduate students consti-tuted 40 per cent of the University's student population. In this respect, graduate students had almost doubled in the initial period of Graduate School development. But what elements of the Warwick culture helped to promote this development? First, the responsive character of the institution was essential. Many of the developments involved bringing together a range of staff: academics, members of the Estates Department and Hospitality Services were involved with wardens and students in designing student accommodation. Similarly, promoting international student recruitment relied upon links between members of the International Office and academics, while the provision of library facilities relied upon links being made between professional librarians, academic staff and postgraduate students. A key feature of Graduate School development involved academics in existing departments and faculties being persuaded that graduate education was important to the future of the University. However, the academic activities needed financial support. In this context, the centrally driven resource allocation system was crucial to the development of the Graduate School and the provision of postgraduate education and training.

While the resource allocation system in many universities has been devolved, in Warwick it has remained centralized through the Estimates and Grants Committee (known locally as E&G). Embedded within the Warwick culture is the role of the Estimates and Grants Committee (a committee that I subsequently chaired in the last four years I was at Warwick as Senior Pro-Vice-Chancellor). The Estimates and Grants Committee lies at the heart of Warwick's success as it brings together research and teaching bids from departments for academic positions. In these circumstances, E&G was, in my view, a means of developing graduate education. Initially, the working group to establish the Graduate School had suggested that the new chairman of the Board of Graduate Studies should be ex-officio on a range of University committees but not a member of the Estimates and Grants Committee. As I had been on E&G as a Faculty Board Chairman I understood its centrality in enhancing academic development, especially when chairs of departments were informed about additional academic resources including requests for new academic positions. This was a time when key objectives in the University could be reinforced through the allocations process. Accordingly, I argued that I would only chair the Graduate School if I continued as a member of the Estimates and Grants Committee as in my view this was central to the success of the Graduate School. With the Graduate School represented on E&G questions could be raised about the use of staff resources to develop graduate education in every department within the University. In this respect, I worked with the then Chair of the Estimates and Grants Committee, Professor Roger Whittenbury, to shape the ways in which graduate teaching and supervision could be developed alongside undergraduate teaching and research across the University. In this context, graduate recruitment was assisted through the provision of additional resources for graduate students and in turn special incentives were provided to recruit international students to boost the size of the postgraduate population and in turn to reinforce and develop the size of academic departments. Growth within the University could partly be attributed to the development of the graduate student base and a set of staff resources to deliver postgraduate programmes. But in turn, the development of the Warwick Graduate School also meant that the culture of the University was reinforced whereby leading edge research was communicated to students registered on masters and doctoral programmes.

Some implications

The two examples that I have provided of academic development at Warwick illustrate the key features associated with several developments: first, the opportunity that was given to all academics to act as 'product champions' to develop an area as they desired; second, the importance of working in teams where no distinction was drawn between academic and administrative staff; third, the way in which a responsive culture has been developed; and fourth, the development of the entrepreneurial culture.

Many of these features are the hallmarks of academic development at Warwick. If we turn to the development of the Warwick Manufacturing Group, the Business School, research groups developed within departments, the hiring of academic staff, and the movement of senior staff from other universities to Warwick, we find a number of common factors. All of these developments reinforce the Warwick 'can do' culture. They are the result of product champions who use the culture to shape academic developments. But what of the future? As always universities in the twenty-first century are moving into uncharted territory, but Warwick is well placed, having embraced the promotion of high-quality research leading to high-quality teaching and service to the local community. In this respect, lifelong learning is a theme that Warwick can take up and, in turn, graduate education – arguably one of the greatest manifestations of lifelong learning – is a key feature in its development. Second, opportunities to expand nationally and internationally through research and teaching mean that Warwick is well placed to take up these opportunities. Finally, universities will need to collaborate and enter into partnerships if they are to compete on a national and international stage. In this respect Warwick has already established itself in a range of groups and networks including a partnership with my own University in the creation of a Leicester–Warwick Medical School. All these developments take Warwick in new directions but fundamentally I suspect the culture will remain with individuals being given the opportunity to promote academic endeavours in directions of their own choosing. In this respect 'the Warwick way' is the culture of the institution. It is the product of its members advancing research and teaching in equal measure. However, the University relies upon groups of academic and administrative staff working together to sustain and develop the research and teaching within the institution.

References

1. M.L. Shattock (1994) *The UGC and the Management of British Universities.* Buckingham: Open University Press; R.G. Burgess (1991) Working and researching at the limits of knowledge, in M.L. Shattock (ed.) *Making a University: A Celebration of Warwick's First Twenty Five Years*, pp. 95–112 and 115–16. Coventry: University of Warwick.

2. E.P. Thompson (1970) *Warwick University Limited.* Harmondsworth: Penguin.
3. Burton R. Clark (1998) The Warwick way: transformation in an English research university, in *Creating Entrepreneurial Universities.* Oxford: Pergamon Press; D. Palfreyman (1989) The Warwick way: a case study of innovation and entrepreneurship within a university context, *Journal of Entrepreneurship and Regional Development,* 1 (2): 207–19.
4. M.L. Shattock (1994) op. cit., p. 43.
5. R.G. Burgess (ed.) (1984) *The Research Process in Educational Settings: Ten Case Studies.* Lewes: Falmer Press; R.G. Burgess (ed.) (1990) *Learning from the Field.* London: JAI Press.
6. R.G. Burgess (1998) The Director's tale: developing teams and themes in a research centre, in G. Walford (ed.) *Doing Research about Education,* pp. 154–69. London: Falmer Press.
7. Ibid.

18

Conclusion: Triumph and Retreat

Peter Scott

Introduction

There are two parallel, but incompatible, stories to be told of British higher education. The first is one of triumph – and that word is not too strong to describe what has been achieved. Since 1960, and in particular since the mid-1980s, Britain has acquired a system of mass higher education – partly by crooked design and partly in a fit of absent-mindedness – but a system that still retains many of the admirable qualities of an elite system. For instance, there continues to be a close and creative embrace between teaching on the one hand and research and scholarship on the other, a strong and continuing commitment to undergraduate education, and a still vital tradition of academic 'intimacy' reflected in teaching styles, patterns of pastoral care and personal relationships between staff and students. For a moment – and perhaps only a moment – at the beginning of the twenty-first century British higher education enjoys the best of both worlds. In scope and structure it has become the largest producer of graduates in Europe, and the British people enjoy unprecedented levels of access to higher education which come close to matching those available to our fellow-European citizens; the historical underdevelopment of British higher education, in quantitative terms, has been overcome. But in its institutional and academic cultures the British system still embodies a commitment to excellence which extends far beyond a dying nostalgia for elitist norms and penetrates deeply into the daily practices of higher education.

British universities and colleges are now delicately balanced between old and new. Innovation has been embraced, but tradition preserved. Perhaps that balance cannot be held. Two 'falls' are possible. Either the curiously elite–mass system which has emerged in Britain in the past two decades will prove incapable of further expansion and adaptation and, as a result, be outflanked by novel and rival forms of higher education that are mass in spirit as well as form and which reject the old academic culture; or that system will slough off its elite characteristics as memories of the 'golden time' fade, budgets decline and more abrasive and urgent imperatives emerge – in an awful phrase, 'dumbing-down'. These possibilities will be considered later in this chapter. But, for the moment, the achievement of British higher education deserves to be celebrated. One (negative?) form of British exceptionalism – the underdevelopment of higher education in terms of participation, with access fiercely and inequitably rationed – has been replaced by another (positive?) form of exceptionalism – much higher levels of participation have been achieved that approximate to participation levels in other developed countries, without seriously compromising the integrity of traditional academic culture. That is British higher education's first story.

The second story is one of retreat and even defeat. In 1960 British higher education was regarded as exceptional in another sense; although overwhelmingly dependent on public funding, it enjoyed a very high level of autonomy. Buffered from the state by that uniquely British institution, the University Grants Committee (UGC), the traditional universities were able to determine their own teaching programmes and academic awards with far greater freedom than universities in the rest of Europe and, unlike many American universities, their budgets could not (easily) be tampered with by politicians. Once the government had agreed the block grant to universities (and until the 1960s the Treasury accepted the UGC's own estimate of the financial needs of the universities), political involvement was at an end. It was the responsibility of the UGC, the members of which although appointed by the government were chosen from the academic great-and-good, to distribute that grant to individual universities. The favourite metaphor was of politicians leaving the money on a tree-stump in the forest to be collected later by the UGC. Ministers received almost no advance warning of the UGC's allocations as late as 1981 when deep, and selective, cuts were made in university budgets which inevitably had loud political reverberations.[1]

The autonomy supposedly enjoyed by traditional universities in Britain has almost certainly been exaggerated by foreign scholars who were comparing the British regime with much cruder and more directly enforced forms of accountability in their own countries, by vice-chancellors and other senior academics in whose interest it was to sustain an 'autonomy' myth and, most powerfully and painfully, with the benefit of hindsight and in full knowledge of how sharply that autonomy was to be eroded in subsequent years. The exceptional degree of autonomy apparently possessed by British universities during the high noon of the UGC era (between the early 1950s and early 1960s) probably reflected two special factors which could not be sustained indefinitely – first, the collusive character of post-war elites, political, administrative and academic; and second, the strong political consensus that prevailed during this period and which has been described, in general terms, as 'the end of ideology' and, in a specifically British context, as 'the post-war settlement'. It is also important to remember that large parts of British higher education lay outside the UGC sector; the polytechnics (now the 'new' universities) remained subject to local authority control until 1989 and teacher training was always tightly policed by the Department for

Education of Science (and its successors, the Department for Education and now the Department for Education and Employment).[2]

But, whether exaggerated or not, that autonomy has been sharply eroded in the past two decades. The UGC was abolished by the Education Reform Act of 1988, paradoxically the same piece of legislation that freed the polytechnics from local authority control and set them on the road to achieving university status. But, long before, the UGC had ceased to be a buffer between government and universities, and instead had come to be regarded as an instrument of the state. The independence of the UGC was compromised not only by its own behaviour but also by external events, notably the establishment of the National Advisory Body (NAB) in 1982 to coordinate the activities of the so-called 'public sector' of higher education. (The language was revealing; universities were still officially described as the 'autonomous sector'.) The UGC was succeeded by the Universities Funding Council (UFC) and the NAB by the Polytechnics and Colleges Funding Council (PCFC). In 1992 when the binary division between universities and polytechnics was abandoned and the latter became universities, the UFC and PCFC were replaced by a unified agency, the Higher Education Funding Council for England (HEFCE). Separate funding councils were established in Scotland and Wales. As a result of these rapid shifts in acronymic authority during the 1980s and 1990s British higher education ended the century with its autonomy sharply curtailed and subject to increasingly intrusive accountability regimes. A retreat certainly and probably a defeat.

Michael Shattock has been intimately associated with both stories – of triumph and retreat – in his capacity as a university administrator, in effect one of the most influential university leaders of his generation, and also as a scholar of higher education. For more than 20 years he was in a commanding position at the University of Warwick, an institution which craftily manoeuvred between innovation and tradition, openness and elitism, and translated the ambiguities inherent in the nature of Britain's elite–mass system into outstanding institutional success. But his influence extended more widely. Through his involvement with the Society for Research into Higher Education (SRHE), his editorship of *Higher Education Quarterly* (HEQ) and, perhaps most significantly, as a leading animator of the Leverhulme series of seminars on the future of higher education in the early 1980s, he not only chronicled and analysed but actively charted the progress of British higher education towards wider access and greater engagement with enveloping society.[3] However, Michael Shattock was also closely involved with the decline and fall of the UGC system – again both as an active participant (for example, in relation to the future of University College, Cardiff in the mid-1980s) and as a scholar (he is the author of the only non-sentimental account of the UGC).[4] So in his achievement as an administrator and his contribution as a scholar he was close to – indeed, part of – the two stories of British higher education.

The remainder of this chapter is divided into three sections. The first is a snapshot of British higher education 'before the Fall', that 'golden time' that began in the late 1950s and stumbled to a close in the 1970s before coming to an abrupt halt with the election victory of Margaret Thatcher at the end of that decade. The second is an account of British higher education today – in terms both of size, scale, scope and structure, and of key issues such as the expansion of student numbers and the assurance of academic quality. The third is a speculation about the future of the system, returning to the question posed at the beginning of this introduction: is Britain's elite–mass system capable of further extension and reform without damaging its essential academic culture, or are we approaching the end of the road?

Post-war higher education: a golden time?

The ethos of British higher education in the third quarter of the twentieth century is now difficult to recall, even though it is within the memory of older members of staff still working in universities but now approaching retirement. To many of them it represents a world that has been lost, and this is an impression that has been transmitted to their younger colleagues. As a result higher education in the 1960s is observed too often through the lens of nostalgia. The final years of the century, Thatcher-to-Blair, saw the sunset of younger brighter hopes for a renaissance of higher education at once liberal, academic and open, an amalgam of Nobel prize-winning science and extra-mural outreach which had been the spirit of that 'golden time'. This undertow of might-have-beens, and of regret, helps to explain why so little satisfaction has been taken in the achievement of mass higher education and the remarkable survival of an authentic academic culture. This was not the way we imagined this goal would be reached: on 'their' terms rather than our own. So it is important to paint a realistic picture of higher education a generation ago.

Higher education was then a much smaller and more fractured system. By the mid-1960s there were 45 universities but many were new and most were small. The grass had barely grown on the greenfield campuses of the first generation of 'new' universities such as Sussex, York, Lancaster and Warwick (the so-called Shakespearean or Baedeker universities), so recently building sites; the technological universities had only just begun to throw off the inhibitions and constraints of their further education past; and even the old civics, then as now the heartland of the university system, had only just begun to outgrow their provincial roots. Only Oxford and Cambridge, then much more numerically significant than they later became, were at that time much as they are now (and even this assessment must be heavily qualified, certainly in the case of the latter). Like much of post-war British society, universities were still recognizably Victorian institutions. Only yesterday it seemed 'scholarship boys' had boarded trams clanking through smoggy streets and 'gilded youth' struggled to recover the tempo and mores of a lost pre-war world. Even as late as 1971 there were only 176,000 students in these 45 universities, fewer than the total of students on higher education courses in further education colleges in 2000. 'Advanced further education', still as its label suggests more closely aligned with the world of technical education than an elitist university sector, had only recently emerged onto the wider terrain of higher education; the first polytechnics, created by amalgamating existing colleges of technology and art and design, were designated at the end of the 1960s. Even including teacher training, the non-university sector only enrolled a total of 120,000 students. It was very much the junior, and often unrecognized, partner. 'Higher education' was still an awkward neologism which had had little general currency before the 1963 Robbins Report.[5]

Yet what the higher education system lacked in size, scope and coherence, it made up for in self-confidence. That self-confidence took two main forms. The first is summed up in A.H. Halsey's celebrated phrase, 'donnish dominion'.[6] Nationally the universities still enjoyed the best of all possible worlds – public patronage (and on an increasingly generous scale) and institutional autonomy. It was not until the later 1960s that the UGC took the first tentative steps towards sector-wide planning by issuing a so-called 'letter of guidance', although already in the 1950s the committee had attempted, discreetly, to steer the development of individual universities. Institutionally they were ruled by alliances of senior professors (who dominated Senates), ambitious and often charismatic vice-chancellors and a new administrative class (which was rapidly becoming professionalized); civic and commercial elites, although still represented on courts and councils, no longer played an active role in the governance of universities. In the new polytechnics, of course, different conditions applied. But even here directorates and, less sure-footedly, academic boards emerged to challenge municipal rule. In both university and non-university sectors academic trade unions had begun to wield greater influence as the trade union movement approached its climax in the late 1960s. The appearance of students as a political class in the wake of the New Left-inspired agitation of that decade also disturbed the elite equilibrium of higher education – but only briefly. The long-lasting impact of student revolt was not on the internal governance of universities but on their public reputation. Well into the 1970s they remained self-governing communities, academic oligarchies, still insulated from the political and market pressures which were to overwhelm higher education a decade later.

The second form taken by higher education's self-confidence – arrogance to some – was the extraordinary flowering of a new intelligentsia. The very word, Russian with strong French connotations, describes a socio-cultural formation traditionally seen as antithetical to English empiricism and unnecessary in the light of the tight affinities between academic and politico-administrative elites. But, in the 1950s and with gathering force in the 1960s, Britain acquired an intellectual class very different from the Bloomsburyite 'men of letters' and the traditional academic caste of the pre-war era. First, this class was professional rather than privileged; many of its members were 'scholarship boys' who benefited from the opening up of secondary education after the 1944 Education Act, and most insisted on seeing intellectual life as an expert rather than gentlemanly activity. Second, it was predominantly located in higher education rather than in newspapers and periodicals or publishing houses. Third, its centre of gravity was in the new social sciences rather than either the liberal arts or physical sciences (the great age of physics was almost over before the expansion of higher education got properly under way). Intellectuals were no longer regarded as dilettante polymaths. As the social sciences swept through the universities of the 1950s and 1960s, more rigorous standards of investigation were applied to political and social questions and a new and rather un-English interest in theory developed. The battle between the 'two cultures' of the arts and the sciences, between Leavis and Snow (in essence a rerun of the contest between Arnold and Huxley 80 years before), took on new and radical forms as cultural studies emerged under the aegis of Richard Hoggart and historians such as Keith Thomas and Edward Thompson began to explore new social and cultural themes. 'Science' no longer belonged to physical scientists; instead a 'scientific', or expert/professional, culture invaded traditional domains, realms of thought, once confined to elite intuition.

These two, perhaps opposed, forms of self-confidence help to explain the peculiar ethos of higher education between 1950 and 1970: on the one hand elitist, even defensive, in the context of institutions, structures and systems; on the other open-minded, even radical, in the academic sphere. Many academics were determined to change our views of nature, society and ourselves (and even to change the world in a more directly revolutionary sense), but they were as determined to preserve the privileged status of their profession and their institutions. It is this curious combination of radicalism, even utopianism, and conservatism that characterized higher education's 'golden time'. Today, of course, the positions seem to be reversed. Higher education is now accessible to mass student populations; it more-or-less willingly accepts the responsibilities (and also opportunities) represented by this much closer engagement with society and the economy; it has been prepared to adapt subject identities, professional practices, research priorities, teaching styles to further the cause of social openness. But the intellectual crackle of the 1960s has subsided into silence; over-zealous accountability and well-intentioned systematization have led too often to a new sense of academic closure. The-world-we-have-lost is not all myth. It has a grit of uncomfortable truth.

Higher education in 2001: brave new world?

British higher education at the beginning of the twenty-first century is a truly mass system with 1.8 million students and an age participation index of 33 per cent. If Martin Trow's taxonomy of elite–mass–universal higher education is accepted, the British system ceased to be an elite system in the mid-1980s and is now moving rapidly towards becoming a universal system.[7] If the 'tone' of many universities and colleges does not support this description of British higher education as an unambiguously mass, still less a near-universal, system, there are a number of explanations.[8] The first, and simplest, is that mentalities are slower to change than structures. Just because it does not yet feel like a mass system does not mean that it is not a mass system. Time will remedy the dissonance. The second explanation is that Trow's taxonomy is essentially quantitative and was developed in a different time (the 1960s) and place (America). It may fail to capture the dimensions of qualitative change, less linear and more sinuous, ambiguous and even regressive. It may also give insufficient weight to the differences between American and British academic cultures, and also between the third quarter of the twentieth century, when welfare-statism was still in the ascendant (even in free-market America) and a confident modernity went unchallenged, and the cusp years between the twentieth and twenty-first centuries, when the state is widely regarded as the 'problem' not the 'solution' and institutional self-confidence has been undermined by the ambivalences of postmodernity. The third explanation, which I prefer to emphasize although the other two are certainly valid, is that a hybrid system of higher education has developed in Britain, mass in scale and structure but elite (even intimate) in its core values and many of its research and teaching practices. Whether this hybrid mass–elite system is a stable formation, or merely a moment of equipoise, will be discussed in the conclusion.

Students

To explore these questions further it may be useful to take a statistical snapshot of British higher education. Of the 1.8 million students more than half (53 per cent) are women. At first sight this appears unambiguous evidence of a successful social revolution; in higher education's 'golden time' between 1950 and 1970 less than a third of students were women. Higher education, having abandoned its traditional 'male' culture, has become a 'feminine' space. Or has it? Without belittling the importance of the impact of the gender revolution on universities and colleges, less may have changed than the headline statistics suggest. First, the increasing proportion of women students is partly explained by the incorporation of nursing and other professions allied to medicine (both traditionally dominated by women) into mainstream higher education. Like-for-like comparisons suggest more limited gains by women. Second, there is evidence not of integration but of polarization between men and women students. Proportionately fewer men are studying traditional arts disciplines, especially languages; more men are enrolled on engineering, mathematics and physics courses. Third, among academic staff men still outnumber women by two to one (84,000 compared to 43,000). Worse still, women are overrepresented in lower grade part-time posts.

The gender balance, of course, is only one measure of the openness of higher education. The data about the social origins of students are more problematical. First, 'class' has fallen out of favour as a categorization – in stark contrast to the 1960s when class was the dominant categorization. This downplaying of class reflects political rhetoric, if not social reality. The former Conservative Prime Minister John Major talked of a 'classless society', and the New Labour Prime Minister Tony Blair addresses his appeal to 'middle England'. Second, class is a volatile category, subject to the vagaries of self-description and also volatile shifts in occupational categories (which remain the basis for defining 'class' despite the dissolution of the old industrial economy). The middle class is expanding but also becoming more diffuse. However, two broad messages are plain. First, although the number of students has tripled during the past three decades, there has been only a limited shift in the class composition of the student body. British higher education has become a mass system because participation rates among the spreading middle class are now 'universal' (in Trow's terminology) while among the working class access to higher education has remained an 'elite' experience confined to the academically able and the highly motivated. Second, working-class students are heavily concentrated in less prestigious institutions. The student mix in elite universities has changed remarkably little since the 'golden time' of the 1960s; to the extent that the system has become more open it has been because of the addition of new institutions with wider student constituencies. As well as gender and class ethnicity is a measure of openness. Here the record is much better. Students from ethnic minorities comprise 13 per cent of the total, almost double the proportion of non-white citizens in Britain as a whole. But, again, two qualifications must be registered. First, as with working-class students, ethnic minority students tend to be concentrated in newer and less prestigious institutions (although, interestingly, not to the same extent). Second, only 4 per cent of the staff in higher education are drawn from ethnic minority communities.

Academic culture

A statistical snapshot of British higher education also reveals the perhaps surprising persistence of traditional academic patterns. Of the 1.8 million students almost four-fifths are studying on non-degree and first-degree courses. More than half are studying full-time for first degrees. Despite the spread of interdisciplinary programmes made possible by new modular (and semester) structures a surprisingly high proportion of students are still following specialized, often single-subject, courses. Full-time specialized undergraduate education continues to be at the heart of British higher education in the year 2001, as it was during its 'golden time'. Of the 22 per cent who are postgraduates growth has been most rapid among two groups. The first group comprises students enrolled on programmes that enrich and supplement undergraduate study rather than representing a distinctively postgraduate phase of higher education. In many cases the one-year taught master's, in effect, is the fourth year of undergraduate education. The alleged debasement of the currency of masters' degrees was a major pre-occupation of the Harris report on postgraduate education.[9]

A more positive interpretation perhaps is that masters' degrees are increasingly being used to 'stretch' the standard three-year duration of bachelors' degrees, partly to conform more closely to the four- (or more) year standard which prevails in the United States and most of the rest of Europe but largely to take account of the increasing sophistication of academic knowledge and/or the demands of professional practice. The second group comprises students enrolled on essentially post-experience programmes such as Master of Business Administration (MBA) courses; some do not have first degrees, and in most cases there has been a significant gap since their undergraduate study. Although many universities have established front-office graduate schools, there is little sign that the British system is poised to develop the powerful graduate and professional schools characteristic of American higher education which challenge the hegemony of conventional academic departments. Finally PhD students make up only 6 per cent of the total. Recruitment to research degrees has not been buoyant and there has been a significant expansion of 'professional' doctorates with significant taught elements.

Further evidence of British higher education's stubborn attachment to elite ways is provided by the very high levels of completion that still characterize the system. Despite the doubling of student numbers between the mid-1980s and mid-1990s and the erosion of exceptionally generous standards of student support, non-completion rates only crept up from 14 to 18 per cent.[10] This reflects three things. First, non-completion is firmly regarded as 'wastage'; the pint is seen as half-empty not half-full; despite the widespread adoption of credit accumulation and transfer systems, the standard view is still that students who do not receive the qualification which was their original goal are 'failures', and that this 'failure' implies a waste of taxpayers' money. Such a view is characteristic of an elite rather than mass system. Second, this restrictive view of 'success' has been reinforced by the introduction of new accountability regimes, notably the development of institution-by-institution performance indicators. The so-called 'audit society' has profoundly conservative effects, because old criteria are used to measure new aspirations. Too little attention has been paid to this systematic bias against innovation. Third, most academics in British higher education continue to see their relationships with their students in personal, even paternalistic, terms; non-completion by the latter is regarded as amounting to failure by the former. The attention paid to the 'student experience' in the British system may partly reflect a new emphasis on students as consumers and on 'customer service', but it also represents a reworking of traditional assumptions about academic intimacy, ultimately embodied in the ideal of the Oxbridge tutorial system, which seems out of place in a truly mass system.

Structure

During its 'golden time' the structure of British higher education was, at best, binary in the sense that the new polytechnics had a secure, but subordinate, place in the system; at worst, it was fractured in the sense that not only did the system lack a coordinated structure, but it also lacked a shared identity. In 2001 neither is any longer true. First, the British system, like the Australian and Swedish, is post-binary in structure. This sets it apart from the majority of other European higher education systems, most of which are still organized along binary lines maintaining a strict demarcation between universities and other higher (vocational) education institutions, and from most state systems in the United States, which tend to be stratified into research universities awarding doctorates, comprehensive state universities concentrating on bachelors' and masters' degrees, and community colleges offering two-year associate-degree programmes. Although unified in the sense that all higher education institutions regardless of title are funded according to the same criteria subject to the audit and assessment regimes, the system is not uniform. Although the former polytechnics (and Scottish central institutions) became universities in 1992, a significant number of non-university institutions remain. Some of these institutions, notably the independent art colleges, are content with being outside the university sector; others aspire to university status and feel they are stigmatized as second-class institutions. In addition a large number of further education colleges offer some higher education programmes, often part-time and generally at sub-degree level. However, more than three-quarters of students are now enrolled in universities, which are the dominant institutional type.

Second, British higher education is now pluralistic rather than fractured. The coherence of the total system is not in doubt; 'higher education' is no longer an administrative neologism but a commonly understood category (frequently but confusingly used interchangeably with 'universities'); its frontiers are reasonably clear – for the moment (the demarcation with further education, although a small issue at present, is likely to grow in importance – and annoyance); common funding formulae and assessment criteria have stimulated a sense of shared interest. Of course, important differences of mission persist. The university sector comprises at least seven distinct institutional types:

(i) Oxford and Cambridge – sui generis;
(ii) the University of London;
(iii) the old 'civics' established in the Victorian period, mainly in the North and Midlands;
(iv) the 'redbricks', founded in the first half of the twentieth century, generally in the South;
(v) the new universities built on greenfield sites during the 1960s;
(vi) the technological universities, the former colleges of advanced technology; and
(vii) the 'new' universities of the 1990s, i.e. the former polytechnics.

This classification excludes Scotland (four 'ancient' universities) and Wales (another federal university like – and unlike – London). New forces of variation are at work. The effects of successive Research Assessment Exercises, and the parallel outcomes of research council priorities, have led to an increasingly selective allocation of research funding; more than 80 per cent of the funding goes to less than 20 per cent of the institutions. 'Clubs' of vice-chancellors have emerged to reflect the competing perspectives of different types of university – the 'Russell Group' for research universities on the one hand; the Coalition of Modern Universities, representing the former polytechnics, on the other. There is pressure from some quarters to introduce a neo-binary system, based on the models of stratification provided by American states such as California and Wisconsin.

Again, a snapshot of institutions may help to clarify the degree to which the structure of British higher education has genuinely evolved from being a binary to become a post-binary and from being a fractured 'system' to become a pluralistic system. There are 176 publicly funded higher education institutions in the United Kingdom – 137 in England, 21 in Scotland, 14 in Wales and four in Northern Ireland. In addition more than 400 further education colleges offer some higher education courses. In England there are 81 universities (dividing the University of London into its 16 constituent schools) and 46 other institutions. However, although the split between universities and others is roughly two-to-one, students are split nine-to-one between the two types of institution. Universities range in size from The Open University (more than 50,000 full-time equivalent students) to institutions with fewer than 5000; some higher education colleges have fewer than a thousand students. Core funding for research ranges from £80 million a year in the case of Cambridge down to less than £250,000 in the case of some 'new' universities. The dimensions of 'difference' could easily be extended. But to do so might lead to a misleading conclusion – that there can, or may, be a return to the loosely and hierarchically arranged collection of dissimilar institutions characteristic of higher education's 'golden time' (before the binary system bit). The overall impression is of heterogeneity but not of dissolution. Although diversity is celebrated, centrifugal forces are kept in check.

Autonomy and accountability

The main reason why these forces are kept in check is that British higher education is now a highly managed system. The three higher education funding councils for England, Scotland and Wales exercise a degree of control and surveillance over the system which would have been unimaginable in the 1960s. This takes three main forms. First, funding formulae are detailed, explicit and transparent; the days when the UGC exercised 'informed prejudice' are long gone. To the extent that it is the responsibility of institutional managers to maximize their funding council income their room for exercising discretion is limited. Similar incentives also apply across the system which tends to promote uniformity. Therefore, not only is uniformity directly mandated by the government – for example, universities are unable to charge higher-than-standard fees to British and other European Union students because any additional income would simply be clawed back from their core funding and also because the government has taken legal powers to prevent institutions charging so-called top-up fees; uniformity is also indirectly encouraged by the application of common funding formulae and standard system-wide criteria.

Second, the funding councils, prompted by the government, have developed a range of initiatives. Increasingly extra public expenditure is not added to core funding for general distribution but instead is dispersed through special initiatives which reflect political priorities. As a result institutions must bid for additional student numbers, the total number and overall mix of which have been prescribed in advance, or for extra funding for projects designed to widen participation, again within a prescribed pattern, or to the Higher Education Reach-Out to Business and the Community (HEROBaC) fund to support knowledge-transfer activities. There has even been a move to earmarking special funding – for example, for information technology and other infrastructure – which is calculated on a pro rata basis and is not actually released to institutions until they have submitted agreed plans to their funding councils. The growth of these initiatives, although still a small proportion of the total public funding available to universities, represents a significant breach in the principle of a block grant. Third, the funding councils carry out a range of assessments, either directly as in the case of the Research Assessment Exercise, or through the Quality Assurance Agency for Higher Education (QAA) as with reviews of teaching quality. Some are used to determine future funding levels; all have significant behavioural impacts on institutions. In addition the funding councils have developed a range of performance indicators on matters such as wastage rates – which are published and, again, have a serious impact on external perceptions of institutions and on their behaviour and cultures.

Control and surveillance are also exercised by other public agencies, notably the QAA (which is – technically – responsible to the universities as well as the government). Assessments of teaching quality by the QAA have proved to be more controversial than research assessment – partly because they do not (currently) determine funding levels and, therefore, can be regarded as redundant, but mainly because research has always been seen as a public activity policed by peer review (of which the RAE can be seen as an elaboration) while teaching is still regarded as a private, even intimate, exchange between teachers and students into which formal assessments are a crude and unwelcome intrusion. For this last reason there has been controversy about how the results of teaching quality assessments (or, as they are to be labelled in future, subject reviews) should be reported. The QAA, backed by the government, has successfully argued for overall 'grades' to be awarded, while the universities as represented by their vice-chancellors preferred a more opaque system of reporting which could not readily be translated into published league tables of institutional performance.

The proliferation of such league tables is a symptom of a further way in which the autonomy of higher education has been constrained; the emergence of new and more vocal 'stakeholders'. The rise of consumerism, and the reconceptualization of higher education as a provider of 'academic services', have compromised the old arguments for institutional autonomy. Universities have always been used to working in partnership with traditional professional bodies, such as the engineering institutions, many of which in practice are dominated by academic-practitioners. But the increasing emphasis on more generic forms of vocationalism, unconstrained by these traditional professional identities, has obliged universities to listen (and defer?) to new voices, some of which have been orchestrated through employer-dominated quangos. This has proved a much less congenial experience. The overall balance sheet is clear. Although there have been modest gains in autonomy, these have been more than offset by new demands for accountability – from the state and its agencies, and from a diversity of 'stakeholders'. Higher education today is substantially less free than it was during its 'golden time'.

Intellectual life

It is a bold claim that the intellectual life of British higher education is less vibrant than it was during its 'golden time' – and one that must be hedged around with many caveats and qualifications. First, although, as I argued earlier, it was during this period that universities became the home of a new class of 'intellectual' academics especially in the social sciences, intellectual life continued to take place outside higher education. Indeed it is possible that, as the possibilities of academic life narrowed through the 1980s and 1990s (because of internal over-specialization as well as external political assaults), a process of dispersal succeeded the process of concentration that had once made universities such exciting places; intellectual life flowed back into publishing and the media and also into new arenas such as think-tanks, activist groups, new social movements and even management consultants.

Second, the particular intellectual quality of higher education in the 1960s reflected the combination of social utopianism and scientific and technological triumphalism that characterized the post-war years. That spirit, condemned retrospectively as naïve and arrogant, died with its age. Nor did it revive with the approach of a new millennium as some optimists expected. In 2001 intellectual life is both more realistic (and limited?) and more pessimistic, as critiques of meta-narrative increase, meanings are deconstructed, the limits (not only of growth but of everything) become more visible and 'risks' of all kinds proliferate. It is hardly surprising that this more sombre spirit has infected academic life in higher education. Third, of course, generalizations across so many disciplines, subdisciplines and specialisms are hazardous; in many cases it can be argued that contemporary disciplinary cultures far exceed in subtlety and vitality the primitive cultures of the 1960s.

Nevertheless, the claim is still made – and there are grounds for supporting it. One reason, of course, is that during the 1980s there was a direct political assault on the social sciences, which perhaps had become too closely linked to the centre-left welfare-statism against which the triumphant New Right had rebelled. The most dramatic episode was the failed attempt to abolish the Social Sciences Research Council (SSRC) and the successful insistence that 'science' be expunged from its title which was changed to the Economic and Social Research Council (ESRC). However, such politically motivated assaults have not been repeated. A second, and sustained, reason is that the research councils have emphasized directed research programmes at the expense of responsive grants (rather as the higher education funding councils have developed targeted initiatives). Processes such as Technology Foresight have encouraged research councils to articulate key 'themes', which are then translated into directed programmes. As a result other research topics have been deprioritized. The primary motive for this shift was a genuine desire to build bridges between research communities and 'user' communities and to break down archaic demarcations between theory and practice and between 'pure' and 'applied' research; but a secondary motive was the need to protect the position of the research councils against charges of ivory-towerism and irrelevance. The downgrading of the academic heads of research councils to the role of 'chief executive' supervised by non-academic chairmen, largely drawn from the business community, and the appointment of a director-general of the Research Councils, emphasized their incorporation within a more heterogeneous and more instrumental 'knowledge' enterprise.

The Research Assessment Exercise may have had a similarly dampening effect on research in universities funded from core budgets, the other half of the dual-support system which, of course, was designed to stimulate creativity by providing funding for open-ended non-thematic research.[11] Although the RAE has certainly increased the volume of research outputs and the productivity of researchers and, arguably, has enhanced the quality of research (in a narrow technical sense), it has probably undermined the vitality of higher education's research effort. First, it has discouraged experimentation, especially in interdisciplinary domains. Better safe than sorry – if a five-star grade is at stake. The funding councils have attempted to remedy this bias towards conformity by undertaking a 'fundamental review' of the RAE, but this bias is inherent in any system dependent on peer review. Second, by concentrating research funding in fewer institutions, the RAE has reduced the sites of experimentation. As radical thought is more likely to flourish on the less heavily policed periphery, this has had serious consequences. Moreover, the reduction in research sites, like a loss of species diversity, tends to reduce the vitality of the research ecosystem. Finally, the judgements and preferences articulated through the RAE tend – naturally – to mirror the priorities developed within the research councils, which again has tended to reduce variety within the research system.

However, there have also been gains. If the autonomy of research and scholarship in higher education has been compromised, the main cause is the emergence of a so-called Knowledge Society. In other words it is a symptom of success, not evidence of failure. Because 'knowledge' is not only a key economic resource but also a determinant of social forms (and even personal identities), its 'production' cannot be left in the hands of autonomous institutions and unaccountable individuals; instead it must be steered and planned. Nor any longer can a valid distinction be made between 'academic' knowledge production, rightly the responsibility of autonomous institutions, and other forms of knowledge production, for which no such valid claims can be made. If such arguments appear to be a counsel of necessity, obligations that universities cannot evade but nevertheless are unwelcome, other more positive arguments are available. For example, it is conventionally assumed that the best and most creative research is done by disinterested researchers working in autonomous institutions insulated from the pressures of politics and the market. But that may no longer be true – if it ever was. The best and most creative research may now be done in contexts of application (and implication), in public places where the heterogeneity of knowledge production is exposed rather than in autonomous spaces from which all forms of contestation that do not conform to scholarly and scientific practice are excluded.[12]

In summary, British higher education at the turn of the century has almost five times as many students as it had at the mid-point of the 'golden time' back in the 1960s. However, its degree of social openness has not matched this fivefold increase. In key respects its academic culture continues to be conservative, not least in the weight attached to full-time specialized undergraduate education and its comparative underdevelopment in graduate education. It enjoys significantly less autonomy and is subject to increasingly intrusive forms of accountability. Finally, it has lost the intellectual verve (and naïvety) characteristic of higher education in the 'golden time' – but has successfully incorporated more open and inclusive notions of research and knowledge production.

Future prospects

The over-arching question facing British higher education at the beginning of a new century is whether the elite–mass system that has developed, raggedly and perhaps absent-mindedly, over the past two decades is capable of further extension and elaboration or whether it has reached the limits of its potential. The answers to more detailed questions – on structure, funding and quality – depend on the answer given to this big question. For example, if the burden of future growth in student numbers is likely to lie elsewhere, there is little point in tinkering with the structure of higher education – or different approaches to funding and quality regimes will (or should) be taken depending on whether higher education is still regarded essentially as a public service or is to be treated in future as a semi-privatized sector of the 'knowledge industry'.

The scale and scope of future expansion are the key. The government, through the Prime Minister, is committed to raising participation to 50 per cent from the present level of 33 per cent. The Department of Education and Employment, intriguingly, was reluctant to endorse this ambitious target. The most important drivers of expansion appear to be largely external to the higher education system; one is certainly the government's commitment to raising standards in schools (clearly improved access to higher education plays a significant role in shaping aspirations), and another is the perceived need to meet the skills needs of a knowledge-based economy. Two components of the government's emerging strategy for future expansion reflect these drivers. The first is the commitment to establishing a two-year foundation degree. Although vocationally focused, this new degree would be more general than the existing range of sub-degree qualifications aimed at training technicians. A better comparison, perhaps, is with the first cycle of higher education in many other European countries. The second is the establishment of alternative institutions uncluttered with the 'academic' baggage which burdens existing universities. The best example is the University for Industry (UfI), now Learn Direct. The UfI has been conceived of, first, as a marketing and branding operation (to stimulate demand not satisfied by existing higher education and provision) and, second, as a model of new methods of course delivery that make much greater use of communication and information technology. Some of the expansion may also be channelled through other forms of 'virtual' university, either joint ventures by existing universities or public–private partnerships, or through corporate universities.

Such developments are relevant to the evolving structure of higher education. It is possible to envisage a new binary division – not a hierarchical division between more and less noble higher education institutions, but between public-sector public-service higher education on the one hand and on the other a growing sector of new providers, whether novel vehicles like the UfI, spin-offs of traditional institutions, public–private alliances or corporate universities. If this happened, the relationship between the two halves of this neo-binary system would be crucial – rivalry or synergy? Seen in this light the restructuring of the existing system may be seen as a secondary issue. However, there are increasingly centrifugal pressures within the unified system created when the old binary system was abandoned in the early 1990s and the polytechnics became universities. First, the restructuring debate is important. Should British higher education be remodelled on the lines of the California or Wisconsin systems, despite the very significant historical, spatial and legal differences, or will novel and 'softer' forms of collaboration between institutions emerge? The latter is certainly a more desirable, and maybe a more likely, outcome. Second, the devolutionary dynamic. The most high-profile example, of course, is the abolition of tuition fees for Scottish-domiciled students in Scottish universities. But equally significant, although less immediately divisive, is the emergence of a stronger regional dimension in England following the creation of regional development agencies (RDAs).

Third, the future organization of research remains unresolved. The traditional dual-support system which was intended to represent a balance between core funding provided by the funding councils and project and programme funding channelled through the research councils has been progressively undermined – by the RAE which has 'externalized' the universities' 'internal' research priorities on the one hand; and on the other the increasingly dirigisme and instrumentalism of the research councils – under pressure from the Office of Science and Technology (OST). The funding councils are fighting a dogged battle to defend their stake in research by conducting a 'fundamental review' of the RAE (partly a re-engineering of the process but largely a rejustification). But the research funding transparency review has shown that they must fight on two fronts simultaneously – against the Treasury determined to increase accountability for different funding streams (without necessarily recognizing that separate accounting encourages separate – operational – development); and the OST and the Department of Trade and Industry (DTI) which have by no means given up the struggle to dominate the research agenda in the larger interests of enhancing national competitiveness, promoting social inclusion and meeting other political priorities. The eventual outcome remains unclear. But the implications of this continuing uncertainty about the future of research funding on the character of institutions and so the shape of the system are very important.

The future pattern of funding in British higher education is similarly clouded. At present the system has an overall annual income of £11.6 billion – of which £4.5 billion comes from the funding councils, just under £3 billion in fees, £1.7 billion in research grants and a little more, about £2 billion from other operating income. The precise public/private split is difficult to calculate because both fees and research income are split between public and private income streams. But there can be no doubt that the state, in its many forms, is the majority stakeholder in higher education – and likely to remain so indefinitely despite the encouragement universities have received to diversify their income. More than half – £6.5 billion – of the system's total expenditure of £11.3 billion goes on staff. In the past decade, and probably for the next, higher education funding has been characterized by two trends. The first is a remarkable increase in productivity (or, from the perspective of higher education, reduced real-terms budgets and lower unit costs). This has amounted to 35 per cent since 1989, a significant achievement because very little of this efficiency gain can be attributed to investment in new technologies and almost all to more productive use of academic labour and better management systems. The second is a shift away from block to specific grants. Instead of being able to determine their own expenditure policies institutions must now account separately for research and teaching expenditure and also bid for initiative funding (such as for widening participation, learning and teaching enhancement, research infrastructure, additional student numbers, and so on). Such expenditure is then audited to ensure that it was spent on these activities.

In the short and medium term both these trends are likely to continue – the former, efficiency gains, perhaps on a reduced scale; the latter, almost certainly, on an increased scale. The medium- to long-term outlook, however, remains obscure. The prospects for a significant uplift in public expenditure on universities is bleak. The government, nominally Labour, is committed to low taxation (because it fears the electoral consequences) and, in any case, has priorities that are more insistent although not more important. But, because the government is nominally Labour, the prospects for more radical forms of privatization are also slight. Certainly a wholesale move towards either allowing institutions to charge higher fee levels, and impose other user charges, or channelling public expenditure on higher education through students by means of vouchers seems unlikely unless there is a significant change in the political climate. The most probable future funding scenario, therefore, is of a system still largely dependent on public expenditure and subject to perennial 'efficiency gains', but increasingly encouraged to form entrepreneurial alliances with the private sector and to generate more non-state income. Although less probable, more radical approaches to higher education funding cannot be entirely discounted. Certainly the traditional pattern of 'free' higher education available to all those who were willing and qualified, the Robbins formula influenced by the National Health Service, was dismantled with remarkable ease during the 1990s – first, by the Conservative government replacing student grants by loans, and then by the new Labour government's imposition of tuition fees.

The question posed at the start of this chapter – can Britain's elite–mass system survive? – is of more than local significance. It matters not only in Britain, where the transition to a mass–universal system implied by Tony Blair's commitment to a 50 per cent participation rate would place great strains on existing normative and organizational structures, but also for the wider potential for building a democratic system of higher education. In the United States very high levels of participation have been produced by the incorporation of all types of post-secondary education within a highly stratified higher education system; in (nearly all) the rest of Europe expansion has taken place within traditional binary structures which protect, and privilege, the role of universities. Only in Britain perhaps has a genuine attempt been made to increase social opportunities for higher education through a system that retains traditional academic attributes in nearly all institutions, and not just in a segregated elite sector. It is a bold, if unconscious, experiment that so far has been a success. There is no compelling evidence to suggest that this success cannot be sustained.

References

1. R. Berdahl (1959) *British Universities and the State.* Berkeley, CA: University of California Press; J. Carswell (1985) *Government and the Universities in Britain: Programme and Performance 1960–1980.* Cambridge: Cambridge University Press.
2. J. Pratt (1997) *The Polytechnic Experiment.* Buckingham: SRHE/Open University Press.
3. Society for Research into Higher Education (1983) *Excellence and Diversity,* final report of the Leverhulme inquiry into the future of higher education. Guildford: SRHE.
4. M. Shattock (1994) *The UGC and the Management of Universities.* Buckingham: Open University Press.
5. Committee on Higher Education (1963) *Higher Education* (Robbins Report). London: HMSO.
6. A.H. Halsey (1992) *Decline of Donnish Dominion.* Oxford: Clarendon Press.
7. M. Trow (1973) *Problems in the Transition from Elite to Mass Higher Education.* Berkeley, CA: Carnegie Commission on Higher Education.
8. P. Scott (1995) *The Meanings of Mass Higher Education.* Buckingham: SRHE/Open University Press.
9. M. Harris (Chairman) (1996) *A Review of Postgraduate Education.* Bristol: Higher Education Funding Council for England (with CVCP and SCoP).
10. Higher Education Funding Council for England (1999) *Performance Indicators in Higher Education 1996–97, 1997–98,* Report 99/66. Bristol: HEFCE.
11. P. Scott (2000) The impact of the research assessment exercise on the quality of British science and scholarship, *Anglistik,* Spring.
12. H. Nowotny, P. Scott and M. Gibbons (2000) *Re-thinking Science: Knowledge Production in an Age of Uncertainties.* Cambridge: Polity Press.

APPENDIX: M.L. Shattock: A Bibliography of Major Published Works and Unpublished Reports 1969–2000, compiled by Dr J.W. Nicholls

Books

1983   (Editor) *The Structure and Governance of Higher Education*. Programme on the Study into the Future of Higher Education, L9; Research into Higher Education Monographs, 52. Guildford: SRHE.

1983   (Editor) *Resource Allocation in British Universities* (with G. Rigby). Research into Higher Education Monographs, 56. Guildford: SRHE.

1991   *Dimensions of Evaluation in Higher Education: Report of the IMHE Study Group on Evaluation in Higher Education* (with U. Dahllof, J. Harris, A. Staropoli and R. in't Veld). Higher Education Policy Series, 13. London: Jessica Kingsley.

1991   (Editor) *Making a University*. Coventry: University of Warwick.

1994   *The UGC and the Management of British Universities*. Buckingham: SRHE/Open University Press.

1996   (Editor) *The Creation of a University System*. Oxford: Blackwell.

Articles and chapters in books

1970   A changing pattern of university administration, *Universities Quarterly*, Summer: 310–20.

1976   Financial constraints on universities: when the pips begin to squeak, in C. Flood Page and M. Yates (eds) *Power and Authority in Higher Education*, pp. 62–70. Guildford: SRHE.

1977   The factors influencing student choice of university (with P. Walker), *Research in Education*, 18: 67–73.

1978   Administrative and governmental structures in growing universities, *Overseas Universities*, October: 35–40.

1979   Factors influencing entry at a university, a polytechnic and a college of education (with P. Walker, J. Cunnington and M. Richards), *Higher Education Review*, Summer: 36–46.

1979   Retrenchment in US higher education: some reflections on the resilience of the US and UK university systems, *Education Policy Bulletin*, 7 (2): 149–67.

1980   Access to higher education (Review Article), *Higher Education*, 9: 101–4.

1981   Demography and social class: the fluctuating demand for higher education in Britain, *European Journal of Education*, 16 (3–4): 381–92.

1981   University resource allocation procedures: responses to change, *International Journal of Institutional Management in Higher Education*, OECD/IMHE, 5 (3): 199–205.

1982   Higher education: a suitable case for treatment, *The Education Policy Bulletin*, 10 (1): 69–81.

1982   How should British universities plan for the 1980s?, *Higher Education*, 11: 193–210.

1982   Mobilising private interest and local support for the development of science parks, in J. Gibbs (ed.) *The Needs of New Technology Based Enterprises*, pp. 91–101. Commission of the European Communities. Infobrief. Luxembourg: SARL.

1984   British higher education under pressure: politics, budgets and demography and the acceleration of ideas for change 1979–83, *European Journal of Education*, 19 (2): 201–16.

1984   The British University Grants Committee 1919–83: changing relationships with government and the universities (with R. Berdahl), *Higher Education*, 13: 471–99 [Reprinted in 1985, in I. McNay. and J. Ozga (eds) *Policy Making in Education: The Breakdown of Consensus: A Reader*. Oxford: Pergamon Press, and in Brazilian Association for the Advancement of Science (ed.) *International Perspectives on Higher Education*.]

1984   Tertiary education in the eighties: paths to reward and growth (Review Article), *Studies in Higher Education*, 9 (2): 203–5.

1984   The UGC idea in international perspective (with R. Berdahl), *Higher Education*, 13: 613–18.

1985   Investment Factors in British Science Park Development, in J. Gibbs (ed.) *Science Parks and Innovation Centres: Their Economic and Social Development*, pp. 149–59. Commission of the European Communities. Oxford: Elsevier.

1985   The Leverhulme Programme of Study into the Future of Higher Education: its implications for higher education and management and policy in the United Kingdom, *International Journal of Institutional Management in Higher Education*, OECD/IMHE, 9 (1): 142–9.

1986   False images but a renewed promise, in S. Bosworth (ed.) *Beyond the Limelight: Essays on the Occasion of the Silver Jubilee of the Conference of University Administrators*, pp. 202–13. Reading: CUA. [Reprinted as: False images but a renewed promise in universities' contribution to industrial and technological advance, *Studies in Higher Education*, 12 (1): 23–37.]

1986   The UGC and the maintenance of 'standards' in the British university system, in G. Moodie (ed.) *Standards and Criteria in Higher Education*, pp. 46–64. Buckingham: SRHE/Open University Press.

1987   Is it simply the government or is it society? *University of Leeds Review*, 30: 185–95.

1987   The last days of the University Grants Committee, *Minerva*, 25 (4): 471–85.

1988   Financial management in universities: the lessons of University College, Cardiff, *Financial Accountability and Management*, 4 (2): 99–112.

1989   Higher Education and the Research Councils, *Minerva*, 27 (2–3): 195–222. [Reprinted in C. Cunningham, P. Gummett and Sir Robin Nicholson (eds) *Science and Technology in the United Kingdom*, pp. 44–69. London: Longman.]

1989   Thatcherism and British higher education: universities and the enterprise culture, *Change*, 21 (5): 30–40.

1989   The universities as charities: private giving and the role of the state in 'the advancement of learning', in A. Ware (ed.) *Charities and Government*, pp. 169–90. Manchester: Manchester University Press.

1990   Elemente einer Universitätsverfassung – Management, akademische Selbstverwaltung und Hochschulpolitik in einem wettbewerbsorientierten Umfeld. Carl Bertelsmann-Preis Symposium 1990, pp. 73–84. Gutersloh: Bertelsmann.

1991   The evaluation of universities' contribution to society (with U. Dahllof, J. Harris, A. Staropoli and R. in't Veld), in *Dimensions of Evaluation in Higher Education*, pp. 57–86. Higher Education Policy Series, 13. London: Jessica Kingsley.

1991   Financial pressures and their effect on quality in British universities, in G. Moodie (ed.) *Quality and Access in Higher Education: Comparing Britain and the United States*, pp. 102–15. Buckingham: SRHE/Open University Press.

1991   Governance: an overview, in T. Schuller (ed.) *The Future of Higher Education*, pp. 78–81. Buckingham: SRHE/Open University Press.

1991   The pre-history of the University, in M. Shattock (ed.) *Making of a University*, pp. 9–22. Coventry: University of Warwick.

1992   The university of the twenty-first century. The internal and external threats to the university, *Minerva*, 30 (2): 130–47.

1994   Balancing priorities in the foundation of a new university: the performance of British universities created in the 1960s, in U. Dahloff and S. Selander (eds) *New Universities and Regional Context: Uppsala Studies in Education*, pp. 101–13. Uppsala: Upsaliensis Academiae.

1994   Optimising university resources, in *A University Policy for Europe, Conference Report in CREaction*, 104: 181–9.

1995   The university of the future, *Higher Education Management*, 7 (2): 157–65.

1996   Tertiary education at the beginning of the twenty-first century, *PEB Exchange: Newsletter of the Programme on Educational Building*, 27: 9–12.

1997   Governance and accountability in the 2020 era, *Perspectives: Policy and Practice in Higher Education*, 1 (1): 18–32.

1997   The management implications of the new priorities, *Higher Education Management*, 9 (2): 27–34.

1997   University–industry research and training partnerships: the Warwick example, *Industry and Higher Education*, 11 (3): 164–7.

1998   The academic divide, *Guardian*, 10 March.

1998   Dearing on governance: the wrong prescription, *Higher Education Quarterly*, 52 (1): 35–47.

1998   Doing well but needs to do better: cannot rest on its laurels (Invited Editorial), *Times Higher Education Supplement*, 14 August. [Reprinted in 1999, in *International Higher Education* 15: 24–6.]

1998   New Labour: not so new prospects for higher education, *International Higher Education*, Boston College Center for International Higher Education, 11: 11–12.

1998   Shape of things to come, *Guardian*, 3 March.

1999   Governance and management in universities: the way we live now, *Journal of Education Policy*, 14 (3): 271–82.

1999   The impact of a new university on its community: the University of Warwick, in H. Gray (ed.) *Universities and the Creation of Wealth*. Buckingham: SRHE/Open University Press.

1999   La capacitat emprenedora i l'exit academic. La Universitat de Warwick, model per a les universitats ambicioces, *Revista Economica de Catalonia*, 37: 119–25.

1999   Managing modern universities, *The Stakeholder*, Public Management Foundation, 3 (3): 30–1. [Reprinted in *Perspectives Policy and Practice in Higher Education*, 4 (2): 33–4.]

2000   Governance and management, in A. Smithers and P. Robinson (eds) *Further Education Re-formed: Shaping the Future*, pp. 89–102. Millennium Education Series. London: Falmer Press.

2000   Strategic management in European universities in an age of increasing institutional self-reliance, *Tertiary Education and Management*, 6 (2): 93–104.

Reports on higher education issues

1969   Report for the Inter-University Council on Higher Education Over-
        seas (IUC), *Administrative Assistance to African Universities,* December.
1969   *Report of the President's Planning Commission on the Future of Higher
        Education in Kenya,* for the Government of Kenya, October (Joint
        Secretary to the Commission).
1974   *Report on the Organisation and Management of the University of Indo-
        nesia,* for UNESCO (Project 045), July.*
1976   *Report on the Establishment of a University in the United Arab Emirate,*
        for the British Council, April.*
1977/78 *Interim and Final Reports of the CUA Group on Forecasting and Univer-
        sity Expansion,* for the CUA (Chairman of the Group), April 1977
        and April 1978.
1980   *The Funding and Organisation of Courses in Higher Education: Interim
        Report on Overseas Student Fees,* First Report from the House of
        Commons Education, Science and Arts Committee, Volume 1
        Report HMSO HC 552-1, April (Specialist Adviser on Higher
        Education to the Committee).
1980   *The Funding and Organisation of Courses in Higher Education,* Fifth
        Report from the House of Commons Education, Science and
        Arts Committee, Volume 1 Report HMSO HC 787-1, September
        (Specialist Adviser on Higher Education to the Committee).
1982   *Biotechnology: Interim Report on the Protection of the Research Base in
        Biotechnology,* Sixth Report from the House of Commons Educa-
        tion, Science and Arts Committee, HMSO HC 289, July (Special-
        ist Adviser on Higher Education to the Committee).
1987   *Report on University College, Cardiff,* for the UGC, February.
        University College, Cardiff, Financial Plan, March.
        University College, Cardiff, Second Financial Plan, May.
        University College, Cardiff, Third Financial Plan, June.
        *Report on the Implementation of Financial Control at University College
        Cardiff,* for the UGC, June.*
1989   *Report of a Review Commission for the National University of Lesotho*
        (Sims Commission), January (Member of the Commission).
1990   *Review of the Planning of the University of Cyprus,* March.*
1991   *Review of the Proposed Revision of the National University of Lesotho Act
        and the National University's Statutes,* for the World Bank, February.*
1991   *Review of the University of Malta* (Warwick HE Group), for the
        British Council, May.
1992   *Second Review of the Planning of the University of Cyprus,* September.*
1994   *Derby College: Wilmorton: Report of an Enquiry into the Governance
        and Management of the College,* for the FEFC, November.*
1994   HEFCE Joint Working Group on Performance Indicators, *Report
        of the Sub Group on Indicators of Financial Health,* March (Chair-
        man of the Group).

1994   *The University of the West Indies: A New Structure – The Regional University in the 1990s and Beyond.* Report of the Chancellor's Commission on the Governance of UWI (Member of the Commission), July.

1995   *University of Cyprus: Report on Staffing Needs,* March.*

1995 (Revised and expanded 1998)

CUC Guide for Members of Governing Bodies of Universities and Colleges in England, Wales and Northern Ireland, December 1995 and March 1998 (Secretary of CUC).

1996   *Report on the Administration and Management of the European University Institute, Florence,* November.*

1997   The National Commission on Higher Education (Dearing Commission): invited paper, January.*

1998   *The Governance, Management and Administration of the University: A Report to Queen's University, Belfast* (with David Holmes), January.

1998   *The University of Western Australia: Some After Thoughts* (Report to the Vice-Chancellor) November.*

2000   *University of Cape Town: Report on Governance and Related Management Issues – Refocusing the Machinery to Match the University's Mission,* March.*

Note: * Indicates sole author

Bibliography

Books and monographs

Ainley, P. (1994) *Degrees of Difference: Higher Education in the 1990s*. London: Lawrence and Wishart.

Annan, N. (1999) *The Dons: Mentors, Eccentrics and Geniuses*. London: HarperCollins.

Association of Business Schools (1999) *Pillars of the Economy: Developing World Class Management Performance*. London: ABS.

Bargh, C., Scott, P. and Smith, D. (1996) *Governing Universities: Changing the Culture?* Buckingham: SRHE/Open University Press.

Barnett, R. (1997) *Higher Education: A Critical Business*. Buckingham: SRHE/Open University Press.

Barnett, R. (1999) *Realizing the University in an age of super-complexity*. Buckingham: SRHE/Open University Press.

Bell, E. (1996) *Counselling in Higher Education*. Buckingham: Open University Press.

Beloff, M. (1969) *The Plateglass Universities*. London: Secker and Warburg.

Berdahl, R. (1959) *British Universities and the State*. Berkeley, CA: University of California Press.

Berquist, W. (1992) *The Four Cultures of the Academy*. San Francisco, CA: Jossey-Bass.

Bess, J. (1988) *Collegiality and Bureaucracy in the Modern University*. New York, NY: Teachers College Press, Columbia University.

Bickerstaffe, G. (1998, 1999) *Which MBA? A Critical Guide to the World's Best Programmes*, 10th and 11th edns. London: The Economist Intelligence Unit.

Birnbaum, R. (1988) *How Colleges Work: The Cybernetics of Academic Organization and Leadership*. San Francisco, CA: Jossey-Bass.

Birnbaum, R. (2000) *Management Fads in Higher Education: Where They Come From, What They Do, Why They Fail*. San Francisco: Jossey-Bass.

Blanchard, K. and Johnson, S. (1983) *The One Minute Manager*. London: Willow.

Blaxter, S., Hughes, T. and Tight, M. (1998) *The Academic Career Handbook*. Buckingham: Open University Press.

Blundell, R. *et al.* (1997) *Higher Education, Employment and Earnings in Britain*. London: Institute for Fiscal Studies.

Braun, D. and Merrien, F. (1999) *Towards a New Model of Governance for Universities? A Comparative View*. London: Jessica Kingsley.

Brecher, B., Fleischmann, O. and Halliday, J. (eds) (1996) *The University in a Liberal State*. Aldershot: Ashgate Publishing (Avebury Series).

British Council (1998) *The Export Earnings of Welsh Higher Education and Their Impact on the Welsh Economy*. Cardiff: British Council.

Brooks, A. (1997) *Academic Women*. Buckingham: SRHE/Open University Press.

Brown, P. and Scase, R. (1994) *Higher Education and Corporate Realities: Class, Culture and the Decline of Graduate Careers*. London: UCL Press.

Bryce, T. and Humes, W. (eds) (1999) *Scottish Education*. Edinburgh: Edinburgh University Press.

Burgess, R. (ed.) (1984) *The Research Process in Educational Settings: Ten Case Studies*. Lewes: Falmer Press.

Burgess, R. (ed.) (1990) *Learning from the Field*. London: JAI Press.

Burgess, R. (ed.) (1997) *Beyond the First Degree*. Buckingham: SRHE/Open University Press.

Buzzell, R., Quelch, J. and Bartlett, C. (1992) *Global Marketing Management: Cases and Readings*. Reading, MA: Addison Wesley.

Caplan, P.J. (1994) *Lifting a Ton of Feathers: A Woman's Guide to Surviving the Academic World*. Toronto: University of Toronto Press.

Cardwell, D.S.L. (1972) *The Organisation of Science in England*. London: Heinemann Educational.

Carswell, J. (1985) *Government and the Universities in Britain: Programme and Performance 1960–1980*. Cambridge: Cambridge University Press.

Carter, I. (1990) *Ancient Cultures of Conceit: British University Fiction in the Post-war Years*. London: Routledge.

Cave, M. *et al.* (1997) *The Use of Performance Indicators in Higher Education: The Challenge of the Quality Movement*. London: Jessica Kingsley.

Clapp, B.W. (1982) *The University of Exeter: A History*. Exeter: University of Exeter Press.

Clark, B. (1998) *Creating Entrepreneurial Universities: Organizational Pathways of Transformation*. Oxford: Pergamon Press.

Cobban, A. (1988) *The Medieval English Universities: Oxford and Cambridge to c1500*. Aldershot: Scolar Press.

Constable, J. and McCormick, R. (1987) *The Making of British Managers*. London: British Institute of Management with the Confederation of British Industry.

Cornford, F. ([1908] 1993) *Microsmographica Academia: Being a Guide for the Young Academic Politician*. Cambridge: MainSail Press.

Council for Industry and Higher Education (1999) *Partnership for Excellence: A 'Confederacy Model' for HE/FE Partnerships*. London: CIHE.

Courrey, M. and Jackson, H. (1991) *Making Equal Opportunities Work*. London: Pitman.

Court, S. (1996) *Dictionary of Higher Education*. London: AUT.

Cowell, D. (1984) *The Marketing of Services*. Oxford: Butterworth-Heinemann.

Crainer, S. and Dearlove, D. (1998) *Gravy Training: Inside the World's Top Business Schools*. Oxford: Capstone.

Cuthbert, R. (ed.) (1996) *Working in Higher Education*. Buckingham: SRHE/Open University Press.

Daiches, D. (ed.) (1964) *The Idea of a New University: An Experiment in Sussex*. London: Andre Deutsch.

Daniel, J. (1996) *Mega-Universities and Knowledge Media: Technology Strategies for Higher Education*. London: Kogan Page.

David, M. and Woodward, D. (eds) (1998) *Negotiating the Glass Ceiling: Careers of Senior Women in the Academic World*. London: Falmer Press.

Davies, A. (1986) *A Very Peculiar Practice*. London: Coronet.

Davies, A. (1988) *A Very Peculiar Practice: The New Frontier*. London: Methuen.

Dearlove, J. (1995) *Governance, Leadership and Change in Universities*. Paris: UNESCO (IIEP).

Dougill, J. (1998) *Oxford in English Literature: The Making and Undoing of 'The English Athens.'* Ann Arbor, MI: University of Michigan Press.

Dover, K. (1994) *Marginal Comment*. London: Duckworth.

Doyle, P. (1994) *Marketing, Management and Strategy*. Hemel Hempstead: Prentice Hall.

Duke, A. (1996) *Importing Oxbridge: English Residential Colleges and American Universities*. New Haven, CT: Yale University Press.

Eggins, H. (ed.) (1997) *Women as Leaders and Managers in Higher Education*. Buckingham: SRHE/Open University Press.

Eliot, C. (1909) *University Administration*. Cambridge, MA: Harvard University Press.

Emberley, P. (1996) *Zero Tolerance: Hot Button Politics in Canada's Universities*. London: Penguin.

Engel, A. (1983) *From Clergyman to Don: The Rise of the Academic Profession in Nineteenth Century Oxford*. Oxford: OUP (Clarendon Press).

Evans, G. (1999) *Calling Academia to Account: Rights and Responsibilities*. Buckingham, SRHE/Open University Press.

Follett, B.K. (1997) University research: how should limited funds be deployed? *Technology, Innovation and Society*, 13: 17–19.

Ford, P. (1996) *Managing Change in Higher Education: A Learning Environment Architecture*. Buckingham: SRHE/Open University Press.

Franks, Lord (1964–65) *University of Oxford: Hebdomadal Council Commission of Inquiry*. Oxford: OUP.

Gilmore, D. (ed.) (1997) *Brand Warriors*. London: HarperCollins.

Gledhill, J. (1999) *Managing Students*. Buckingham: Open University Press.

Goodlad, S. (1995) *The Quest for Quality: Sixteen Forms of Heresy in Higher Education*. Buckingham: SRHE/Open University Press.

Gordon, R. and Howell, J. (1959) *Higher Education for Business*. New York, NY: Columbia University Press.

Gray, H. (1999) *Universities and the Creation of Wealth*. Buckingham: SRHE/Open University Press.

Gregory, J. (1998) *Marketing Corporate Image*. Chicago, IL: NTC.

Halsey, A. (1992) *Decline of Donnish Dominion: The British Academic Professions in the Twentieth Century*. Oxford: Clarendon Press.

Hamel, G. and Prahalad, C. (1994) *Competing for the Future*. Boston, MA: Harvard Business School Press.

Handy, C. (1985) *Understanding Organizations*. Harmondoworth: Penguin.

Handy, C., Gow, I., Gordon, C., Randlesome, C. and Moloney, M. (1987) *The Making of Managers*. London: National Economic Development Council with the British Institute of Management and the Manpower Services Commission.

Hardy, C. (1996) *The Politics of Collegiality: Retrenchment Strategies in Canadian Universities*. Montreal: McGill-Queen's University Press.

Hardy, T. (1895) *Jude the Obscure*. London: Osgood and McIlvane.

Harrison, B. (ed.) (1994) *History of the University of Oxford: Volume VIII, The Twentieth Century*. Oxford: Oxford University Press.

Harrop, S. (1994) *Decade of Change: The University of Liverpool 1981–1991*. Liverpool: Liverpool University Press.

Harvey, L. (1997) *The Student Satisfaction Manual.* Buckingham: SRHE/Open University Press.

Harvey, L. and Knight, P. (1996) *Transforming Higher Education.* Buckingham: SRHE/Open University Press.

Hobson, D. (1999) *The National Wealth: Who Gets What in Britain.* London: HarperCollins.

Hooley, G., Saunders, J. and Piercy, N. (1998) *Marketing Strategy and Competitive Positioning.* Hemel Hempstead: Prentice Hall.

Hudson, M. (1995) *Managing Without Profit: The Art of Managing Third-sector Organisations.* London: Penguin.

Hughes, T. (1861) *Tom Brown at Oxford.* London: Macmillan.

Humfrey, C. (1999) *Managing International Students.* Buckingham: Open University Press.

Ives, E. (2000) *The First Civic University: Birmingham 1880–1980.* Birmingham: University of Birmingham Press.

Jary, D. and Parker, M. (1998) *The New Higher Education: Issues and Directions for the Post-Dearing University.* Stafford: Staffordshire University Press.

Jenkins, S. (1995) *Accountable to None.* London: Penguin.

Jobber, D. (1998) *Principles and Practice of Marketing.* Maidenhead: McGraw-Hill.

Johnes, J. and Taylor, J. (1990) *Performance Indicators in Higher Education.* Buckingham: SRHE/Open University Press.

Jones, D.R. (1988) *The Origins of Civics Universities: Manchester, Leeds and Liverpool.* London: Routledge.

Kane, T.J. (1999) *The Price of Admission: Rethinking How Americans Pay for College.* Washington, DC: Brookings Institution Press, and New York, NY: Russell Sage Foundation.

Kapferer, J-N. (1997) *Strategic Brand Management.* London: Kogan Page.

Kelly, T. (1981) *For Advancement of Learning: The University of Liverpool 1881–1981.* Liverpool: Liverpool University Press.

Kennedy, D. (1997) *Academic Duty.* Cambridge, MA: Harvard University Press.

Kotler, P. (1994) *Marketing Management: Analysis, Planning, Implementation and Control,* 8th ed. London: Prentice Hall.

Kotler, P. and Fox, K. ([1988]1994) *Strategic Marketing for Educational Institutions.* Englewood Cliffs, NJ: Prentice Hall.

Letwin, S. (1992) *The Anatomy of Thatcherism.* London: Fontana.

Lewis, M. (1997) *Poisoning the Ivy: The Seven Deadly Sins and other Vices of Higher Education in America.* New York, NY: Sharp.

Liston, C. (1999) *Managing Quality and Standards.* Buckingham: Open University Press.

Martin, J. and Samels, J. (1997) *First Among Equals: The Role of the Chief Academic Officer.* Baltimore: Johns Hopkins University Press.

Martin, R. (1998) *Chalk Lines: The Politics of Work in the Managed University.* Durham, NC: Duke University Press.

Micklethwait, J. and Wooldridge, A. (1996) *The Witch Doctors: What the Management Gurus are Saying, Why it Matters and How to Make Sense of it.* London: Heinemann.

Moore, W. (1968) *The Tutorial System and its Future.* Oxford: Pergamon Press.

Nelson, C. and Watt, S. (1999) *Academic Key Words: A Devil's Dictionary for Higher Education.* London: Routledge.

Newman, J. ([1852] 1965) *The Idea of a University.* London: Dent.

Nilson, T.H. (1998) *Competitive Branding.* Chichester: Wiley.

Nowotny, H., Scott, P. and Gribbons, M. (2000) *Re-thinking Science: Knowledge Production in an Age of Uncertainties.* Cambridge: Polity Press.

O'Brien, G. (1998) *All the Essential (Half-) Truths about Higher Education.* Chicago, IL: University of Chicago Press.

Palfreyman, D. and Warner, D. (1998) *Higher Education and the Law: A Guide for Managers.* Buckingham: SRHE/Open University Press.

Palfreyman, D., Thomas, H. and Warner, D. (1998) *How to Manage a Merger . . . or Avoid One.* Leeds: Heist Publications.

Pattison, M. (1868) *Suggestions on Academical Organisation.* Edinburgh: Edmonston and Douglas.

Paxman, J. (1991) *Friends in High Places: Who Runs Britain?* London: Penguin.

Perkin, H. (1989) *The Rise of Professional Society.* London: Routledge.

Pierson, F. (1959) *The Education of American Businessmen.* New York, NY: McGraw-Hill.

Pratt, J. (1997) *The Polytechnic Experiment.* Buckingham: SRHE/Open University Press.

Proctor, M. (1957) *The English University Novel.* Berkeley: University of California Press.

Radford, J. and Raaheim, K. (1997) *Quantity and Quality in Higher Education.* London: Jessica Kingsley.

Ramsden, P. (1998) *Learning to Lead in Higher Education.* London: Routledge.

Readings, B. (1996) *The University in Ruins.* Cambridge, MA: Harvard University Press.

Richards, J. (ed.) (1997) *Uneasy Chairs: Life as a Professor.* Lancaster Unit for Innovation in HE: University of Lancaster.

Robinson, P. (1994) *Snapshots from Hell: The Making of an MBA.* London: Nicholas Brealey.

Rose, J. and Ziman, J. (1964) *Camford Observed.* London: Victor Gollancz.

Rosenzweig, R. (1997) *The Political University: Policy, Politics and Presidential Leadership in the American Research University.* Baltimore, MD: Johns Hopkins University Press.

Rothblatt, S. (1968) *The Revolution of the Dons.* London: Faber and Faber.

Ryan, A. (1998) *Liberal Anxieties and Liberal Education.* New York, NY: Hill and Wang.

Sanderson, M. (1972) *The Universities and British Industry 1850–1970.* London: Routledge.

Sanderson, M. (1975) *The Universities and the Nineteenth Century.* London: Routledge.

Scott, P. (1995) *The Meanings of Mass Higher Education.* Buckingham: SRHE/Open University Press.

Sharpe, T. (1976) *Porterhouse Blue.* London: Pan.

Sharpe, T. (1995) *Granchester Grind.* London: André Deutsch and Secker and Warburg.

Shattock, M. (ed.) (1991) *Making a University: A Celebration of Warwick's First Twenty Five Years.* Coventry: University of Warwick.

Shattock, M. (1994) *The UGC and the Management of Universities.* Buckingham: SRHE/Open University Press.

Shattock, M.L. (2000) Strategic management in European universities in an age of increasing institutional self-reliance, in *Tertiary Education and Management,* 6 (2): 93–104.

Silver, H. and Silver, P. (1997) *Students: Changing Roles, Changing Lives.* Buckingham: SRHE/Open University Press.

Slaughter, S. and Leslie, L. (1997) *Academic Capitalism: Politics, Policies, and the Entrepreneurial University.* Baltimore, MD: Johns Hopkins University Press.

Sloman, A. (1963) *A University in the Making: The Reith Lectures 1963.* London: BBC.

Smart, J. (1991) *Higher Education: Handbook of Theory and Research.* New York, NY: Agathon Press.

Smith, A. and Webster, F. (eds) (1997) *The Postmodern University? Contested Visions of Higher Education in Society.* Buckingham: SRHE/Open University Press.

Smith, D. and Langslow, A. (1999) *The Idea of a University.* London: Jessica Kingsley.

Snow, C. (1951) *The Masters.* London: Macmillan.

Soares, J. (1999) *The Decline of Privilege: The Modernisation of Oxford University.* Stanford, CA: Stanford University Press.

Soley, L. (1995) *Leasing The Ivory Tower: The Corporate Takeover of Academia.* Boston, MA: South End Press.

Sporn, B. (1999) *Adaptive University Structures: An Analysis of Adaptation to Socioeconomic Environments of US and European Universities.* London: Jessica Kingsley.

Stewart, J. (1975–78) *A Staircase in Surrey* (a quintet of novels). London: Gullancz.

Tapper, T. and Palfreyman, D. (2000) *Oxford and the Decline of the Collegiate Tradition.* London: Woburn Press.

Tapper, T. and Salter, B. (1992) *Oxford, Cambridge and the Changing Idea of the University: The Challenge to Donnish Domination.* Buckingham: SRHE/Open University Press.

Taylor, P. (1999) *Making Sense of Academic Life: Academics, Universities and Change.* Buckingham: SRHE/Open University Press.

Thompson, E. (ed.) (1970) *Warwick University Limited.* Harmondsworth: Penguin.

Thorley, H. (1998) *Take a Minute: Reflections on Modern Higher Education Administration.* Lancaster: Unit for Innovation in Higher Education: University of Lancaster.

Toth, E. (1997) *Ms Mentor's Impeccable Advice for Women in Academia.* Philadelphia, PA: University of Pennsylvania Press.

Trow, M. (1973) *Problems in the Transition from Elite to Mass Higher Education.* Berkeley, CA: Carnegie Commission on Higher Education.

Trow, M. (1994) *Managerialism and the Academic Profession: Quality and Control.* London: Open University Quality Support Centre.

Vincent, E.W. and Hinton, P. (1947) *The University of Birmingham: Its History and Significance.* Birmingham: Cornish Brothers.

Warner, D. and Leonard, C. (1997) *The Income Generation Handbook,* 2nd ed. Buckingham: SRHE/Open University Press.

Warner, D. and Palfreyman, D. (1996) *Higher Education Management: The Key Elements.* Buckingham: SRHE/Open University Press.

Watson, D. (2000) *Managing Strategy.* Buckingham: Open University Press.

Watson, K., Modgil, C. and Modgil, S. (1997) *Educational Dilemmas: Debate and Diversity. Volume 2: Reforms in Higher Education.* London: Cassell.

Webb, G. (1996) *Understanding Staff Development.* Buckingham: SRHE/Open University Press.

Williams, J. (ed.) (1997) *Negotiating Access to Higher Education.* Buckingham: SRHE/Open University Press.

Articles and chapters in books

Ashton, D. (1988) Are business schools good learning organisations? Institutional values and their effects in management education, *Personnel Review,* 17 (4): 9–14.

Bagilhole, B. (1993) How to keep a good woman down: an investigation of the role of institutional factors in the process of discrimination against women academics, *British Journal of Sociology of Education,* 14: 261–74.

Bitner, M. (1992) Servicescapes: the impact of physical surroundings on customers and employees, *Journal of Marketing*, 56 (2) (April): 57–71.

Bolton, A. (1997) How to succeed in business school leadership by really trying, *Perspectives: Policy and Practice in Higher Education*, 1 (2): 62–5.

Brown, M. and Wolf, D. (1995) Planning for Change, *Higher Education Policy*, 8 (3): 46–8.

Burgess, R. (1991) Working and researching at the limits of knowledge, in M.L. Shattock (ed.), *Making a University: A Celebration of Warwick's First Twenty five years*, pp. 95–112, 115–16. Coventry: University of Warwick.

Burgess, R. (1998) The Director's tale: developing teams and themes in a research centre, in G. Walford (ed.) *Doing Research about Education*, pp. 154–69. London: Falmer Press.

Clark, B.R. (1998) The entrepreneurial university: demand and response, *Tertiary Education and Management*, 4 (1): 5–16.

Clayton, M. (1995) Encouraging the 'Kaizen' approach to quality in a university, *Total Quality Management*, 6 (5–6): 593–601.

Crainer, S. (1997) The concept crisis: too few big ideas to go around? *MBA*, December: 35–9.

Davies, S. and Glaister, K. (1996) Spurs to higher things: mission statements of UK universities, *Higher Education Quarterly*, 50 (4): 261–94.

Dearlove, J. (1995) Collegiality, managerialism and leadership in English universities, *Journal of Tertiary Education and Management*, 1 (2): 161–9.

Deem, R. (1998) New managerialism in higher education: the management of performance and cultures, *International Studies in the Sociology of Education*, 8 (1): 47–70.

Follett, B.K. (1997) University research: how should limited funds be deployed? *Technology, Innovation and Society*, 13: 17–19.

Gledhill, J. (1996) Student management, in D. Warner and D. Palfreyman, *Higher Education Management: The Key Elements*. Buckingham: SRHE/Open University Press.

Goldman, M. (1996) The case against 'practicality' and 'relevance' as gauges of business schools: responding to challenges posed by criticisms of business school research, *Journal of Management Inquiry*, 5 (4): 336–49.

Higher Education Quarterly (1988) Special edition on Dearing, 52 (1).

Kemp, I. and Seagraves, L. (1995) Transferable skills – can higher education deliver?, *Studies in Higher Education*, 20 (3): 315–28.

Leslie, D. (1996) Strategic governance: the wrong questions? *The Review of Higher Education*, 20 (1): 101–12.

Leslie, L. and Rhoades, G. (1996) Rising administrative costs: seeking explanations, *Journal of Higher Education*, 66 (2): 187–212.

Lewis, L. and Altbach, P. (1996) Faculty versus administration: a universal problem, *Higher Education Policy*, 9 (3): 255–8.

Lock, A. (1996) The future of the MBA in the UK, *Higher Education*, 31 (2): 164–85.

McGee, C. and Chandler, G. (1998) Benchmarking in student administration: an Australian university's experience, *Perspectives: Policy and Practice in Higher Education* 2 (2): 38–44.

McNair, S. (1999) Liberal adult education: contemporary definitions and practice, in Cambridge, UK: *Liberal Adult Education: Towards a Contemporary Paradigm*, Occasional Paper 25, pp. 22–9. Universities Association for Continuing Education.

McNay, I. (1995) From collegial academy to corporate enterprise: the changing cultures of universities, in T. Schuller (ed.) *The Changing University*. Buckingham: SRHE/Open University Press.

Moore, T. (1997) The corporate university: transforming management education, *Accounting Horizons*, 11 (1): 77–85.

Palfreyman, D. (1989) The Warwick way: a case study of innovation and entrepreneurship within a university context, *Journal of Entrepreneurship and Regional Development*, 1 (2): 207–19.

Palfreyman, D. (1995/96) Oxbridge fellows as charity trustees, *Charity Law and Practice Review*, 3 (3): 187–202.

Palfreyman, D. (1998/99) Oxford colleges: permanent endowment, charity trusteeship and personal liability, *Charity Law and Practice Review*, 5 (2): 85–134.

Palfreyman, D. (1999) Is Porterhouse really 'a charity'? *Charity Law and Practice Review*, 6 (1): 75–87.

Parasurman, A., Zeithaml, V. and Barry, L. (1985) A conceptual model of service quality and its implications for future research, *Journal of Marketing*, 49 (fall): 41–50.

Ramanzoglu, C. (1987) Sex and violence in academic life or you can keep a good woman down, in J. Hanmer and M. Maynard (eds) *Women, Violence and Social Control*. London: Macmillan.

Rothblatt, S. (1997) An Oxonian 'idea' of a university: J. Newman and 'well-being', *History of the University of Oxford: Volume VI, Nineteenth-Century Oxford, Part 1*, Chapter 9. Oxford: Oxford University Press.

Ryan, A. (1999) 'The American way', *Prospect*, Aug/Sept: 24–30.

Ryder, A. (1996) Reform and UK higher education in the enterprise era, *Higher Education Quarterly*, 50 (1): 54–70.

Sandbach, J. and Thomas, A. (1996) Sources of funding and resource allocation, in D. Warner and D. Palfreyman (eds) *Higher Education Management*, pp. 47–65. Buckingham: SRHE/Open University Press.

Scott, P. (1989) Higher education, in D. Kavanagh and A. Seldon (eds) *The Thatcher Effect*, pp. 198–212. Oxford: OUP.

Scott, P.(1996) The future of continuing education, in M. Zukas (ed.) *The Purposes of Continuing Education*, Proceedings of the 1996 UACE Annual Conference, pp. 23–32. Leeds: Universities Association for Continuing Education.

Scott, P. (2000) The impact of the Research Assessment Exercise on the quality of British science and scholarship, *Anglistik*, 11: 129–43.

Shapiro, B. (1988) What the hell is 'marketing oriented'? *Harvard Business Review*, Nov–Dec: 119–25.

Shattock, M. (1999) The impact of a new university on its community: the University of Warwick, in H. Gray (ed.) *Universities and the Creation of Wealth*. Buckingham: SRHE/Open University Press.

Shattock, M.L. (2000) Strategic management in European universities in an age of increasing institutional self-reliance, *Tertiary Education and Management*, 6 (2): 93–104.

Sizer, J. (1992) Accountability, in B. Clark and G. Neave (eds) *The Encyclopaedia of Higher Education*. Volume 2: Analytical Perspectives, pp. 1305–13. Oxford: Pergamon.

Sizer, J. and Cannon, S. (1999) Autonomy, governance and accountability, in J. Breenan, J. Fedorowitz, M. Huber and T. Shaw (eds) *What Kind of University?* Buckingham: SRHE/Open University Press.

Sizer, J. and Mackie, D. (1995) Greater accountability: the price of autonomy, *Higher Education Management*, 7 (3): 323–32.

Slapper, G. (1997) Judging the educators: forensic evaluation of academic judgement, *Education and the Law*, 9 (1): 5–12.

Tapper, T. and Palfreyman, D. (1998) Continuity and change in the collegial tradition, *Higher Education Quarterly* 52 (2): 139–61.

Taylor, R. (1998) Lifelong learning policy in England, in R. Taylor and D. Watson (eds) *Lifelong Learning Policy in the United Kingdom 1997/98*, pp. 5–11. Cambridge: UACE.

Thomas, H. (1997) The unexpected consequences of financial devolution, *Higher Education Review*, 29 (3): 7–21.

Tight, M. (1996) The re-location of higher education, *Higher Education Quarterly*, 50 (2): 119–37.

Tight, M. (1999) Education, education, education! The vision of lifelong learning in the Kennedy, Dearing and Fryer reports, *Oxford Review of Education*, 24 (4): 482–85.

Warner, D. (1999) An academic and/or an administrative career, *Perspectives: Policy and Practice in Higher Education*, 3 (1): 16–18.

Warren, R. (1994) The collegiate ideal and the organisation of the new universities, *Reflections on Higher Education*, 6: 34–55.

Watson, D. (1997) Conclusion: UACE and the future, in R. Taylor and D. Watson (eds) *From Continuing Education to Lifelong Learning: A Review of UACE Strategy and Objectives*, Occasional Paper 20, pp. 151–3. Cambridge: Universities Association for Continuing Education.

Watson, S. (1993) The place for universities in management education, *Journal of General Management*, 19 (2): 14–42.

Woodrow, M. (1999) The struggle for the soul of lifelong learning, *Widening Participation and Lifelong Learning*, 1 (9): 9–12.

Reports

Cadbury Report (1992) *Report of the Committee on the Financial Aspects of Corporate Governance*. London: Stock Exchange.

Committee on Higher Education (1963) *Higher Education: Report of the Committee Appointed by the Prime Minister Under the Chairmanship of Lord Robbins 1961–63*, Cm 2154 (Robbins Report). London: HMSO.

Committee on Standards in Public Life (Nolan Committee) (1996) *Local Spending Bodies*, Second Report, Cm 3270. London: HMSO.

Committee of University Chairmen (1995) *Guide for Members of Governing Bodies of Universities and Colleges in England, Wales and Northern Ireland*. Bristol: Higher Education Funding Council for England.

Committee of University Chairmen (2000) *Progress Report of the Working Party on Effectiveness of University Governing Bodies*. Warwick: CUC.

Committee of Vice-Chancellors and Principals (1985) *Report of the Steering Committee for Efficiency Studies in Universities* (Jarratt Report). London: CVCP.

Crawford, R. (ed.) (1997) *A Future for Scottish Higher Education*. Glasgow: Committee of Scottish Higher Education Principals (COSHEP).

Davis, D. (1995) *Performance Indicators: An Overview of Their Use in Selected Commonwealth Countries*. London: Commonwealth Higher Education Management Service (CHEMS).

Duke, C. (1996) *Research in Continuing Education: Summary of Publications Generated by Research Funded by the UFC in the Period 1990 to 1994*, Occasional Paper 19. Leeds: Universities Association for Continuing Education.

European Universities Continuing Education Network (1998) *Interim Report on the THENUCE Project.* Paris: EUCEN.

Field, J. and Moseley, R. (1999) *Promoting Vocational Lifelong Learning: A Guide to Good Practice in the HE Sector*, HEFCE 98/46. Bristol: HEFCE.

Hambley, E. (1998) *Personal Liability in Public Service Organisations: A Legal Research Study for the Committee on Standards in Public Life.* London: The Stationery Office.

Harris, M. (Chairman) (1996) *A Review of Postgraduate Education.* Bristol: Higher Education Funding Council for England (with the Committee of Vice-Chancellors and Principals and Standing Conference of Principals).

Higher Education Funding Council for England (1992) *Continuing Education Policy Review*, Bristol: HEFCE.

Higher Education Funding Council for England (1993) *Continuing Education*, Circular 18/93. Bristol: HEFCE.

Higher Education Funding Council for England (1998) *The Evaluation of the Funding for the Development of Continuing Vocational Education*, Report 98/44, Bristol: HEFCE.

Higher Education Funding Council for England (1999) *Higher Education Reach-out to Business and the Community Fund: Funding Proposals*, Consultation 99/16. Bristol: HEFCE.

Higher Education Funding Council for England (1999) *Performance Indicators in Higher Education 1996–97, 1997–98*, Report 99/66. Bristol: HEFCE.

Higher Education Funding Council for England (1999) *Profiles of Higher Education Institutions*, Circular 99/68. Bristol: HEFCE.

Higher Education Funding Council for Wales (1999) *Profiles of Higher Education Institutions in Wales.* Cardiff: HEFCW.

Higher Education Funding Council for Wales (1999) *The Scope for Institutional Mergers at the Higher Education Level.* Cardiff: HEFCW.

Higher Education Statistics Agency (1999) *Resources of Higher Education Institutions 1997/98*, Cheltenham: HESA.

Hobsons (1997) *Distance Learning and Supported Learning in the UK.* London: Hobsons.

Independent Committee of Inquiry into Student Finance (1999) *Student Finance: Fairness for the Future* ('Cubie Report'). Edinburgh: Independent Committee of Inquiry into Student Finance.

Lund, H. (1998) *Joining Hands: A Survey of Non-academic Collaboration Between Commonwealth Universities.* London: Commonwealth Higher Education Management Service (CHEMS).

McNicoll, I.H. (1995) *The Impact of the Scottish Higher Sector on the Economy of Scotland.* Glasgow: COSHEP.

McNicoll, I., Kelly, U. and McLellan, D. (1999) *Economic Aspects of Scottish Higher Education Institutions: Report to the Committee of Scottish Higher Education Principals.* Edinburgh: COSHEP.

National Audit Office (1997) *Governance and Management of Overseas Courses at Swansea Institute of Higher Education*, Report of the Comptroller and Auditor General, HC 222 Session 1996–97, Jan. London: HMSO.

National Audit Office (1997) *University of Portsmouth*, Report of the Comptroller and Auditor General, HC4 Session 1997–98, Jan. London: HMSO.

National Audit Office (1998) *The Management of Building Projects at English Higher Education Institutions,* H 542 Session 1997–98. London: The Stationery Office.

National Audit Office (1998) *Scottish Higher Education Funding Council Investigation of Misconduct at Glasgow Caledonian University,* Report of the Comptroller and Auditor General, HC 680 Session 1997–98, Jan. London: The Stationery Office.

North (1997) *Commission of Inquiry: Report.* Oxford: OUP.

Riley Research (1999) *Clearing 1999: Benchmarking Advertising and Marketing.* Nottingham: Riley Research.

Sawbridge, M. (1996) *The Politics and Organisational Complexity of Staff Development of Academics: A Discussion Paper,* Occasional Green Paper No 14. Sheffield: UCoSDA.

Schofield, A. (1998) *Benchmarking in Higher Education: An International Review.* London: Commonwealth Higher Education Management Service (CHEMS) and Paris: UNESCO.

Scottish Higher Education Funding (1996) *National Committee of Inquiry into Higher Education: Submission of Evidence from the SHEFC.* Edinburgh: SHEFC.

Scottish Higher Education Funding Council (1998) *Financial Memorandum between the Scottish Higher Education Funding Council and the University of Aberdeen.* Edinburgh: SHEFC.

Scottish Higher Education Funding Council (1999) *Guide for Members of Governing Bodies of Scottish Higher Education Institutions and Good Practice Benchmarks,* Circular Letter HE05/99. Edinburgh: SHEFC.

Scottish Higher Education Funding Council (1999) *Corporate Plan 1999–2003.* Edinburgh: SHEFC.

Scottish Higher Education Funding Council (1999) *The Guide for Members of Governing Bodies of Scottish Higher Education Institutions and Good Practice Benchmarks.* Edinburgh: SHEFC.

Scottish Higher Education Funding Council (2000) *Funding for the Future: Stage 2 Consultation Paper on the Funding of Teaching,* Consultation paper HEC01/00. Edinburgh: SHEFC.

Society for Research into Higher Education (1983) *Excellence and Diversity,* Final report of the Leverhulme Inquiry into the Future of Higher Education. Guildford: SRHE.

Universities Funding Council and Polytechnics and Colleges Funding Council (1991) *Report of the Joint UFC/PCFC Working Group.* London: UFC and PCFC.

University of Wales (1997) *The Impact of the Higher Education Sector on the Welsh Economy: Measurement, Analysis and Enhancement.* Cardiff: University of Wales.

Wales European Taskforce (1999) *Proposals for a National Economic Development Strategy: A Consultation Document.* Cardiff: National Assembly for Wales. (Also see www.wales.gov.uk/polinifo/european/neds/cntnts/e.htm)

Websites and other material

Acherman, H. (1998) Central strategic governance and decentralised accountable leadership: the case of the University of Amsterdam. Paper presented to the EAIR/IMHE Conference, Amsterdam, October.

American Association of University Women: www.aauw.org

Authers, J. (1997) Extending the learning curve, *Financial Times,* 22 September.

Bradshaw, D. (1998) Changing places: deans' posts hard to fill, *Financial Times,* 20 April.

Bradshaw, D. (2000) Deans take on dot-com interests, *Financial Times*, 10 January.

Butterworth, J. (1982) *Annual Report 1980–81*, Coventry: University of Warwick.

Carnall, C. (1999) Executive education briefing for ABS Executive, Paper ABS/99/03/07, June (unpublished).

Dearlove, D. (1999) Modern ideas hit old buffers, *Times*, 4 October.

Donkin, R. (1994) Initials that stand for main board advance, *Financial Times*, 20 July.

Fieldhouse, R. (1997) Report on the process and progress of accreditation and mainstreaming of continuing education in the pre-1992 English and Welsh universities. Unpublished paper, Universities Association for Continuing Education.

Financial Times (1999) Top 50 business schools, 25 January.

Financial Times (2000) MBA 2000, 24 January.

Higher Education Statistics Agency (HESA) (1998) *Students in Higher Education Institutions 1996/97*. Cheltenham: HESA.

Hodges, L. (2000) Fear not . . . the professor has a cunning plan, *Independent*, Education Section, 2 March.

MBA Newsletter (1999) 8 (2): 1–8 and 8 (4): 7.

Miles, D. (1996) The development of management education. Second unpublished lecture, De Lissa Lecture, Kingston University, 25 April.

National Association for Women in Education: www.nawe.org

1994 Group (1999) *Research and Education for the Future*. Colchester: 1994 Group.

O' Leary, J. (1999) Boom time for British MBAs, *Times*, 7 May.

Rowland-Jones, A. (1962) Basic principles of the University of Essex development plan. Unpublished paper, University of Essex Library: Special Collections.

Ruggles-Brise, J. (1960) *Proposal for University of Essex*, submitted by the Promotion Committee for consideration by the University Grants Committee, Essex Library, Special Collections.

Sandler, B.R. and Hall, R. (1986) *The Campus Climate Revisited: Chilly for Women Faculty, Administrators and Graduate Students*. Washington, DC: Association of American Colleges and Universities. (See www.aacu-edu.org/Initiatives/psew.html for further information.)

Shatter the Glass Ceiling: www.theglassceiling.com

Stamp, R. (1996) Marketing orientation in higher education. Unpublished MA thesis, Nottingham Business School, Nottingham Trent University.

Sunday Times (1999) University Guide. London: *Sunday Times*.

Times (1999) The good university guide, 23 April.

Times Higher Education Supplement (1996) League table of excellence, 20 December.

University of Essex (1962) *First Report of the Academic Planning Board to the Promotion Committee*, University of Essex Library, Special Collections.

Wild, R. (1999) Is it time to tie the corporate knot? *Guardian*, 2 March.

Women in Higher Education: www.wihe.com

Index

(References to figures and tables are in bold)

The Society for Research into Higher Education

The Society for Research into Higher Education (SRHE) exists to stimulate and coordinate research into all aspects of higher education. It aims to improve the quality of higher education through the encouragement of debate and publication on issues of policy, on the organization and management of higher education institutions, and on the curriculum, teaching and learning methods.

The Society is entirely independent and receives no subsidies, although individual events often receive sponsorship from business or industry. The Society is financed through corporate and individual subscriptions and has members from many parts of the world.

Under the imprint *SRHE & Open University Press*, the Society is a specialist publisher of research, having over 80 titles in print. In addition to *SRHE News*, the Society's newsletter, the Society publishes three journals: *Studies in Higher Education* (three issues a year), *Higher Education Quarterly* and *Research into Higher Education Abstracts* (three issues a year).

The Society runs frequent conferences, consultations, seminars and other events. The annual conference in December is organized at and with a higher education institution. There are a growing number of networks which focus on particular areas of interest, including:

Access	Learning Environment
Assessment	Legal Education
Consultants	Managing Innovation
Curriculum Development	New Technology for Learning
Eastern European	Postgraduate Issues
Educational Development Research	Quantitative Studies
FE/HE	Student Development
Funding	Vocation at Qualification
Graduate Employment	

Benefits to members

Individual

- The opportunity to participate in the Society's networks

- Reduced rates for the annual conferences
- Free copies of *Research into Higher Education Abstracts*
- Reduced rates for *Studies in Higher Education*
- Reduced rates for *Higher Education Quarterly*
- Free copy of *Register of Members' Research Interests* – includes valuable reference material on research being pursued by the Society's members
- Free copy of occasional in-house publications, e.g. *The Thirtieth Anniversary Seminars Presented by the Vice-Presidents*
- Free copies of *SRHE News* which informs members of the Society's activities and provides a calendar of events, with additional material provided in regular mailings
- A 35 per cent discount on all SRHE/Open University Press books
- Access to HESA statistics for student members
- The opportunity for you to apply for the annual research grants
- Inclusion of your research in the *Register of Members' Research Interests*

Corporate

- Reduced rates for the annual conferences
- The opportunity for members of the Institution to attend SRHE's network events at reduced rates
- Free copies of *Research into Higher Education Abstracts*
- Free copies of *Studies in Higher Education*
- Free copies of *Register of Members' Research Interests* – includes valuable reference material on research being pursued by the Society's members
- Free copy of occasional in-house publications
- Free copies of *SRHE News*
- A 35 per cent discount on all SRHE/Open University Press books
- Access to HESA statistics for research for students of the Institution
- The opportunity for members of the Institution to submit applications for the Society's research grants
- The opportunity to work with the Society and co-host conferences
- The opportunity to include in the *Register of Members' Research Interests* you Institution's research into aspects of higher education

Membership details: SRHE, 3 Devonshire Street, London
W1N 2BA, UK. Tel: 020 7637 2766. Fax: 020 7637 2781.
email: srhe@mailbox.ulcc.ac.uk
world wide web: http://www.srhe.ac.uk./srhe/
Catalogue: SRHE & Open University Press, Celtic Court,
22 Ballmoor, Buckingham MK18 1XW. Tel: 01280 823388.
Fax: 01280 823233. email: enquiries@openup.co.uk